Software Industry–Oriented Education Practices and Curriculum Development:

Experiences and Lessons

Matthew Hussey
Dublin Institute of Technology, Ireland

Bing Wu
Dublin Institute of Technology, Ireland

Xiaofei Xu
Harbin Institute of Technology, China

Senior Editorial Director:	Kristin Klinger
Director of Book Publications:	Julia Mosemann
Editorial Director:	Lindsay Johnston
Acquisitions Editor:	Erika Carter
Development Editor:	Myla Harty
Production Editor:	Sean Woznicki
Typesetters:	Deanna Jo Zombro
Print Coordinator:	Jamie Snavely
Cover Design:	Nick Newcomer

Published in the United States of America by
Engineering Science Reference (an imprint of IGI Global)
701 E. Chocolate Avenue
Hershey PA 17033
Tel: 717-533-8845
Fax: 717-533-8661
E-mail: cust@igi-global.com
Web site: http://www.igi-global.com

Library of Congress Cataloging-in-Publication Data
Software industry-oriented education practices and curriculum development: experiences and lessons / Matthew Hussey, Bing Wu and Xiaofei Xu, editors.
    p. cm.
  Includes bibliographical references and index.
  ISBN 978-1-60960-797-5 (hbk.) -- ISBN 978-1-60960-798-2 (ebook) -- ISBN 978-1-60960-799-9 (print & perpetual access) 1. Software engineering--Study and teaching. 2. Computer software industry. 3. Business and education. 4. Academic-industrial collaboration. I. Hussey, Matthew. II. Wu, Bing, 1962- III. Xu, Xiaofei, 1962-
  QA76.758.S656165 2011
  005.1071--dc22
                    2011012987

British Cataloguing in Publication Data
A Cataloguing in Publication record for this book is available from the British Library.

All work contributed to this book is new, previously-unpublished material. The views expressed in this book are those of the authors, but not necessarily of the publisher.

Table of Contents

Section 1
Introduction to Industry Oriented Software Education

Section 2
International Higher Education Institution-Industry Co-Operation Models

Section 3
Curriculum Issues

Section 4
International Academic Quality Assurance

Section 5
E-Learning and Support Tools

Detailed Table of Contents

Section 1
Introduction to Industry Oriented Software Education

This introductory chapter outlines the evolution of the collaboration on industry-oriented undergraduate software programmes between the Dublin Institute of Technology (DIT) in Ireland and the Harbin Institute of Technology (HIT) in China that led to the annual series of China-Europe Symposia on Software Industry-Oriented Education and largely to the concept of this book. The chapter also provides a review of key elements in industry-oriented higher education and the quality assurance processes required to underpin it at undergraduate and postgraduate programmes and postgraduate research levels. The discussion is set in the context of the fundamental and global significance of software engineering and the software industry to industry as a whole and to society in general.

Section 2
International Higher Education Institution-Industry Co-Operation Models

The development, practicalities, and outcomes of the so-called EMERSION project, an international (Irish/United Kingdom/Chinese) collaboration, within the European Union Asia-Link programme (2003-2006), to develop and implement a software industry-oriented undergraduate degree programme within the School of Software in HIT, are described in this chapter. This collaboration was an extremely active one, adapting an undergraduate programme from DIT, with features from the University of Wolverhampton (UW), for implementation in HIT. This involved an ambitious human resource development of the teaching and administrative staff in HIT, characterised by extensive China-Europe staff exchanges. A fully documented curriculum with new content and industry interactions, specifying teaching, learning, and assessment modes and elaborating a systematic quality assurance system was developed and matched to the cultural and regulatory systems in China. Important spin-offs were a series of research projects in HIT, DIT, and UW evaluating and optimising these processes relating to industry-oriented software education. There were also significant academic developments in the software programmes offered in DIT and UW resulting from the intensive creative work on the project by staff members of these institutions.

Chapter 3

Yanqing Wang, Harbin Institute of Technology, China

This chapter describes in detail the valuable experiences arising from the Europe-Harbin collaborations and insights in China; particularly in Harbin Institute of Technology (HIT) relating to devising and establishing viable and sustainable co-operation mechanisms between the School of Software and local and national software industries. The mutual benefits to the various stakeholders in software education - the higher education institution, the industries, the local and national government, and the students - are explored in detail and shown to argue strongly for active and continuous institution-industry co-operation. The extensive range of related activities already developed by HIT has proven extremely enterprising and, not surprisingly, beneficial and quite inspiring for the students.

Chapter 4

David Chen, IMS-University of Bordeaux 1, France
Bruno Vallespir, IMS-University of Bordeaux 1, France
Jean-Paul Bourrières, IMS-University of Bordeaux 1, France
Thècle Alix, IMS-University of Bordeaux 1, France e

The theme of this chapter is an adventurous international (French/Chinese) collaborative Master's degree programme of Harbin Institute of Technology (HIT) and the University of Bordeaux 1 (UB1) in France. This programme draws together production engineering and software engineering based on the complementary strengths of the two institutions, that of HIT in computer sciences and software engineering and that of UB1 in enterprise modelling and interoperability, and production systems science and engineering. This is a thoroughly international programme in that all students spend two semesters of the four in both China and France. It is also thoroughly industry-oriented in that all students spend two semesters in industrial placements in China, France, or elsewhere in the world.

Section 3
Curriculum Issues

Chapter 5

Tugrul Esendal, De Montfort University, UK
Simon Rogerson, De Montfort University, UK

This chapter presents an interesting approach to developing and delivering software engineering curricula with strong industry orientation to produce ethical professional software engineers. A substantial module on software development is described, covering issues such as software quality framework and measurement tools, professionalism and professional conduct, licensing and self-regulation frameworks, social impact, risk analysis, remedies for failures, and other professional aspects of software engineering. Furthermore, the enterprising teaching/learning throughout involves a strong element of active student participation, both in groups and individually, including learner-matched pathways and other mechanisms.

Chapter 6

Yushan Sun, Harbin Institute of Technology at Wehei, China

The development processes for a progression of industry-oriented software engineering modules for inclusion in general undergraduate computer science programmes in the Wehei campus of HIT are described in detail in this chapter. These modules cover introductory software engineering, object-oriented software design, software architecture and design patterns, and software quality assurance and testing. In the overall process of developing these modules by the teaching team, the sequencing of the material and the relationships between the modules are carefully examined to avoid unnecessary duplication and help ensure smooth connectedness between them. The so-called bottom-up teaching approach chosen also assists in achieving a holistic induction to software. Each class session begins with an introduction to key concepts in a software coding/design assignment that the students then complete in the middle of the session, ending with a thorough class discussion. A case study is presented relating to the iterative development in the classroom setting of the strategic and tactical decisions, and the resulting software, to sort an integer array. This is a hands-on process involving active student participation.

Chapter 7

Gary Hill, University of Northampton, UK
Scott Turner, University of Northampton, UK

The topic of this chapter is a module that emphasises the core value of problem-solving for software engineers in industry and advocates the pro-active introduction of a session in problem-solving to help develop this ability at an early stage in the undergraduate programme preparatory to the introduction to programming. The approach advocated is one based on programming robots to solve certain challenging practical problems followed by graphical programming to simulate the same problem-solving tasks implemented earlier with the robots. A number of individual and group case studies are presented, and very high student involvement and satisfaction are reported due to the visual nature of the teaching/learning.

Chapter 8

A persuasive case for including a detailed industry-oriented module on structured parallel programming within undergraduate and postgraduate degree programmes in software engineering is set out in this chapter. Because the computer and telecommunications industries are rapidly developing and exploiting multi-core processing units, the demand of those and other industries for software engineers with parallel programming skills and abilities to fully exploit these devices is also rapidly growing. In response, a valuable introductory module with three strands, parallel architectures, structured parallelism, and parallel programming, is described in this chapter.

Chapter 9

The theme of this chapter emphasises the importance of active pedagogy and active learning by students, in this case for the development of expertise in the software systems for enterprise resource planning. These systems are used to organise and integrate the full range of business processes, including, very frequently, change management processes. They can encompass a wide range of technical developments as well as organizational and human resource implications. The module developed begins with the initial analysis by the class group of the major factors involved in choosing an appropriate enterprise resource planning software system and proceeds through the physical preparation of the computer laboratory workplace, and the assignment of tasks and schedules to the different student work groups. The next phase consists of producing comprehensive worksheets on the range of functional and technical practices (so-called closed practices) to be managed in the system and then to create the framework for developing new functionalities and practices (so-called open practices). The final phase of the module is the development and implementation of a set of objective evaluations with appropriate weightings. Thus, this chapter introduces a profoundly industry-oriented theme, with extensive technical and software content but also with extensive social functionalities relating to the workforce and the customers of the enterprise.

Chapter 10

This chapter presents a wide-ranging discussion on the fundamental values and necessity for co-operation between the software industry and the higher education institutions in the provision of software education to the future designers and managers of the complex software systems that will underpin the next generation of industrial and societal processes. The chapter also introduces comprehensive approaches to and preparations for the development of industry-oriented undergraduate and postgraduate software engineering programmes, with strong software industry/university co-operation, duly accredited by authoritative international agencies.

Section 4
International Academic Quality Assurance

Chapter 11

Earlier chapters refer in some detail to quality assurance, but this chapter provides a comprehensive description and analysis of the vital need for quality assurance at the international level in higher software education to ensure the production of skilled engineers that can be relied on to produce world-class software for the world market. The presentation is in the context of the increasing internationalization of software education and the increasing requirements of national and international authorities for the assurance of quality of software and therefore of software engineers. The chapter proposes seven prime factors, motivation, purpose, team, environment, method, fitness and safety, which provide a guiding framework for delivering quality and assessing that quality. It discusses the particular considerations and methods used across the globe to achieve these goals in international inter-cultural programmes, and it argues that the seven factors are invaluable in this form of software education.

Section 5
E-Learning and Support Tools

Chapter 12

This chapter describes an ambitious, comprehensive Web-based system for training software students in IT project management. A special feature of the approach is the development of a personalised competency catalogue for each student, which, together with a parallel reference competency map of the required outcomes (knowledge and skills) of the training course, identifies the gap between these and allows the design of a personalised course for the student. Furthermore, the educational content of the system, which is competency-based, is built into an ontological structure which allows the development of large numbers of different personalised learning paths. This would have valuable application in undergraduate and postgraduate programmes, and also in a wide range of lifelong learning situations, a vital aspect of the continuing professionalism of software engineering.

Foreword

Education is changing. It has become a global activity; it is enjoyed and pursued by millions of people around the world, and it is widely recognised as vital for our future well-being and prosperity. University level education is, in particular, promoted by governments across the globe as the means by which we can move our societies forward. Coupled with this, there is increasing recognition that universities need to work closely with industry and business partners to ensure that the education we offer meets the current and future skill needs of our people. These concepts are relevant to all industries, but are particularly important to the software industry.

This book draws on the experience of international experts who are working at the interface between universities and the software industry. The authors have a wealth of real practical experience of working in this important area, and this is very evident within this text. The book proposes a series of strong and important arguments for the development of a new form of industry-oriented software education, which produces curricula that go beyond the theoretical and develop within our future graduates the practical software skills needed to develop and drive the tools of our future economies. A number of different models of curricula are proposed and discussed by the authors: each of these has been implemented with different degrees of industry interaction. The models draw from projects which straddle eight countries across Europe and China, and present the reader with practical examples of advanced university curriculum development and novel teaching and learning practices. Throughout the book, there is an emphasis on the highest quality educational programmes, based upon world-class quality assurance models.

The authors have worked together on a significant Europe-China programme which enabled university staff from the two continents to work together on novel models of university-industry collaboration, and through this, to develop new state of the art software curricula. The book is the culmination of the project, and draws together the unique experiences of the authors in a text which is a very significant piece of work in the field of global university-industry collaboration.

This work will be of interest to academics, students, and practitioners, not only from computer science and software, but also from any discipline developing vocational skills within their graduates. The chapters are thought-provoking and helpful for designers and developers of software educational programmes, including taught undergraduate, postgraduate, and research programmes. It will also be of interest and use to technical managers, human resource specialists, and trainers who work within the software industry and those industries heavily reliant on software for their operation. The book offers significant insights for strategic planners in government higher education policy, and for those who work at the strategic level in our universities across the world.

This book is timely, and its lessons are vitally important if we are to enable our software and other industries to move forward and provide the competitive future of our global economy. I personally greatly enjoyed reading the work of my colleagues and look forward to seeing the lessons within put into practice by others.

Peter Smith
University of Sunderland, UK

Peter Smith: *Professor of Computing at the University of Sunderland, United Kingdom. Ph. D. from the University of Sunderland (1981). Held several teaching, research and management positions within the university. Published over 200 refereed papers on subjects within computing, management and diversity, and has spoken at conferences throughout the world. Supervised and examined over 100 doctoral students. Worked on, and managed several large research projects, many of which involved industrial collaborations. Fellow of the British Computer Society, the Royal Society of Arts and the Higher Education Academy.*

Preface

This book recounts the experiences of academics in Europe and Asia over the past decade in developing and implementing international models for higher education in software engineering that would be thoroughly informed by and oriented to the requirements of the broad software industry. In that the software industry underpins and drives the continuing global revolution in industry, commerce, and society in general, the formation of the highest quality software professionals is of global significance.

The technological and societal changes underway pose fundamental challenges to higher education institutions in every country. Probably the broadest response these institutions have been developing is a deeper and more active involvement with more sections and layers of society than ever before. In particular, the development of a professional industry-oriented approach to higher education constitutes a significant strand of that response.

WHERE TOPIC FITS IN THE WORLD TODAY

A primary objective of industry-oriented software education is the development of highly skilled, highly educated, and highly employable software professionals, capable of developing effective applied software systems of the best quality for the global software industry. They will contribute to the enhancement and further professionalization of the software industry. They will contribute to enhancing the role of the institutions of higher education in enhancing this key industry and industry in general, through industry-institution-society research and development partnerships and a myriad other mechanisms, through enhanced professionalism, through national and international collaborations, through the development of applications throughout the full range of disciplines in the higher education institutions and, indeed, through the appropriate application of the industry-orientation to the disciplines.

TARGET AUDIENCE

It is hoped that the insights and experiences in these chapters will be of assistance to educationalists and academic programme designers across the world involved in industry-oriented software education seeking to produce appropriately skilled graduates for this global industry. They will also help leaders and policy makers in academic institutions and relevant local and national government departments. They will particularly provide useful ideas and guidance to managers of industrial interactions with academic institutions, including recruiters of software graduates, as well as managers of academic interactions with industry.

At the coal-face of programme and curriculum design incorporating purposeful industry-orientation, these chapters will offer examples, lessons, advice, and guidance, including the provision of appropriate quality assurance of the academic, industry, and academic/industrial interface elements of programmes and their integration in practice, to ensure the achievement of international standards of excellence in their graduates entering this globalised industry.

IMPORTANT ELEMENTS IN EACH CHAPTER

This book consists of twelve stand-alone chapters grouped into five broad, sometimes overlapping sections.

Section 1 comprises the introductory chapter 1, which outlines the evolution of the collaboration on industry-oriented undergraduate software programmes between the Dublin Institute of Technology (DIT) in Ireland and the Harbin Institute of Technology (HIT) in China that led to the annual series of China-Europe Symposia on Software Industry-Oriented Education and to the concept of this book. The chapter also provides a review of key elements in industry-oriented higher education and the quality assurance processes required to underpin this at undergraduate and postgraduate programme levels and in postgraduate research. The discussion is set in the context of the fundamental and global significance of software engineering and the software industry to industry as a whole, and to society in general.

Section 2 contains three chapters dealing with the overall theme of operational, integrated, industry-oriented software degree programmes, with emphasis on the measures taken to copper-fastening their industry orientation.

The development, practicalities, and outcomes of the so-called EMERSION project, an international (Irish/United Kingdom/Chinese) collaboration, within the European Union Asia-Link programme (2003-2006), to develop and implement a software industry-oriented undergraduate degree programme within the School of Software in HIT, are described in chapter 2. This collaboration was an extremely active one devoted to adapting an undergraduate programme from DIT, with features from the University of Wolverhampton (UW) for implementation in HIT. This involved an ambitious human resource development of the teaching and administrative staff in HIT, characterised by extensive China-Europe staff exchanges. A fully documented curriculum with new content and industry interactions, specifying teaching, learning, and assessment modes and elaborating a systematic quality assurance system was developed and matched to the cultural and regulatory systems in China. Important spin-offs were a series of research projects in HIT, DIT, and UW evaluating and optimising these processes relating to industry-oriented software education. There were also significant academic developments in the software programmes offered in DIT and UW resulting from the intensive creative work on the project by staff members of these institutions.

Chapter 3 presents a valuable description of the experiences in China and particularly in HIT to devise and establish viable and sustainable co-operation mechanisms between the School of Software and local and national software industries. The mutual benefits to the various stakeholders in software education - higher education institutions, industries, local and national governments, and the students - are explored in detail and shown to argue strongly for active and continuous institution-industry co-operation. The extensive range of related activities already developed by HIT have proven extremely enterprising and, not surprisingly, beneficial and quite inspiring for the students.

The theme of chapter 4 is an adventurous, international (French/Chinese), collaborative Master's degree programme of HIT and the University of Bordeaux 1 (UB1) in France. This draws together production engineering and software engineering based on the complementary strengths of the two institutions, that of HIT in computer sciences and software engineering and that of UB1 in enterprise modelling and interoperability, and production systems science and engineering. This is a thoroughly international programme in that all students spend two semesters of the four in both China and France. It is also thoroughly industry-oriented in that all students spend two semesters in industrial placements in China, France, or elsewhere in the world.

Section 3 has a selection of six chapters detailing experiences in China, the United Kingdom, and Turkey of developing and delivering software engineering modules with strong industry orientation as elements within general computing degree programmes.

Chapter 5 presents an interesting approach to developing and delivering software engineering curricula with strong industry orientation to produce ethical professional software engineers. A substantial module on software development is described, covering issues such as software quality framework and measurement tools, professionalism and professional conduct, licensing and self-regulation frameworks, social impact, risk analysis, remedies for failures, and other professional aspects of software engineering. Furthermore, the teaching throughout involves a strong element of active student participation, both in groups and individually, including learner-matched pathways and other mechanisms.

The development processes for a progression of industry-oriented software engineering modules for inclusion in general undergraduate computer science programmes in the Wehei campus of HIT is described in chapter 6. These modules cover introductory software engineering, object oriented software design, software architecture and design patterns, and software quality assurance and testing. In the overall process of developing these modules by the teaching team, the sequencing of the material and the relationships between the modules are carefully examined to avoid unnecessary duplication and help ensure smooth connectedness between them. The so-called bottom-up teaching approach chosen also assists in achieving a holistic induction into software. Each class session begins with an introduction to key concepts in a software coding/design assignment that the students then complete in the middle of the session, which ends with a thorough class discussion. A case study is presented relating to the iterative development of the strategic and tactical decisions in the classroom setting, and the resulting software, to sort an integer array in a hands-on process involving active student participation.

The topic of chapter 7 is a module that emphasises the crucial ability of problem-solving for software engineers in industry and advocates the pro-active introduction of a session to develop this ability among the students at an early stage in the undergraduate programme and preparatory to the introduction to programming. The approach advocated is one based on programming robots to solve certain challenging practical problems followed by graphical programming to simulate the same problem-solving tasks implemented earlier with the robots. A number of individual and group case studies are presented, and very high student involvement and satisfaction are reported due to the visual character of the teaching/learning.

A persuasive case for including a detailed, industry-oriented module on structured parallel programming within undergraduate and postgraduate degree programmes in software engineering is set out in chapter 8. Because the computer and telecommunications industries are rapidly developing and exploiting multi-core processing units, the demand of those and other industries for software engineers with parallel programming skills and abilities to fully exploit these devices is also rapidly growing. In response, an introductory module with three strands, parallel architectures, structured parallelism, and parallel programming is described in this chapter.

The theme of chapter 9 also emphasises the importance of active pedagogy and active learning by students, in this case for the development of expertise in the software systems for enterprise resource planning. These systems are used to organise and integrate the full range of business processes, including, very frequently, change management processes. They can encompass a wide range of technical developments as well as organizational and human resource implications. The module developed begins with the initial analysis by the class group of the major factors involved in choosing an appropriate enterprise resource planning software system and proceeds through the physical preparation of the computer laboratory workplace, and the assignment of tasks and schedules to the different student work groups. The next phase consists of producing comprehensive worksheets on the range of functional and technical practices (so-called closed practices) to be managed in the system and then to create the framework for developing new functionalities and practices (so-called open practices). The final phase of the module is the development and implementation of a set of objective evaluations with appropriate weightings. Thus, this chapter introduces a profoundly industry-oriented theme with extensive technical and software content, but also with extensive social functionalities relating to the workforce and the customers of the enterprise.

Chapter 10 has a wide-ranging discussion on the fundamental values and necessity for co-operation between the software industry and the higher education institutions in the provision of software education to the future designers and managers of the complex software systems that will underpin the next generation of industrial and societal processes. The chapter also introduces comprehensive approaches to and preparations for the development of industry-oriented undergraduate and postgraduate software engineering programmes.

Section 4 has one chapter on the key issue of quality assurance in international software education.

Earlier chapters refer in some detail to quality assurance, but Chapter 11 provides a comprehensive description and analysis of the vital need for quality assurance on the international level in higher software education to ensure the production of skilled engineers that can be relied on to produce world-class software for the world market. The presentation is in the context of the increasing internationalization of software education and the increasing requirements of national and international authorities for the assurance of quality of software and therefore of software engineers. The chapter proposes seven prime factors, *motivation, purpose, team, environment, method, fitness,* and *safety,* which provide a guiding framework for delivering quality and for assessing that quality. It discusses the particular methods used across the globe to achieve these goals, particularly in international inter-cultural programmes, and explains how the seven factors are invaluable in the quality characterization of such programmes.

Section 5 is concerned with e-learning and support tools.

Here, there is one chapter, chapter 12, which describes an ambitious, comprehensive, Web-based system for training software students in IT project management. A special feature of the approach is the development of a personalised competency catalogue, which, together with a parallel reference competency map of the required outcomes (knowledge and skills) of the training course, identifies the gap between these and allows the design of a personalised course for each student. Furthermore, the educational content of the system, which is competency-based, is built into an ontological structure, which allows the development of large numbers of different personalised learning paths. This would have valuable application in undergraduate and postgraduate programmes, and also in a wide range of lifelong learning situations, a vital aspect of the continuing professionalism of software engineering.

HOW THIS BOOK IMPACTS THE FIELD AND CONTRIBUTES TO THE SUBJECT MATTER

This book has a global perspective for the holistic education of the student software engineers and professionals who will construct the next phase of the profoundly global software industry.

Each chapter describes compelling experiences from many countries and derives fundamental lessons on the profound value of software industry-oriented higher education. Most of the chapters define and re-define software industry-oriented education, but generally focus on the software industry as a partner, collaborator, and certainly as an inspiration in constructing the form and content of the education and training being provided.

Significant course modules and complete undergraduate and postgraduate programmes are described in their origins and initial development, in the evolution of their teaching and learning philosophies, in their implementation and quality assurance, and in their evaluation by cohorts of students. The book is full of experiences, practical research investigations, helpful insights and lessons, as well as directions and guidelines in this work. Throughout, the efforts by the developers of these course modules and overall programmes to grow a range of forms of co-operation with the software industry so as to capture the applied real-life nature, and the essence of the industrial practice of software development in the different countries are described in detail.

The central thrust and argument is to inform fellow academics in every country across the world of the value and, indeed, necessity of this approach to the education and formation of the next generation of software professionals who will shape the coming knowledge economy and society. This argument is also directed to the software industry which can and must have a major strategic role in this educational task.

Most fundamentally, the book is dedicated to the students of software and to the development of the most suitable, most fruitful, and most productive educational and training programmes that will enable them to contribute capably, creatively, and with integrity throughout their careers to shaping the global knowledge society.

Matthew Hussey
Dublin Institute of Technology, Ireland

Bing Wu
Dublin Institute of Technology, Ireland

Xiaofei Xu
Harbin Institute of Technology, China

Section 1
Introduction to Industry Oriented Software Education

Chapter 1
Introduction to the Broad Concepts Underlying this Book

Matthew Hussey
Dublin Institute of Technology, Ireland

ABSTRACT

This introductory chapter presents general suggestions on the concept of quality-assured industry-oriented higher education in software engineering that relate to and underpin the other chapters in the book. The body of work reported here was based initially on the close co-operation since 2002 between Dublin Institute of Technology in Ireland and Harbin Institute of Technology in China, and on the subsequent development and propagation of this co-operation across Europe and China. The experiences described come from a range of countries, France, Spain, Germany, United Kingdom, Romania and Turkey, as well as China and Ireland. They capture many of the interesting and valuable lessons of these past eight years of thinking and research and development relating to international software industry-oriented higher education in the broad context of the global striving towards the knowledge economy. They make the case for a strong role for software industry-oriented higher education in the production of the software architects, developers, and engineers required for the future.

INTRODUCTION

There is a deep-going review and re-engineering of higher education, its roles and institutions, underway throughout the world. Technological and societal changes are buffeting the universities and other higher education institutions, having revealed shortcomings in their services to the communities and societies in which they exist and on which they depend for their continued vitality (Beckman et al., 1997; Jaakkola et al., 2008; Kral & Zemlicka, 2008). Together with international and national agencies, the higher education institutions have been struggling to fully comprehend

DOI: 10.4018/978-1-60960-797-5.ch001

the forces of change and their implications and to forge new roles and identities as major shapers of the intellectual leadership of the changing society in every country (Dearing, 1997; OECD, 1995; World Bank, 2000).

A key force in driving these changes in society and in education is the rapidly developing computing and software industries, with their deep and often revolutionary working out in almost every aspect and corner of society. A knowledge economy and a knowledge society of unknown depth and extent are being forged across the world. Within this context, the development of the hardware systems and the practical and creative software required is dynamic in nature and the software industry itself, rather than the higher education institutions, plays the fundamental role in this process. The discipline of software development is thoroughly world-wide and the software industry is thoroughly globalized. For the optimum development of the software industry and of society into the future, higher education institutions need to produce graduates at primary and postgraduate degree levels that are well matched to the needs of local and international industry as well as being in tune with the needs of society in general. The central argument of this book is that in order to do so, these institutions need to be oriented to the software industry and engaged in a wide range of collaborations with the industry, involving their students and staff. This also requires a close and committed engagement by the software industry with the educational institutions. And there is need for the dynamic academic/industrial programmes to be fully quality assured through assessment and monitoring by external and international academic and industrial experts and peers.

In this regard, new and some old and neglected models of higher education with potentially improved matching to the needs of society are being developed, re-developed and evaluated.

The Dublin Institute of Technology Higher Education Model

The Dublin Institute of Technology (DIT) and its predecessor colleges have an historical legacy of over 120 years of higher education provision with an applied, technological, vocational, professional and industry-oriented emphasis mainly for young people in Ireland, but increasingly for those in other countries in Europe and beyond as well. In the past, this emphasis has prepared young people for technician and graduate employment in a wide range of scientific, engineering, service and business areas. DIT helped to serve as midwife in Dublin and Ireland for the revolutions in electricity, telecommunications and electronics, water and sewage, transport, construction, chemicals and pharmaceuticals, hospital laboratory and clinical technologies, retail and wholesale business and management and others since 1887. It has done so through producing skilled personnel for the workforce that introduced and maintained these emerging technologies by offering relevant and up-to-date industry-oriented education, training and research programmes (Duff et al., 2000).

DIT has strongly retained this industry-oriented approach to higher education in the current phase of industrial, social and economic development that has been fuelled by the information technology/communications revolution of the past thirty years (DIT, 2006, 2007). In now seeking to meet the challenges posed by the emerging knowledge economy, not only is DIT striving to continue to meet the immediate demands of its local community and economy, but is also continuing to broaden its perspective to meet the needs of Ireland as a player in the broader European Union (EU) and global community (Forfás, 2007). This challenge is formidable and is impacting upon all aspects of higher education policy and delivery. It requires that the higher education institutions absorb all the lessons of earlier successes to guide the re-engineering that is underway.

The Collaboration Between DIT and Harbin Institute of Technology

Some initial re-engineering steps at institution level and implementation level are already underway within DIT. In the area of IT education significant enhancements to the content, structure and delivery of the programmes offered, have been made and continue to be made to meet the needs of the IT industry in Ireland. The international collaboration it has established with Harbin Institute of Technology (HIT) in Harbin in the north of China is a significant indicator of its wider perspective on the global community (Lawless et al., 2007).

The Chinese government facilitated this collaborative link and has been interested since 2001 in the track-record of DIT in education oriented to the IT industry. This interest arose particularly in the context of that government's strategic decision in 2001 to establish thirty five National Pilot Schools of Software throughout China. In particular, two of the outstanding highlights of this collaboration inspire this book. These were the 3-year (2003–2006) European Union Asia-Link project, termed the EMERSION project (involving the University of Wolverhampton from the United Kingdom as a third partner), and the establishment in 2004 of the annual (2005–2010) China-Europe International Symposia on Software Industry-Oriented Education (CEISIE).

The EMERSION Project

This project was devised to investigate the adaptation of DIT's productive approach to software industry-oriented education at home in Ireland to the conditions and situation in Harbin in China. It was viewed in China as a pilot experiment in the Chinese government's efforts to reform its traditional, mainly theoretically based, higher education system for software engineering so as to better meet the rapidly evolving industrial, economic and social challenges of the knowledge economy in China (Lawless et al., 2007; Ministry of Education, 2001; Wen, 2003).

Investigating and devising the best mechanisms to achieve high quality industry-oriented education in general, has been the main corporate focus of DIT throughout its existence, including this recent collaboration with China. The achievement of the EMERSION project has been to successfully develop an industry-oriented education model for software education in China. This success was based on the experience of all the partners and their willingness to clearly identify the challenges and requirements in China, and then to develop and implement a comprehensive model to meet them. This project has provided many striking lessons to those involved and these lessons can be of great value to the wider higher education community facing similar challenges.

The CEISIE Symposium Series

The first two sessions of the ground-breaking series of China-Europe International Symposia on Software Industry-Oriented Education took place in Harbin in 2005 and 2006, and the third was held in Dublin in 2007 (Proceedings, 2005; Wu et al., 2007). The fourth annual session, in 2008, was held in GuangZhou and the fifth was in Bordeaux in France in 2009 (Proceedings 2009; Wu & Bourrrières, 2010). In 2010 the symposium returned to China to Xi'an (Proceedings, 2010) and the seventh session is scheduled for Wolverhampton in 2011.

The main overlapping themes of these symposia, broadly corresponding to the themes that echo throughout this book, comprise the following, frequently broadly overlapping, topics:

- the nature of the modern software industry
- evaluation and innovation in software education
- education for the knowledge economy and society
- internationalization of software education

- skills development for modern service industry and enterprise application software
- education for IT management
- the knowledge, skills and ethics requirements for software professionals
- the role of industry as stakeholders in computing education
- research underpinning industry oriented software education (IOSE)
- the ethos of IOSE
- student placement issues
- models for IOSE and co-operation between industries and software education institutions
- curricula for IOSE
- quality evaluation and assurance in IOSE
- e-learning and support tools.

These symposia have had attendances of more than 100 on each occasion, with participants from every continent. They have also had a wide range of significant international sponsors and supporters including:

- Higher Education Department of the Ministry of Education (China)
- Harbin Institute of Technology (China)
- Dublin Institute of Technology (Ireland)
- University of Wolverhampton (United Kingdom)
- Ministry of Higher Education and Research (France)
- Higher Education Authority (Ireland)
- European Virtual Laboratory for Enterprise Interoperability (France)
- Mairie de Bordeaux (France)
- Centre National de Recherche Scientifique (France)
- EU-Asia-Link Programme (European Commission)
- HIT ShouChuang Co. Ltd.
- Langchao Group Genersoft Co. Ltd.
- Beijing Kingsoft Software Co. Ltd.
- Microsoft Research Asia

- Enterprise Ireland
- China Software Industry Association
- Computer Education, China
- Xi'an Software Park (China)
- IT Future Centre, Advantage (United Kingdom)
- Heilonjiang Computer Federation (China).

The Appendix to this chapter, provides a detailed list of the authors, university affiliations and the titles of the presentations in each of the first six symposia.

THE SOFTWARE INDUSTRY AND HIGHER EDUCATION INSTITUTIONS TODAY

Industry underpins society to a large extent through the provision of products and services to the market as well as employment and income for citizens. In its widest connotation, industry includes manufacturing and service industries, agriculture, art and culture, business, commerce, trade, transport, and also government, inter-governmental and international agencies, and all of these depend on and exploit constantly developing technologies and automated systems. Most industries have international ramifications, with operations spanning the globe operating on a 24-hour basis. Probably the quintessential globalized industry is the dynamically changing software industry and this requires a workforce with intellectual and creative depth, and a commitment to lifelong skill development and learning so as to enable those involved to cope with and master the changing technological, functional and behavioural demands across the increasingly globalised world (Friedman, 2005). But the fact that the software industry underpins, supports and helps shape virtually all other industries and even societal structures, indicates its deeply strategic nature for the future.

In response to this dynamic flux in industry, the economy and society in general, the higher education institutions have framed a range of responses. At the insistence of their governments, they have opened their doors to wider participation, to more academically weak students, to more mature students, to students with disabilities and to students from other countries. In consequence they have undergone a phase of rapid growth and expansion that still has to be evaluated thoroughly. Another consequence has been the development of quality assurance procedures by the institutions to seek to guarantee to students, governments, future employers and society in general that the academic standards achieved and the skills and competencies acquired by students and graduates in the larger mass higher education institutions are comparable to or superior to those achieved in previous generations (Duff et al., 2000). For instance, within the particular context of Irish higher education, it is notable that the development of effective quality assurance systems has been a significant aspect of recent reviews of higher education, now required under legislation (EUA, 2006: OECD, 2004). More generally still, the higher education institutions have also begun to engage in frequent self-study and strategic planning, seeking to extend and deepen their involvement in and active engagement with the widest range of elements and layers of society. One fruitful model for this newer, wider engagement is the development and implementation of industry-oriented education programmes, as described and advocated in this book in relation to the software industry.

SOFTWARE INDUSTRY-ORIENTED EDUCATION

The main initial outcome sought of software industry-oriented higher education is the achievement of a smooth and efficient transition from recent graduate to productive employee, and ultimately to entrepreneur/employer. The idea is to minimise the frequent need for extensive and expensive on-the-job training of the new graduate recruit to the workplace. The subsequent transition of the employee to entrepreneur, individually or with a team of colleagues, should also be considerably facilitated.

For success, the processes of industry-oriented education must be characterised by the development and implementation of an education quality assurance/enhancement system with suitable procedures and a strong industry involvement, aimed at achieving a number of key programme learning outcomes, including

- acquisition of relevant expertise, theoretical and practical, to the standard normally required for the particular degree award
- awareness/experience of working in the industry context and the full range of related boundary conditions
- documented practical experience of working in multi-level teams
- management competency in individual and collective projects
- possession of discipline, sense of responsibility and integrity
- good inter-personal communication skills and acceptable personal and social behaviour for working in an industry setting
- commitment to professional and career development and lifelong learning
- possession of a personal portfolio indicating many of these attributes
- awareness of the global and societal context of the industry.

An approach encompassing these attributes offers rewards to the new graduates, to the higher education institutions, to the industries they serve, as well as to general social cohesion in society. The young graduates are sharply attuned to the professional industry environment. The institutions tend to provide relevant programmes and research, and produce employable industry-oriented graduates.

The co-operating industries involved are in a good position to recruit better-prepared and more productive employees as well as acquiring a wider intellectual hinterland and the potential for relevant and fruitful research and development outcomes.

IMPLEMENTATION MECHANISMS FOR INDUSTRY-ORIENTED EDUCATION

The main services provided by higher education institutions are higher education and training in relevant skills and competencies, principally but not exclusively to primary degree level. Shorter education and training programmes, and increasingly, more advanced postgraduate degree level programmes are also important natural parts of their armoury of services. Postgraduate research programmes leading to higher degrees are vital to the knowledge generation as well as the knowledge/skill teaching functions of these institutions. Commercial research, development and consultancy services to industry, government and society are also provided to some extent by higher education institutions, generally as income-generating enterprises.

The interactions between a higher education institution and industrial companies can be manifold and may include:

- interactive collaboration in research, consultancy and other projects
- seamless direct relationships through industry representation in teaching and research programme planning and implementation, student and staff internship/placement in companies, industry staff placement in the institution, research/development co-operation, etc.
- indirect relationships through government and other think-tanks, national and other strategic planning processes, professional, accreditation and standards bodies, etc.

- involvement of authoritative representatives of industrial companies at all stages (planning, validation, implementation, assessment, review and change, of taught and research programmes, overall institutional reviews and strategic planning processes) in the quality assurance procedures of the higher education institution as outlined above.

Another significant area for such constructive quality-assured interaction with industry is the recruitment, induction, training, and continuing development of the relevant staff of the higher education institution, and particularly the process of forming and developing the team to deliver each programme. Recruitment of teaching staff for the programme with senior experience in relevant industries can be very advantageous. Building and maintaining the cohesion, general agreement on the industry-oriented approach and constructive participation of all the stakeholders in the programme team are vital for success.

These interactions need to be carefully managed, collectively agreed and fully documented. In particular the associated documentation should unambiguously reflect the interactive and constructive nature of the relationship between the higher education institution and the industry that underpins the industry-oriented education model.

The ultimate employment of the graduates and their employers' evaluation of their work performance should provide a definitive indicator of the success of the industry-oriented education model, and indeed indications on ways to continuously enhance the model.

QUALITY ASSURANCE IN INDUSTRY-ORIENTED EDUCATION

Ensuring an ethos of quality enhancement is particularly vital for industry-oriented education and must be the joint aim of all involved. This ethos must pervade all aspects of the educational programme and so it is necessary that all stakeholders, students and academic and administrative staff of the higher education institution, industry staff and governmental authorities, take responsibility for the quality of their individual components but also for the integration of all of the components. Teamwork is a basic requirement. The quality assurance system of procedures and structures is a framework to facilitate this teamwork amongst the stakeholders (Duff et al., 2000).

Quality Assurance in Taught Courses and Programmes

Quality assurance procedures first come into play at the stage of proposing a new programme and constructing the case for the programme by the development team. This case needs to be based on industry and society developments and needs and on the availability of requisite resources. Authoritative input from industry and other professional and government agencies is essential in establishing a firm foundation for the programme. The case must itemize and give evidence for the industry needs, the feasibility of the programme objectives, the learning outcomes and how these match the industry and society needs, the industry support for the programme and the resources both human and physical required to offer the programme.

After the proposed programme has been given outline approval by the higher education institution the development team has to develop and document the complete curriculum for the programme. The programme document must provide the aims and learning outcomes for each stage and each module, the detailed syllabus for each module including teaching, learning and assessment strategies, the arrangements for industry input, and guidelines for specific aspects of the programme (e.g. student handbook for each stage, industrial placements, final year and other projects, etc.).

Assistance, advice and involvement by industry representatives in the process of drafting this document is essential.

The programme must next be validated by an independent panel of experts, with authoritative members from both the institution and industry. This validation panel visits and inspects the institution, meets the programme team and considers the proposal in detail. When the proposal is adjudged satisfactory, possibly after the inclusion of recommendations by the panel, the panel recommends that the programme be approved to be offered to students and that successful students on the programme be eligible for the degree or other award of the higher education institution.

The programme management committee, with academic and industry members, manages the overall delivery of the programme as specified in the programme document. Assessments of the students provide vital corrective feedback within the quality assurance system and are administered as specified in the programme document under the regulations of the institution. External examiners are an essential element of external peer review in relation to assessments and both academic and industrial external examiners should be are appointed to emphasize and ensure the industry orientation of the programme and its learning outcomes.

The assessment board, a formal meeting of all internal and external examiners involved, determines each student's results for the overall assessment process for a given stage of the programme, guided by the general institution assessment regulations, any specific additional regulations specified in the programme document and the principles of natural justice and equity.

The operation of the programme should be evaluated annually. The programme management committee reviews the implementation of the programme, including student, staff and industry feedback as well as the assessment results and the report of each external examiner on the assessment processes and their observations on the programme in general. The key outcome of this review is an annual report containing an evaluation of the current implementation of the programme, a summary of the assessment results with comments and suggestions by the external examiners and industry collaborators, the key feedback observations of students, staff and industry representatives involved, and an action plan for improvements in the implementation of the programme.

The overall programme is also evaluated periodically, usually once every two to five years. This should involve a root-and-branch self-study and evaluation of the programme and its implementation, taking into account its success in fulfilling the requirements of the relevant industry (industrial placements, learning outcomes, numbers of graduates), the changes underway in the industry, the student feedback received, the feedback from industry on students in placement and graduates employed, the outcomes of the lecturer evaluation processes in the programme, and comparison with similar programmes in other institutions at home and abroad. It should also involve a review of the industry it serves and other relevant local and national developments by the programme management committee. A reviewed programme document is prepared and submitted to an independent review panel and examined in a similar manner to the initial validation, for continuing approval as a degree or other award programme.

Quality Assurance in Research Programmes

Industry-oriented postgraduate research programmes must be subjected to a broadly similar framework of quality assurance procedures, with industry involvement at all key points. In this case the stages at which industry collaboration and peer review are vital for corrective feedback and other quality assurance activities include

- elaboration of an appropriate research plan
- agreement on any requisite terms of ethical approval, confidentiality and intellectual property rights
- the formation and continuing development of the supervision team of staff from the higher education institution and the industrial companies involved
- provision of access to equipment and work stations
- the annual report and evaluation of the progress of the research
- evaluation of the thesis preparatory to submission
- assessment of the thesis and the *viva voce* by external academic and industry examiners
- feedback from the student on the research experience
- feedback for industry on the student in placement and of the graduate employed
- the preparation of papers on the work for publication
- the further industrial exploitation of the outcomes of the research.

CONCLUSION

The collective agreement on the industry-orientation and on the quality assurance framework by the staff members of the higher education institution and of the industrial companies participating, is key to the success and continuing enhancement of industry-oriented education. This requires strong commitment and leadership by the presidents and deans of the institutions and the directors of the companies, as well as time and dedication on the part of staff.

Every effort must be made to maintain constructive, friendly, flexible, helpful and non-exploitative dialogue and goodwill between the relevant staff of the institution and the industrial companies involved. Issues of ethics, confidentiality, intellectual property and academic freedom must be agreed at an early stage in these interactions. Dialogue between institution and industry should be supported by an appropriate partnership agreement whose terms of reference are such that neither side dictates the direction but listens to advice and acts by mutual agreement wherever possible (Carroll et al., 2005). Ultimately however, the responsibility for academic standards must rest with the higher education institution concerned as there may be sound pedagogical reasons why certain courses of action may not be appropriate within the academic context.

The industry-oriented approach outlined throughout this book in relation to the software industry, while still a work-in-progress, has been shown to be extremely fruitful and applicable as much in China as in Ireland and many other countries in Europe.

It offers significant potential for enhancing the engagement between higher education institutions and industry and society in general. It offers considerable social rewards. It can make a significant contribution to the fundamental re-engineering processes underway within the higher education institutions and significant assistance in managing and ameliorating the dislocating processes of technological change within society.

REFERENCES

Beckman, K., Coulter, N., Khajenouri, S., & Mead, N. (1997). Collaborations: Closing the industry–academy gap. *Institute of Electrical and Electronic Engineering (IEEE). Software, 14*(6), 49–57. doi:10.1109/52.636668

Carroll, D., Lawless, D., Hussey, M., O'Leary, C., Mtenzi, F., Gordon, D., & Collins, M. (2005). Stakeholders in the quality process of software engineering education. In *Proceedings of the 2nd China-Europe International Symposium on Software Industry-Oriented Education.* [New Series]. *Journal of Harbin Institute of Technology, 12*, 88–93.

Dearing, R. (1997). *Higher education in the learning society.* London, United Kingdom: National Committee of Inquiry into Higher Education.

Dublin Institute of Technology (DIT). (2006). *Handbook for academic quality enhancement.* Dublin, Ireland: Dublin Institute of Technology.

Dublin Institute of Technology (DIT). (2007). *Regulations for postgraduate study by research* (4th ed.). Dublin, Ireland: Dublin Institute of Technology.

Duff, T., Hegarty, J., & Hussey, M. (2000). *The story of the Dublin Institute of Technology.* Dublin, Ireland: Blackhall.

Duff, T., Hegarty, J., & Hussey, M. (2000). *Academic quality assurance in Irish higher education: Elements of a handbook.* Dublin, Ireland: Blackhall.

European Universities Association (EUA) Institutional Evaluation Programme. (2006). *EUA reviewers' report: Review of quality assurance in Dublin Institute of Technology.* Brussels, Belgium: European Universities Association.

Forfás. (2007). *5th report of the expert group on future skills needs- tomorrow's skills needs: Towards a national skills strategy.* Dublin, Ireland: Forfás.

Friedman, T. L. (2005). *The world is flat: A brief history of the twenty-first century.* New York, NY: Farrar, Straus & Giroux.

Jaakkola, H., Henno, J., & Rudas, I. J. (2006). IT curriculum as a complex emerging process. In [Washington, DC: Institute of Electrical and Electronic Engineering.]. *Proceedings of the Institute of Electrical and Electronic Engineering International Conference on Computational Cybernetics, ICCC,* 1–5. doi:10.1109/ICCCYB.2006.305731

Kral, J., & Zemlicka, M. (2008). Engineering education - a great challenge to software engineering. In *Proceedings of the 7th Institute of Electrical and Electronic Engineering/Advanced Cellular Internet Service International Conference on Computer and Information Science (ICIS 2008)* (pp. 488-495). Washington, DC: Institute of Electrical and Electronic Engineering.

Lawless, D., Wu, B., Carroll, D., Gordon, D., Hussey, M., O'Leary, C., et al. O'Shea, B. & Xu, X. (Eds.). (2007). *An industry-oriented model for software education in China: Adapting an Irish model to Chinese conditions*. Dublin, Ireland: Blackhall.

Ministry of Education. (2001). *China, File No. [2001] 3*. Beijing, China: Government of China.

Organization for Economic Co-operation and Development (OECD). (1995). *Education at a glance*. Paris, France: Organization for Economic Co-operation and Development.

Organization for Economic Co-operation and Development (OECD). (2004). *Review of national policies for higher education: Review of higher education in Ireland, examiners' report, EDU/EC (2004) 14*. Paris, France: Organization for Economic Co-operation and Development.

Proceedings of the 2nd China-Europe International Symposium on Software Industry-Oriented Education. (2005). *Journal of Harbin Institute of Technology (New Series), 12 (Supplement)*. Harbin, China: Harbin Institute of Technology.

Proceedings of the 4th China-Europe International Symposium on Software Industry-Oriented Education. (2007). *Acta Scientiarum Naturalium, 46*(2). GuangZhou, China.

Proceedings of the 6th China-Europe International Symposium on Software Industry Oriented Education. (2010). *Computer Education, 9*(117). Xi'an, China.

Wen, J. (2003). *Government work report*. 10th Chinese National People's Congress (NPC). Beijing, China: Government of China.

World Bank. (2000). *Constructing knowledge societies: Challenges for tertiary education*. New York, NY: World Bank.

Wu, B., & Bourrières, J.-P. (Eds.). (2010). Educate adaptive talents for IT applications in enterprises and interoperability. In *Proceedings of 5th China-Europe International Symposium on Software Industry Oriented Education*). Talence, France: University of Bordeaux.

Wu, B., MacNamee, B., Xu, X., & Guo, W. (Eds.). (2007). *Proceedings of the 3rd China-Europe International Symposium on Software Industry-Oriented Education*. Dublin, Ireland: Blackhall.

KEY TERMS AND DEFINITIONS

Academic Quality Assurance: The procedures, involving peer monitoring, review and assessment by internal institutional academics as well as leading by external academics and industry experts (including international academics and other experts) of all aspects (academic, institutional, environmental, etc.) of each educational programme from inception to the production of graduates who must compete on the world stage.

Industry-Oriented Education Model: A higher education programme (principally in software in this book) with a curriculum and module syllabuses that cover the fundamental theory and contain considerable amount of practical implementation work, including projects on real-life industry problems, internship(s) in relevant industries, involvement of industry engineers in lecturing or supervising, etc., with a view to producing graduates who can readily make a smooth transition into the industry as productive employees.

Knowledge Economy: The developing worldwide economy which will strongly rest on knowledge and intelligent analysis and synthesis of knowledge through extensive computer systems to assist in the management of human affairs, and in which the role of the new generations of software engineers will be vital.

APPENDIX: AUTHORS AND TITLES OF PRESENTATIONS AT THE SIX ANNUAL CHINA-EUROPE SYMPOSIA ON SOFTWARE INDUSTRY-ORIENTED EDUCATION (CEISIE) (2005 – 2010)

1st China-Europe International Symposium on Software Industry Oriented Education, Harbin, China, January 2005

Bechkoum, K. (University of Wolverhampton, Wolverhampton), Using a VLE in an e-learning approach to software education

Carroll, D. (Dublin Institute of Technology, Dublin), EMERSION industry-oriented education model: quality assurance system requirements overview

Fu, Y. (Jiaotong University, Shanghai), A progress report on software engineering education of Shanghai Jiao Tong University

Hu, F. (Northwestern Polytechnical University, Xi'an), The innovation of software engineer education -- introduction of Northwestern Polytechnical University software college

Hussey, M. (Dublin Institute of Technology, Dublin), DIT's industry-oriented approach to education, and quality assurance in industry–oriented programmes

Hussey, M. (Dublin Institute of Technology, Dublin), Developing a quality assurance system for the proposed industry-oriented model for education in software development

Le, M., MOT on IT education

Li, H. F., & Li, N. (Harbin Institute of Technology, Harbin), Curriculum for university education of software professionals

Ma, P. J., & Wang, Y. Q. (Harbin Institute of Technology, Harbin), Enriching the education model for software professionals through work placement

Moreton, R. (University of Wolverhampton, Wolverhampton), Quality assurance: the UK context

Moreton, R., & Nash, A. (University of Wolverhampton, Wolverhampton), International business issues for software education

Newton, R. (University of Wolverhampton, Wolverhampton), Industrially relevant software education in the UK

Newton, R., & Bechkoum, K. (University of Wolverhampton, Wolverhampton), The international software environment

Newton, R., Moreton, R., Nash, A., & Bechkoum, K. (University of Wolverhampton, Wolverhampton), A model for managing industrial placements

Shu, L. The quality assurance system of education for software schools

Sun, Y. S., & Meng, X. X. (Harbin Institute of Technology at Wehei, Wehei), Research and implementation on training system of industrial software talents

Wu, B. (Dublin Institute of Technology, Dublin), Education for industry: the structure and practices of the School of Computing in DIT

Xu, X. F. (Harbin Institute of Technology, Harbin), The education model for the requirements of software industry in China

Yao, S. Z. (Beihang University, Beijing), Implementing the practice throughout the software education course

Zhu, Z., Pang, H. & Zhao, X. (Northeastern University, Shenyang), The exploration and practice of training practical software talents facing the requirements of enterprises

2nd China-Europe International Symposium on Software Industry Oriented Education, Harbin, China, January 2006

Cai, K. Y., Lu, W., Hu, F., & Wu, J. S. (Northwestern Polytechnical University, Xi'an), The introduction, absorption and improvements in the software curriculum

Carroll, D., Lawless, D., Hussey, M., O'Leary, C., Mtenzi, F., Gordon, D., & Collins, M. (Dublin Institute of Technology, Dublin), Stakeholders in the quality process of software engineering education

Chang, H. Y. (Sun Yat-sen University, Guangzhou), Planning and practice of the experimental teaching and learning scheme on the major of software engineering

Chen, D. M., Zhu, Z. L., & Gao, X. X. (Northeastern University, Shenyang), Study on model of industry oriented software education,

Chi, L. J., Sun, Y. S., & Wang, K. (Harbin Institute of Technology at Wehei, Weihei), On creating suitable syllabus in guaranteeing promotion of students' technical skills and comprehensive ability

Collins, M., Kelly, P., Lawlor, R., Liu, C., Mtenzi, F., & O'Leary, C. (Dublin Institute of Technology, Dublin), Industry-oriented software education in practice: a case study

Cui, Y. Q., & Rong, X. X. (Shandong University, Jinan), Fuzzy evaluation decision based on e-learning

Du, Y. G. (East China Normal University, Shanghai), Software education quality management system based on ISO9000

Fan, G. X,, Xu, J. C., Ma, P. J., & Xu, X. F. (Harbin Institute of Technology, Harbin), Education of industry-oriented software talents: exploration and practice

Gong, C. H., & Jin, M. (Hunan University, Changsha), Research on conformity practice of information technique and curricula

Gronau, N., Fröming, J., & Schmid, S. (University of Potsdam, Potsdam), Application of knowledge management methods for the improvement of education and training

Journal of Harbin Institute of Technology. 12, Dec 2005 (ISSN 1005-9113)

Kearns, B., & Lawless, D. (Dublin Institute of Technology, Dublin), Open source and software engineering education

Lawless, D., O'Leary. C., Gordon, D., Mtenzi, F., Carroll, D., & Collins, M. (Dublin Institute of Technology, Dublin), Developing an industry-oriented education model for software engineering education

Le Dinh, T., Leonard, M., & Dong Thi, B. T. (University of Geneva, Geneva), Lessons learned in capturing and managing knowledge used in information system development

Li, D., & Su, X. H. (Harbin Institute of Technology, Harbin), To cultivate the skills of problem solving in course 'computer organization'

Li, X. M. (Peking University, Beijing), Undergraduate computing education in China: a brief status and perspective

Liu, S., Xu, X. F., Ma, P. J., & Sun, Y. S. (Harbin Institute of Technology, Harbin), Education quality assurance system of school of software at HIT

Lv, G. X., Wu, Y., & Yao, L. (Harbin Institute of Technology, Harbin), The industrial practice for the software school of HIT

Meng, X. X., Qu, Y., & Li, X. Q. (Shandong University, Jinan), The understanding of the training mode in engineering talents cultivation

Mtenzi, F., Lawless, D., Gordon, D., O'Leary, C., Carroll, D., & Collins, M. (Dublin Institute of Technology, Dublin), Linking research to industrial oriented software education: the EMERSION experience

Nash, A., & Newton, R. (University of Wolverhampton, Wolverhampton), Systems project management and project procurement: critical factors for success

O'Leary, C. (Dublin Institute of Technology, Dublin), Enhancing industry oriented education with embedded real world experience

O'Leary, C., Lawless, D., Gordon, D., Carroll, D., Mtenzi, F., & Collins, M. (Dublin Institute of Technology, Dublin), Industry oriented curriculum design for software engineering

Ouyang, L. B., & Wu, K. S. (Hunan University, Changsha), PBL in team applied to software engineering education

Pan, L. Q., Li, H. F., & Tian, Y. X. (Harbin Institute of Technology, Harbin), An industry-oriented interactive mode for cultivating software talents

Qin, W. Z., Wan, J. Y., & Zhang, D. (Tongji University, Shanghai), Research on 'project-driven' teaching method in software engineering school

Qiu, X. P. (IBM China), What industry can help education: IBM's view and practice

Shao, D., & Luo, B. (Nanjing University, Nanjing), Design of the curricula in software engineering

Shi, H., & Horwood, J. (Victoria University, Melbourne), Development of the flexible learning materials for software development

Su, X. H., Li, D., & Ma, P. J. (Harbin Institute of Technology, Harbin), Ability-training-oriented teaching method in computer graphics course

Sun, Y. S., & Liu, S. (Harbin Institute of Technology at Wehei, Wehei), Teaching in English for Chinese students in computer science

Wu, Y., & Liu, N. Q. (University of Electronic Sciene and Technology of China, Chengdu), Software engineering education with special background

Wu, Y., Yao, L., & Lv, G. X. (Harbin Institute of Technology, Harbin), A simple analysis on teaching and learning skill for software education

Xu, X. F. (Harbin Institute of Technology, Harbin), The approach and practice of software industry oriented education in China

Yang, F., & Zhou, G. T. (University of Heilongjiang, Harbin), The research for and implementation of the reform in the architecture of software engineering courses

Zhang, H. Y., Lu, W., & Li, H. M. (Jiaotong University, Beijing), Software engineering specialty education system research and practice

Zhang, W. D., Qin, W. Z., Zhang, D., & Wang, C. M. (Tongji University, Shanghai), Run the school of software with the spirit of innovation, train practical software talents

Zhu, Z. L., Xu, Z., Li, Y. Q., & Bi. J. (Northeastern University, Shenyang), Service oriented application integration platform based on component technology

Zou. X. (Microsoft Research, Asia), Help students realize their potential: Microsoft perspective

3rd China-Europe International Symposium on Software Industry Oriented Education, Dublin, Ireland, February 2007

Buckley, K. A. & Bentley, H. (University of Wolverhampton, Wolverhampton), Welcome Week - making a good start at university

Carroll, D., Gordon, D., Lawless, D., Hussey, M., O'Leary, C., Mtenzi, F.,& Collins, M. (Dublin Institute of Technology, Dublin), Quality is never an accident: 3D aligned quality assurance

Chen, D., Vallespir, B. & Bourrières J. -P. (University of Bordeaux 1, Bordeaux), Research and education in software engineering and production systems: a double complementary perspective

Chen, D. M., Zhu, Z. L., Na, J. (Northeastern University, Shenyang), Practice teaching system in cultivating software talents

Ding, J. R., Chen, B., Liang, Y. X., & Sun, Y. S. (Harbin Institute of Technology at Wehei, Wehei), Interactive teaching practices on industry-oriented.NET courses

Fan, G. X., Sun, G. D., Chen, H., & Ma, P. J. (Harbin Institute of Technology, Harbin), On experience of industry-oriented education of software talents

Guo, H. Y., Chi, L. J., & Kuai W. J. (Harbin Institute of Technology at Wehei, Wehei), Cultivation of creativity and innovative thinking in students in the teaching of programming languages

Guo, W. H., & Xu, X. F. (Harbin Institute of Technology, Harbin), Utilizing the international teaching resource to support and enhance the education in NPSS at HIT

Gutowska, A., & Bechkoum, K. (University of Wolverhampton, Wolverhampton), The issue of online trust and its impact on international curriculum design

He, Q. G., Wang, K., Sun, Y.,& Ging, J. R. (Harbin Institute of Technology at Wehei, Wehei), On seamless connection to market education model and ERP

Kearns, B., Gordon, D., & Lawless, D. (Dublin Institute of Technology, Dublin), Open source, open sesame: teaching introductory programming using open source software

Li, H., Xu, X. F., Huang, H. J., & Jiang, S. X. (Harbin Institute of Technology, Harbin), Engineering innovation ability oriented MSE education model at HIT

Li, H. F., Xu, X. F., Huang, H. J., Chen, D., Vallespir, B., Bourrières, J. -P., & Doumeingts, G. (Harbin Institute of Technology, Harbin and University of Bordeaux 1, Bordeaux), Multi-culture and multi-discipline MSE educational programme between HIT and UBI

Meng, X. X., Li, X. Q., & Qu, Y. (Shandong University, Jinan), The new scheme and quality control system for developing skills and competencies of software engineering graduates

Nash, A., & Newton, R. (University of Wolverhampton, Wolverhampton), A case study analysis and proposal for operational change within the IT services department of a major organisation

O'Leary, C., & Kelly, P. (Dublin Institute of Technology, Dublin), Student-led instruction: deeper understanding and enhanced skills?

O'Leary, C., Lawless, D., Gordon, D., Carroll, D., Mtenzi, F., & Collins, M. (Dublin Institute of Technology, Dublin), 3D-Alignment as a method for curriculum development and an ethos for industry-oriented education

Pan, L. Q., Duggan, B., & Fitzpatrick, R. (Dublin Institute of Technology, Dublin), Experiences teaching website engagibility to computer science students

Penfold, B. (University of Wolverhampton, Wolverhampton), Using audience voting systems to identify students at risk

Rong, G. P., Shao. D., Zhao, Z. H., & Luo, B. (Nanjing University, Nanjing), A web-based body of knowledge and curriculum management system

Sun, Y. S., Liang, Y. X., Zhang, Y., Chen, B., & Wang, K. (Harbin Institute of Technology at Wehei, Wehei), Industry-oriented curriculum of software engineering series courses in school of software

Tung, F. C., Li, W. P., & Chan, W. (Peking University, Beijing), A software engineering curriculum for logistics/supply chain

Wang, Y. Q., Wang, J. Z., Sui, X. N., & Ma, P. J. (Harbin Institute of Technology, Harbin), Quantitative research on how much students comply with coding standard in their programming practices

Wang, Y. Q., Wei, T., Chen, Z., & Xu, X. F. (Harbin Institute of Technology, Harbin), Student studio and its contribution to incremental industrialization strategy

Wu, B., Xu, X. F., Lawless, D., & Bechkoum, K. (Dublin Institute of Technology, Dublin), EMERSION: Education to meet the requirements of software industry and beyond – establishing, implementing and evaluating an industry-oriented education model in China

Wu, Y., & Yao, L. (Harbin Institute of Technology, Harbin), A model of cultivating industrial talents in software education

Xu, X. F., & Wang, Z. J. (Harbin Institute of Technology, Harbin), Curriculum development on SSME in school of software of Harbin Institute of Technology

Yao, S. Z., Yuan, C. Z., Lin, G. G., & Tan, H. B. (Beihang University, Beijing), The curriculum and practice of the advanced software engineering for MSE

Zhu, Z. L., & Jing, B. (Northeastern University, Shenyang), Web services-based multilayer distributed enterprise information integration system

4th China-Europe International Symposium on Software Industry Oriented Education, Guangzhou, China, January 2008

Acta Scientiarum Naturalium Universitatis Sunyatseni, 46 (Supp. 2), 2007

Bechkoum, K. (University of Derby, Derby), Challenges facing higher education computing and IT departments

Carroll, D. (Dublin Institute of Technology, Dublin), Learing outcome analysis: analysing the design of an academic programme

Chen, D., Doumeingts, G., Vallespir, B., Bourrières, J. -P., & Poler, R. (University of Bordeaux 1, Bordeaux), Interop Master programme on interoperability of enterprise software and applications

Chen, D. M., Zhu, Z. L., & Gao, X. X. (Northeastern University, Shenyang), Secure software education in industry-oriented software talents cultivation

Chen, F., & Lei, H. (University of Electronic Science and Technology of China, Chengdu), Enhancing university-enterprise co-operation by meeting the needs of market – tentative idea about university-enterprose co-operation of software school

Chen, H. P, Li, H. F., Wang, L., Fan, G. X., Huang, H. J., & Xu, X. F. (Harbin Institute of Technology, Harbin), The practice of maintaining the feature of internationalization and industrialization for staff team in School of Software at HIT

Collins, M. (Dublin Institute of Technology, Dublin), Experiences in industry placement – shaping the student's mind in an industry-oriented software engineering curriculum

Franco, D. R., Gasquet Gomez, P., Poler, R., Bas Ortiz, Á., & Gómez, P. (Universidad Politécnica de Valencia, Valencia), Developing a common didactical offer for teaching international operations management in China, Italy and Spain: experiences and lessons learnt.

Gleeson, M., Reynolds, G., & Duggan, B. (Dublin Institute of Technology, Dublin), Web services and next generation workforce

He, Q. G., Ding, J. R., & Xin, G. D. (Harbin Institute of Technology at Wehei, Wehei), Discussion on designing industry oriented curriculum

Hu, Y., Chang, H. Y., & Chao, H. Y. (Sun Yat-sen University, Guangzhou), In order to improve the quality of software talents roundly, construct the software factory of Sun Yat-sen University

Hussey, M., Lawless, D., Wu, B., O'Shea, B., & Carroll, D. (Dublin Institute of Technology, Dublin), A contribution to the concept and philosophy of industry-oriented higher education

Kassel, S., Winkelmann, S., & Tittmann, C. (University of Applied Sciences, Zwickau), Decentralized building of complex software systems – an e-commerce study

Leonard, M. (University of Geneva, Geneva), A framework for service oriented teaching programs

Li, W. J., Chao, H. Y., & Chang, H. Y. (Sun Yat-sen University, Guangzhou), Learning by doing: practice and experience in the teaching of Master of Software Engineering students

Liu, J. (Tianjin University of Finance and Economics, Tianjin), Skill-based teaching model for undergraduate computing education

Liu, S., & Yin, S. J. (Harbin Institute of Technology, Harbin), Teaching experience sharing on course "Software quality assurance testing"

Pan, M. L., & Wu, H. (Sun Yat-sen University, Guangzhou), Practical software engineering training mode based on organisational learning

Poler, R., Sanchis, R., & Lario, F. C. (Universidad Politécnica de Valencia, Valencia), The interope-learning contents on enterprise interoperability

Qin, Z. G., Xia, Q., & Lei, H. (University of Electronic Science and Technology of China, Chengdu), Training software engineering talents: exploration and practice

Qu, Y., Meng, X. X., Li, X. Q., & Zhou, T. (Shandong University, Jinan), Discussion and innovation on the intensive cultivation pattern of software engineering talent

Reynolds, G., & Gleeson, M. (Dublin Institute of Technology, Dublin), Towards the deployment of flexible and efficient learning toolls: the thin client

Rosen, C. C. H., & Aldridge, S. (University of Derby, Derby), The importance of theory in computing curricula

Shao, D., Rong, G. P., Zheng, T., & Zhao, Z. H. (Nanjing University, Nanjing), Capability maturity model for software engineering education

Shu, Z. M., Li, W. J., & Zhou, X. C. (Sun Yat-sen University, Guangzhou), Practice and experience of teaching reform for compiler principle

Teich, T., Milizer, J., Unger, K., Zimmermann, M., & Kassel, S. (University of Applied Sciences, Zwickau), Visualizing supply chain structures and processes to evolve a better understanding for IT-related operations in mySAP ERP

Wan, H., & Li, W. J. (Sun Yat-sen University, Guangzhou), Helping students elicit and analyze service-oriented requirement using SPOM (subject-predicate-object method)

Wang, Y. Q., Su, H. D., Wang, J. Z., & Wang, B. (Harbin Institute of Technology, Harbin), How many students are ready to write quality programs complying with coding standards: a case study

Wang, Y. Q., Yang, F., Liu, P. J., & Collins, M. (Harbin Institute of Technology, Harbin), Quality assurance of peer code review process: a computer science based strategy

Wu, H., & Pan, M. L. (Sun Yat-sen University, Guangzhou), Incentive modes on software practical training education using enterprise's views

Xiong, Y. Y., Yin, D. S., & Li, W. J. (Sun Yat-sen University, Guangzhou), A co-operation of SYSU and EMC2: an example of SIOE

Xu, X. F., & Guo, W. H. (Harbin Institute of Technology, Harbin), How to cultivate the IT talents with international competition ability in the flat world

Xu, X. F., Liu, S., Wang, Z. J., & Huang, H. J. (Harbin Institute of Technology, Harbin), Strategic version on the development of 2nd type specialty services science and enterprise informationization in HIT

Yi, Y., Ma, F. T., Rong, F. L., & Li, X. X (Sun Yat-sen University, Guangzhou), An integrity specification by OO visual modelling of UML – a case study in computing education

Yuan, A. L., Qiao, L. X., & Guo, Q. (Harbin Institute of Technology, Harbin), The research and algorithm design on fuzzy indicator of teaching evaluate system

Zhang, J., Xu, J. L., & Ma, X. N. (Shandong University, Jinan), The research of optimizing the curriculum system of software engineering by course group method

Zhang., F., & Lei, H. (University of Electronic Science and Technology of China, Chengdu), A methodological analysis of IT planning and demand of corporate informationization system

5th China-Europe International Symposium on Software Industry Oriented Education, Bordeaux, France, May 2009

Alix, T., Jia, Z., & Chen, D. (University of Bordeaux 1, Bordeaux), Return on experience of a joint Master programme on enterprise software and production systems

Boudjlida, N., Jacquot, J. P., & Urso, P. (Université Nancy 1, Nancy), Software engineering education by example

Boutjlida, N., & Panetto, H. (Université Nancy 1, Nancy), The basis of interoperability: a curriculum

Boza, J., & Cuenca, Ll. (Universidad Politécnica de Valencia, Valencia), An educative experience of autonomous workgroups in the subject "enterprise computer tools"

Carroll, D. (Dublin Institute of Technology, Dublin), Analysing academic programme alignment: a pairwise comparison approach

Chen, D, & Vallespir, B. (University of Bordeaux 1, Bordeaux), MRPII learning project based in a unified common case-study: simulation, re-engineering and computerization

Jiang, B., Hu, Y., Pan, M. L., & Hu, Y. J. (Sun Yat-sen University, Guangzhou), Seeking after practice teaching mode of software engineering specialty: training high quality software talented person

Jullien, J. M., Martel, C., Vignollet, L., & Wentland, M. (University Claude Bernard, Lyon), EMé. a flexible environment for competences evaluation

Kassel, S., Schumann, C. A., & Winkelmann, S. (University of Applied Sciences, Zwickau), An integrated approach for teaching product data management: preparations for a focal course program of product life cycle management

Li, D. C., Zhu, Z. L., & Liu, Y. X. (Northeastern University, Shenyang), The exploration and practice of the innovative talent cultivation mode in software engineering

Li, H. F., Huang, H. J., Chen, H. P., & Xu, X. F. (Harbin Institute of Technology, Harbin), Knowledge structure and ability configuration of MSE

Li, X. M., X, J. & Xu, S. (University of Electronic Science and Technology of China, Chengdu), A government-university joint training model of software talents

Liu, S., Ma, P. J., & Xu, X. F. (Harbin Institute of Technology, Harbin), To improve MSE dissertation quality through comprehensive process management

Ma, L. J. (Tangshan Industrial Professional Technical College, Tangshan), The exploration and practice of curriculum reform based on the work process of computer network technology specialty

Meng, F. D., Tong, Z. X., & Chen, H. (Harbin Institute of Technology, Harbin), The analysis report on employment of undergraduates from 2006 to 2008 in School of Software at Harbin Institute of Technology

Min, H. Q., Wang, Z. Y., Zuo, B. H., & Xu, Y. (South China University of Technology, Guangzhou), Practice of software engineering postgraduate education

O'Leary, C., & Gordon, D. (Dublin Institute of Technology, Dublin), Creativity and open-ended assessment in system design

O'Leary, C., & Kelly, P. (Dublin Institute of Technology, Dublin), Guidelines for student-as-teacher service-learning projects

O'Sullivan, D., & Dooley, L. (National University of Ireland, Galway), Project based learning in applied innovation

Payne, D., & Toal, M. (Institute of Technology, Tallaght), Detecting plagiarism: do software packages help ?

Peng, Y., Zhang, Y. G., & Xu, J. C. (Harbin Institute of Technology, Harbin), Analysis of bilingual teaching methods for engineering courses in China

Rong, G. P., Shao, D., & Zhao, Z. H. (Nanjing University, Nanjing), Cultivate qualified software engineers usign PSP and TSP

Rosen C.C. H. (University of Derby, Derby), Overcoming student resistance to applying for placement

Ullberg, J., Johnson, P., & Lagerström. R. (Royal Institute of Technology, Stockholm), Education in enterprise architecture analysis: assessing interoperability of service oriented architectures

Wang, Q., Chen, X. C., & Chang, H. Y. (Sun Yat-sen University, Guangzhou), Project based software development training in undergraduate education of software engineering

Wang, Y. Q., & Xu, X. F. (Harbin Institute of Technology, Harbin), Review of our researches and practices under SIOE framework

Wang, Y. Q., Xu, X. F., & Liu, P. J. (Harbin Institute of Technology, Harbin), Institute-industry interaction in educating software talents: an interpenetration approach

Wang, Z. J., Wang, Y. Y., Chen, Y. & Xu, X. F. (Harbin Institute of Technology, Harbin), Enterprise application oriented tentative design of incremental labs for software architecture course

Wei, Z., Tao, Z., Lewis, C. H. M., & Fang, D. F. (Northwestern Polytechnical University, Shanxi), The theory and practice of bilingual teaching in "object-oriented software engineering"

Wu, B., & Bourrière, J. P. (2010). CEISIE2009 5th China-Europe International Symposium on Software Industry Oriented Education, Bordeaux, France. University of Bordeaux 1

Wu, Y., & He, H. (Harbin Institute of Technology, Shenzen campus, Shenzen), Nurturing software engineering professionals of the 21st century by cultivating comprehensive quality

Xu., X. F., Li, H. F., & Guo, W. H. (Harbin Institute of Technology, Harbin), An international Master programme on software engineering at HIT-NPSS

Zhang, T., Zhou, Q. M., & Zhu, Y. A. (Northwestern Polytechnical University, Xi'an), Software engineering curriculum discussion based on CDIO approach

Zhang, Y. P., Zhu, Y., Wu, J. S., & Cai, K. Y. (Northwestern Polytechnical University, Xi'an), Investigation and practical steps to enhance practical project ability of students in human-computer interface design

Zhong, T., Deng, J. H., & Qin, Z. G. (University of Electronic Science and Technology of China, Chengdu), The four-for-one software engineering education practice in UESTC

Zhu, S. X., Zhou, H. Y., & Wang, L. (Harbin Institute of Technology, Harbin), Curriculum framework for embedded engineering direction: exploration on the building of embedded engineering direction in school of software

6th China-Europe International Symposium on Software Industry Oriented Education, Xi'an, China, May 2010

Chen, D., Vallespir, B., Tu, Z. Y., & Bourrières, J. -P. (University of Bordeaux 1, Bordeaux), Towards a formal model of UB1-HIT joint Master curriculum

Chen, P. H., Hsu, W. H., & Fong, D. S. (Tungnan University, Taipei), Two-phase stepwise clustering by a virtual robot deploying in an obstacle region

Esendal, T., & Rogerson, S. (De Montfort University, Leicester), Developing the software professional: a fusion of disciplines

Fan, G. X., Wang, L., & Ma, P. J. (Harbin Institute of Technology, Harbin), Practice of process management of Bachelor students' internship and final project in HIT-NPSS

Gliniorz, R., Kassel, S., Schmucker, D., & Schumann, C. A. (University of Applied Sciences, Zwickau), Electronic and mobile learning courseware development for mechatronic training and education

Huang, M., Liu, Z., Linag, Xu., Lin, L., & Ge, J. P. (Dalian Jiao Tong University, Dalien), Exploration and practice of complex embedded software training model

Huysentruyt, J., & Chen, D. (University of Bordeaux 1, Bordeaux), Joint UB1-HIT Master programme engineering knowledge and engineering education

Jiang, H. (Dalien University of Technology, Dalien), Inspiration of computer science discipline development in American mini research university

Jiang, L. Y., Li, D. C. & Zhu, Z. L. (Northeastern University, Shenyang), Research and practice of the training model of industrialization in embedded software

Li, Y. L. (Henan University, Kaifeng), Research on undergraduate teaching practice for computer application professional

Liang, X., Huang, M., Wu, D., & Dong, C. H. (Dalien Jiao Tong University, Dalien), Research and practice of dual professional and compound software engineering curriculum

Liao, Z. F., Chen, Z. G., Yu, S., & Liu, L. P. (Central South University, Changsha), Research on software engineering one frame with four aspects in practical teaching system

Liu, L. P., & Chen, Z. G. (Central South University, Changsha), Study on the quality assurance and evaluation mechanism in college-enterprise co-operation

Liu, Q. (South China University of Technology, Guangzhou), A multi-objective education model for software engineering graduate

Liu, S., Li, X. Z., & Chen, P. (Dalien Nationalities University, Dalien), Research on employment-oriented IT experience training program

Liu, W. J., Wang, Y. G., Qiu, Y. F., & Qu, H. C. (Liaoning Technical University, Huludao), Application and research of software engineering practical teaching system

McLoughlin, H., & Toolan, F. (University College, Dublin), Name and conquer

O'Leary, C. (Dublin Institute of Technology, Dublin), Matching frameworks: qualifications mapping in Europe and China

Rosen, C. C. H. (University of Derby, Derby), Peer mentoring; an experience report

Sun, W., Zhou, Q., & Dai, l. (SunYat-sen University, Guangzhou), Exploration on teaching experience of software engineering practical training curriculum

Sun, X. D., Chang, H. Y., & Zhang, F. (Sun Yat-sen University, Guangzhou), An E-learning platform based on integrated modeling for personalized and intelligent selection of E-learning resource

Sun, Y. S., & Ding, J. R. (Harbin Institute of Technology at Wehei, Wehei), Application of elaboration theory of instruction in designing syllabus for software architecture and teaching practice

Tan, T., Wang, Y. M., & Li, X. M. (University of Electronic Science and Technology of China, Chengdu), Exploration and practice of international software talents cultivation

Toolan, F., & McLoughlin, H. (University College, Dublin), Discrete mathematics for program construction

Turner, S., & Hill, G. (University of Northampton, Northampton), Innovative use of robots and graphical programming in software education

Wang, C. D., Zhang, H., & Mo, X. L. (Tianjin University of Technology, Tianjin), Emphasis on practice teaching to deepen teaching reform of computer network

Wang, F. Y., Xiao, Y. Y., & Zhang, Y. (Tianjin University of Technology, Tianjin), Research on practice teaching reform on database system curriculum design

Wang, J., Li, X. Q., & Zhou, T. (Shandong University, Jinan), Research and implementation on cultivation and management pattern of engineering talent supported by informationization

Wei, C. Y., & Liu, C. (Qingdao University of Science and Technology, Qingdao), Exploration on embedded system education in communication engineering undergraduate program

Wu, Y., & He, H. (Harbin Institute of Technology, Shenzen campus, Shenzen), A simple discussion on E-commerce teaching and practice

Xu, X. F., Li, H. F., Wang, L., & Guo, W. H. (Harbin Institute of Technology, Harbin), The "MSE+X" programme in software engineering at HIT-NPSS

Xu, Y, Li, D., & Wang, Z. Y. (South China University of Technology, Guangdong), A postgraduate engineering education pattern on software engineering

Yadav, S. S., & Chen, M. X. (Xiamen University, Xiamen), CHECK-IT: internship oriented co-operation in software engineering education

Yang, J., Peng, C. Y., & Ou, Y. T. (South China University of Technology, Guangzhou), Innovation model of the industrialized software curriculum system based on school-enterprise co-operation

Zhang, Y., & Chen, S. Y. (Chongqing University, Chongqing), Cultivating program for software talents based on project driven

Zhang, Y. P., & Huang, Y. T. (Northwestern Polytechnical University, Xi'an), Curriculum reform research of introduction to computer systems

Zheng, W., Zhao, C., Ma, X. L., & Yang, J. J. (Northwestern Polytechnical University, Xi'an), Application of spiral learning method in software engineering study

Zhou, T., Li, X. Q., Li, L. X., & Wang, J. (Shandong University, Jinan), Discussion on talents cultivation of engineering-type software with CDIO education pattern

Section 2
International Higher Education Institution–Industry Co-Operation Models

Chapter 2
EMERSION:
Education to Meet the Requirements of Software Industry and Beyond – Establishing, Implementing and Evaluating an Industry–Oriented Education Model in China

Bing Wu
Dublin Institute of Technology, Ireland

Kamal Bechkoum
University of Northampton, UK

Deirdre Lawless
Dublin Institute of Technology, Ireland

Xiaofei Xu
Harbin Institute of Technology, China

ABSTRACT

China and the European Union both face the challenge of building dynamic and internationally focused knowledge economies. Information Technology (IT) is a key enabler of such economies and IT education must be at the forefront of any strategy to meet the challenges of building them. Recognising this, the School of Computing in Dublin Institute of Technology (DIT), Ireland, the National Pilot School of Software in Harbin Institute of Technology (HIT), China, and the School of Computing and Information Technology in the University of Wolverhampton (UW), United Kingdom, established a collaboration which resulted in the EMERSION (Education to Meet the Requirements of Software Industry and Beyond - Establishing, Implementing and Evaluating an Industry-Oriented Education Model in China) project. This project designed, implemented, and evaluated an education model with an industrial ethos to deliver sustainable, high-quality, and effective IT education in HIT. The project was completed in 2006, and this chapter presents a review of the main lessons that emerged from it.

DOI: 10.4018/978-1-60960-797-5.ch002

INTRODUCTION

China is advancing rapidly to become a competitive and dynamic knowledge economy with a thoroughly international perspective. The European Union (EU) shares a similar aim, having declared at its council meeting in Lisbon in March 2000 that the EU must become the most competitive and dynamic knowledge-based economy in the world capable of sustainable economic growth with more and better jobs and greater social cohesion. Achieving and sustaining such an economy involves many challenges, the central one of which consists of ensuring the quality and effectiveness of IT education.

Educational institutes in the EU and China must therefore be in the forefront of the efforts to meet this challenge. While traditional education models and practices in the higher education sector in China have been very successful in educating students for academic excellence, there have been problems in producing industry-oriented graduates, who can readily fit into the working environment of the Chinese software industry (Chinese Government Report, 2001). The parallel challenge for education institutions in EU countries is to enhance and improve their education programmes to ensure graduates meet the requirements of the software industry and the development of the most competitive and dynamic knowledge-based economy.

Recognising this, the School of Computing, Dublin Institute of Technology (DIT-SoC), the National Pilot School of Software, Harbin Institute of Technology (HIT-NPSS) and the School of Computing and Information Technology, University of Wolverhampton UK (UW-SCIT) initiated a collaboration in 2003 to address this challenge.

The collaboration and co-operation between DIT-SoC and HIT-NPSS had been initially established during the visit to DIT in January 2002 by an Education Delegation led by the Chinese Vice-Minister of Education, Mr. Lu, Fuyuan, where Prof. Xu, Xiaofei the Dean of NPSS-HIT was a delegation member. Impressed in general by the success of the Irish software industry, which was one of the top software exporting countries for some years around that time, and in particular by the industry-oriented quality-assured education ethos and practices as well as the high quality of industry-oriented lecturing staff within the DIT-SoC, Minister Lu invited DIT-SoC to develop collaborations with the Chinese National Pilot Schools of Software, and nominated HIT-NPSS to be the direct Chinese partner in the collaboration. The aim agreed was to pilot the establishment of an industry-oriented education model and lecturing team in the HIT-NPSS, to incorporate industry-oriented education practices.

As this collaboration progressed, the partnership recognized that their aims, objectives and timelines were closely aligned with those of the European Union Asia-Link programme which aimed to promote regional and multilateral networking between higher education institutions in the EU and Asia. There had been a long-term academic relationship between DIT-SoC and UW-SCIT, strongly based on their common high level commitment to an industry-oriented education philosophy and practice, and the three institutions put forward a joint submission to the Asia-Link programme and the EMERSION (Education to Meet the Requirements of Software Industry and Beyond - Establishing, Implementing and Evaluating an Industry-Oriented Education Model in China) project was approved in early 2003. The project was initially intended to run for 3 years from March 2003. However, the official starting date was delayed until July 2003, due to the SARS (Severe Acute Respiratory Syndrome) epidemic of the time.

AIMS AND OBJECTIVES OF THE EMERSION PROJECT

The primary aim of the EMERSION project was to leverage the experience of the project partners to design, implement and evaluate an education model with an industrial ethos to deliver effective, sustainable and high-quality IT education in China. More specifically, the project aimed to focus this model on the IT sector, to help meet the vast demands of the Chinese software industry and, furthermore, to foster positive relations between the EU and China.

Other aims were to contribute to the development of the EU knowledge-based economy by improving understanding of higher education processes and curricula in the software engineering area, to contribute to the emerging global knowledge industry, to increase the exchange of knowledge on leading research practice between the EU and China and assist in increasing EU-Chinese business opportunities through promotion of the project within the EU and China.

The project concerned one priority area in particular of the Asia-Link programme, *Human Resource Development,* with some cross-over activities into the other two priority areas of *Curriculum Development* and *Institutional and Systems Development.* The target groups of the project were the relevant staff of the partner institutions who would be involved in developing and implementing the model, the collaborating staff from different software companies, and the undergraduate and postgraduate students and software professionals who would benefit from the enhanced industry focus of the education model. In particular, establishing a lecturing team within HIT-NPSS with an industry-oriented ethos was identified as one of the most important prerequisites for success in establishing a sustainable industry-oriented education model. Cross-over components in the areas of *Curriculum Development* for industry-oriented curricula and *Institutional and Systems Development* for quality assurance systems and structures were also envisaged as essential.

The sequence of primary objectives set out for the EMERSION project were:

- to introduce an industry-oriented education philosophy and ethos to the management, teaching and support staff of HIT in China
- to establish a well-trained industry-oriented education team in HIT with the support of DIT and UW
- to share the successful industry-oriented education experiences of DIT and UW with HIT
- to demonstrate the industry-oriented teaching practices of DIT and UW through participation of staff from these institutions in the educational activities of HIT
- to develop suitable curricula for both postgraduate and undergraduate levels in HIT, with the emphasis not only on knowledge acquisition but also on developing students' ability to learn, and their creativity, hands-on experience and communication skills
- to enhance the design and practice of project supervision at HIT
- to establish an industry work placement programme in HIT to probe and help address the requirements of the local software industry in the Harbin area
- to establish a quality assurance system suitable for the industry-oriented education philosophy and ethos developed in HIT
- to enhance the research activities of both DIT and UW by establishing a supervision programme using the research skills and experience of HIT
- to further develop the well-established industry-oriented education practice of both DIT and UW by leveraging the skills and knowledge of HIT in advanced research areas
- to evaluate and promulgate the model with its involvement with the software industry in China, for the mutual benefit of trade and collaboration between the EU and China, and

- to create two-way study opportunities between the EU and China.

Collaborative activities to progress each of these objectives were pursued throughout the three years and a number of other significant results/impacts also emerged along the way (EMERSION project management team, 2004, 2005, 2006; Lawless et al., 2007).

SUMMARY OF MAJOR ACTIVITIES WITHIN THE EMERSION PROJECT

The majority of the effort during the project was concentrated on developing an industry oriented curriculum, supported by relevant teaching and learning methods and quality assurance model, and establishing a lecturing team with an agreed industry-oriented ethos and philosophy to implement this curriculum.

Human Resource Development

Through mutual visits of staff, workshops, participation in the full range of teaching activities, considerable effort was expended to establish a well-trained and experienced industry-oriented lecturing team in HIT-NPSS and, to assist in transferring skills acquired during the project from this lecturing team to other members of staff within HIT and beyond, by staff from HIT-NPSS. Within DIT and UW the skills and knowledge of lecturing staff were enhanced through increased knowledge and understanding of higher education processes and curricula in the software engineering area. In all three partner institutions a growing research community developed in the areas of teaching and learning in software engineering, as well as curriculum development for software engineering, that led to joint international peer-reviewed publications. Many mechanisms were provided for the exchange of staff and students between the partner institutions for purposes of research and skills development.

Extent of Staff and Student Exchange

Throughout the project an extensive exchange of staff and students between all three partner institutions was a fundamental feature. This international exchange facilitated considerable cultural interchange and a strong strand of peer review of academic and procedural issues among the participants from the three institutions. The highlights of these exchanges included

- 20 staff in HIT-NPSS received training as part of missions undertaken by DIT and UW staff in HIT
- 50 staff members from other National Pilot Software Schools in China experienced short training sessions delivered by DIT and UW staff in China
- 650 undergraduate students and 150 postgraduate students in HIT experienced the teaching and learning methods of the industry-oriented education model
- 13 staff from DIT and 8 staff from UW travelled to HIT on more than one occasion to participate in teaching and training missions
- 15 staff from HIT travelled to DIT and UW on more than one occasion to engage in training and teaching observation
- 5 members of HIT staff visited DIT and UW to participate in research discussions and training
- 9 MSc students from DIT travelled to UW to receive training and 1 PhD student from UW travelled to DIT to present at the DIT PhD conference
- 20 DIT staff attended a research workshop in DIT and with presentations on the research activities in HIT and UW and 10

UW staff attended the similar research workshop in UW to learn about the research activities of DIT and HIT

- some hundreds of software professionals from more than 20 Chinese companies involved in HIT's industrial placement programme were exposed to the ideas of industrial placement and participated actively in the industrial placement programme
- close to 100 software professionals in China were involved as project supervisors under the industrial placement guidelines developed in the project.

Curriculum Development

A fully-documented honours BSc programme in Computer Science and Software Engineering to be delivered in HIT-NPSS was developed with an industry-oriented ethos, while also integrating Chinese cultural dimensions. The details of the theoretical underpinning, the development and specification of the syllabus, including the industrial aspects, the quality assurance and enhancement procedures, and the measures relating to staff recruitment, training and continuing development, are described in Lawless et al. (2007).

Furthermore, the related undergraduate programmes in DIT and UW were also fundamentally reviewed and revised using the results of the project to reflect new content, new teaching, learning and assessment methods and new quality assurance measures. New undergraduate and postgraduate programmes were also developed in DIT and UW incorporating not only the content of the EMERSION education model but also using the skills developed by staff during the project. In particular a new degree in International IT Management and a new undergraduate module in International Comparative Studies in System Design were established in UW. The latter module is being used by all undergraduate IT courses. The experience gained during EMERSION was also used in the development and validation of an honours BSc

programme in Business Computing, currently delivered in-country in Colombo, Sri Lanka.

Institutional and Systems Development

Developing a new quality assurance system to support the software industry-oriented education model was based on the rich and long-existing academic quality assurance systems and experiences within DIT and UW and incorporated the existing quality assurance processes in HIT. A key activity was taking measures through extended workshops and staff meetings to transfer the lessons learned in the development and implementation of the quality assurance system to a wider audience within HIT, including staff beyond the teaching and administrative staff in HIT-NPSS.

Disseminating Widely the Philosophy and Practicalities of the Model

In addition to the participants presenting results and reviews of the project through academic papers and at government/industry forums/meetings in their home countries and elsewhere (Carroll et al., 2006; Lawless et al., 2004a; Lawless et al., 2004b; Lawless et al., 2005; Lawless et al., 2007; O'Leary et al., 2006a; O'Leary et al., 2006b), the most significant development was the founding in 2005 of the annual China-Europe International Symposium on Software Industry-Oriented Education (CEISIE). The first and second symposia were held in Harbin with a significant support from the Chinese Ministry of Education, the Chinese Software Association, Enterprise Ireland and Advantage West Midlands, UK. In subsequent years this event was held in Dublin, Guangzhou, Bordeaux and Xi'an (Proceedings, 2005, 2007; Wu et al., 2007; Wu & Bourrière, 2010). The next one is to be held in Wolverhampton, United Kingdom, in May 2011 with the main theme of *Green Computing in Higher Education*. These symposia and the collaborative networks developed from them were an invaluable outcome of the EMERSION project.

Broader Institutional and Political Aspects

Within all three partner institutions, the involvement of senior staff in a wide range EMERSION activities was remarkable. All three of the Presidents/Vice-Chancellors of the three institutions visited the partner institutions and attended many project events.

But, surprisingly, the project had a wide political/diplomatic footfall. In Ireland and China different government ministers, particularly from the Education Ministries, sought briefings on the progress of the project and/or attended the China-Europe symposia. Ireland's ambassador to China visited HIT on more than one occasion during the project and received briefings by DIT members in China. The final workshop to report on the outcomes of the project, held in Dublin in 2006, was attended by the ambassadors of China and the United Kingom to Ireland as well as Ireland's ambassador to China.

The interest of the Chinese government was particularly strong throughout the project. Two years before the project began, China had established 35 National Pilot Schools of Software, of which one was in HIT, to address the issues of the knowledge economy in an alternative and more effective way than the some 1800 Schools of Computer Science in Chinese higher education institutions were achieving by traditional academic approaches. The Ministry of Education China had high hopes that a successful EMERSION project would have a significant impact on the reform/ modernisation of the Chinese Education higher system as a whole.

A significant event during the first year of the project was the award of the Honorary Doctorate of Harbin Institute of Technology in October 2003 to Professor Mary McAleese, President of

Ireland. This award was recommended by DIT and HIT and was the first honorary doctorate ever approved by the Chinese Government to be awarded by HIT.

Chinese Ministry of Education and Software Industry Association Evaluation of HIT-NPSS, 2003

In October 2003 a joint team from the Higher Education Department of the Chinese Ministry of Education and the Software Industry Association carried out an interim evaluation of the work of the National Pilot School of Software at HIT and produced the report below (in rough translation).

According to the recommendation of the notice on the mid-term evaluations for National Schools of Software (Higher Education Department [2003, No. 3]) from the Ministry of Education, the China Software Industry Association organized an expert team to make an interim evaluation in the National School of Software at Harbin Institute of Technology from 8 October to 10 October 2003.

The experts received the self-evaluation report of the National School of Software at Harbin Institute of Technology, reviewed the teaching, laboratory, administration, and on- and off-campus environment of the school, held seminars with students, teachers and staff of this and related functional sections of the university, audited the course randomly, and consulted related file material. After detailed discussions, the experts unanimously agreed the following points:

- *The development plan of the National School of Software at Harbin Institute of Technology meets the overall requirements set out for all the national pilot schools of software as well as the actual measures required for the development of the software industry. This National School of Software proposed the ethos of "Internationalization, Industrialization, High Quality, High Speed". The concept* of the teaching guidelines is advanced and has developed specific teaching characteristics. The orientation and aim of educating and producing skilled graduates is clear and definite, and has strong support from the university.

- The international co-operation has made substantial improvement and progress, especially the deep collaboration with Dublin Institute of Technology (DIT). The school successfully brought in the advanced industrial orientation system for developing relevant student skills from DIT, the HIT-DIT joint class has begun courses, and many foreign teachers have been brought in for teaching. One cohort of students has been sent to DIT to take the final two years of their degree courses, and funds have been received from European government projects to assist in this. The internationalization task has made remarkable progress.

- The software enterprises have maintained a close relationship of collaboration and communication, and the development of the industrial practice bases focuses on actual placements and industrial projects, and appears to be producing an active acceleration of the development of industry-oriented skills. Currently, over 150 master's degree students of software engineering are carrying out industrial placement in such industrial practice bases, and are busy with their degree dissertation projects. The management of the work placement base is satisfactory.

- In order to meet the software industry requirements, the school made a high administrative priority of developing industrial software skills among the students. This special orientation and the relevant curriculum and teaching system is new and characteristic. The school has established a strong quality assurance system which permeates all the teaching activities. The

school has developed a staff recruitment and training plan to guarantee a staff percentage with strong industrial experience. The double language (Chinese and English) teaching reached close to 70% in some subject areas, and many excellent foreign original books are used in the teaching in nearly 30 subject and courseware areas. The student workload has already produced some unique features, such as the flourishing enterprise style of student club activities and the very concentrated atmosphere of industrial involvement and orientation.

- The school has established a clear written management scheme, with a complete organizational framework and a range of bylaws, with documentation that is quite comprehensive.

- The two schools, of software and of computer science, cooperate and are improving in parallel, so as to develop together.

We recommend that the school further improve the teaching environment and summarize and document the experience of these developments, so as to disseminate those lessons and accelerate the processes of change and development. There is also a need for the school to actively develop social resources to satisfy the needs arising from growing student and staff numbers.

Chinese Ministry of Education and Software Industry Association Evaluation of HIT-NPSS, 2006

In May 2006 a second team from the Higher Education Department of the Chinese Ministry of Education and the Software Industry Association carried out a further evaluation of the work of the HIT-NPSS and produced the report below (in translation).

According to the recommendation of the notice with regard to the interim evaluations for the

National Schools of Software (Higher Education Department [2006, No. 27]) from the Ministry of Education, the China Software Industry Association organized an expert team to make an evaluation in the National School of Software at Harbin Institute of Technology on 22 May 2006. This team discussed the summary self-study report submitted by the National Pilot School of Software at Harbin Institute of Technology in Beijing, and made an evaluation visit to Harbin Institute of Technology. After a detailed discussion, all the experts agreed as follows:

- *According to the spirit of the [2001] No. 6 document of the Higher Education Department and the national requirement for skilled software graduates for industry, with a strong support from the School of Computer Science, the National Pilot School of Software at Harbin Institute of Technology makes full use of the integrated resources of the university; its teaching ethos of "Interntionalization, Industrialization, High quality, High speed" is advanced, and the central aim of producing highly educated and skilled graduates is clear and well grounded. The school actively pursues the continuous improvement of its approach to lecturing, practical work and innovation. The university provides strong support for the school, and branches have been established in the HIT campuses in Weihai and Shenzhen, each with its own emphasis and character based on local needs and resources. The number of postgraduate students has now reached 675, and the number of undergraduate students 1,645.*

- *The National Pilot School of Software at Harbin Institute of Technology has established a staff complement of high calibre, which is made up of full-time lecturers with industrial experience, basic on-campus part-time lecturers and part-time lecturers from industry from both home and abroad. The structure is reasonable with perhaps a predominance of external supplementary part-time members. At present, the school has 29 full-time lecturers, over 130 part-time lecturers on and off the campus. The school pays special attention to retaining excellent lecturers in the school and has taken a number of effective measures to develop young teachers to ensure a staff with high-level practical software knowledge and skills.*

- *The School established collaborations with a range of enterprises to ensure development of industry-related skills among the students, and this forms the core of its characteristic industry-oriented practical education system. 26 external industrial work placement bases, 3 on-campus practice bases, 3 joint laboratories and over 40 collaborating enterprises have been established. Furthermore, 6 student clubs with industrial and innovation orientations were established, and many regular activities such as the entrepreneur forums and summit meetings between school and enterprises take place. All of these contribute to the favourable environment for the industrial emphasis and play an important role for the enterprises in the development of industrially skilled software graduates.*

- *The School actively develops internationalized teaching on a wide scale, and the co-operation with Dublin Institute of Technology on curriculum system development, in the introduction of new courses, in teacher training, in student exchange and lecturer retention is deep and well-founded. The collaboration with universities in America, Britain and Korea is growing, and the proportion of double language teaching in the school has reached 65%. In the meantime, the school launched and organized two China-Europe International*

Symposia on Software Industry Orientation Education, that have had a wide influence.

- *The School, having considered the skills requirements of the software industry, put the industrialized teaching ethos into the system of education and training of the students and graduates. The teaching plan follows the principle of "five series connected, three directions characterized". The outcome is brilliant and its impact impressive.*

- *The School introduced the European and American style curriculum and teaching quality assurance system and methodology, established the industry-oriented quality assurance system with its specific features, and, as a result, the teaching quality and the quality of the learning and skills acquisition by the students have been assured and steadily improved.*

- *The School set up a student assignment system which favours of the development of industry-relevant skills. The regular activities of student clubs, entrepreneur forums, visits and presentations by IT enterprise representatives on professional career guidance all contribute to the development of the outlook, knowledge and skills sought by industry on a wide scale. The school also has provided funding for poorer students.*

- *The National Pilot School of Software at Harbin Institute of Technology has achieved great progress in the strategy of developing industry-oriented knowledge and skills, in implementing the related teaching plan and practical experience system, international cooperation and communication, as well as industrial placement, and in implementing a rigorous quality assurance scheme in all aspects of this educational experience, thereby creating a uniquely effective system encompassing all of these areas.*

The experts in the evaluation team agreed that the National Pilot School of Software at Harbin Institute of Technology had been very successful. The experts also suggested that the National Pilot School of Software at Harbin Institute of Technology further improve its teaching conditions, and further deepen on-going reforms.

REVIEW OF THE OPERATION OF THE PROJECT

The considerable success of the EMERSION project and, indeed, the continuing vitality of many of the collaborations established during the project are due, in large part, to a well-established unity of purpose and, consequently, a successful and robust partnership between the three institutions and their staff members actively involved. This partnership was also based on trust and mutual respect characterised by good working relations established between all those involved in the management and implementation of the project. Staff members of the three partner institutions were willing to become involved and were generous with the time they gave to the project. The expertise of these staff members, their generosity in sharing this expertise and their willingness to carry out large amounts of work on the project were particular strengths. Another strength was the unanimity among the partners on the drive for excellence and the development and implementation of a robust quality assurance scheme. The direct involvement of senior staff from all partner institutions was a particular benefit. The willingness of the partner institutions to release the human resources beyond contractual commitments was also essential to the success.

Another factor contributing to the fruitful partnership was the clarity established from the start on roles and responsibilities within the project, based on the partners' resources, experience and expertise. In addition to being the lead partner responsible for monitoring and directing the overall project, DIT also took the lead role in activities contributing to the development of the education model and training. UW was responsible for activities requiring the use of technology-supported learning and also contributed to the development of the educational model and the training. HIT represented the *user community* for the educational model and took the lead role in activities related to enhancing cross-partner research. Thus, this allocation of roles and responsibilities reflected the acknowledged expertise of the partner institutions and was readily agreed.

The willingness of HIT staff to change and embrace the new ethos and philosophy and to adopt the teaching and learning practices of the model was a particularly noteworthy strength of the project since it required a considerable amount of additional work on their part. The eagerness of the HIT undergraduate and postgraduate students to embrace the ethos and philosophy of the model was also vital.

In addition, the tripartite partnership was strengthened by a number of noteworthy supporters. The openness and even alacrity of the Chinese software industry to become involved in the education model in HIT made the establishment of the industry placement programme much easier than might have been expected. The project also drew extensive interest from the other National Pilot Schools of Software in China who are keen to adopt and adapt the model developed. The Chinese government (local and provincial) also demonstrated a great deal of interest in the project, which added to the strength of the partnership and its commitment to the objectives of the project.

However, in an international project of this scale problems were unavoidable. The fact that communications had to be done through English placed constraints on the partners from HIT. Only those staff members from HIT with a good command of oral, aural and written English could fully participate in the many discussions and visitations in Europe. However the institutional commitment

of HIT to developing more courses and even programmes to be delivered largely or fully through English, as the international language of business, helped to turn this problem into an inducement to many staff members to use the project to improve their command of English.

Many issues arose in relation to teaching through English both for staff members and students of HIT. The supply, currency and availability of the English textbooks in China are very limited. In software disciplines much advanced material is not available in textbooks anyhow and the books go out of date very rapidly. Bilingual teaching would be most desirable, but lecturers from Ireland and the United Kingdom, working through English, needed to speak very slowly when lecturing. The circulation of class notes in advance of class (on the VLE, WebCT, etc., and preferably with key phrases translated) was found to be vital. Another solution was for the Chinese students to visit Ireland/United Kingdom and spend some time improving their English and their understanding of the spoken language.

The distance, duration and cost of travel between the partners remain major impediments to such collaborative projects. The winning of the Asia-Link grant from the EU was an invaluable contribution to the costs involved, but the time required to travel between China and Europe was always substantial, particularly for staff members with heavy duties in their home institutions. Most of the direct participants gave considerable amounts of their free and vacation time and also other participants provided back-filling for their travelling colleagues. There was, therefore, a considerable amount of voluntary work involved.

Other unexpected issues such as the SARS epidemic that occurred at the start of the project and fluctuations in currency exchange rates had significant impacts on the timetable and sequence of the project as well as on the extent of different projected activities achieved. But the original structure of the project, divided into a large number of activities, many of which could be implemented in parallel and/or in sequence, and the strong partnership ethos that developed among the partners allowed such problems to be resolved satisfactorily.

The partners co-operated and collaborated well but were not able to contribute equally. DIT carried the responsibility for directing the majority of the project with both DIT and HIT being responsible for the execution and UW offering consultation. The steering committee, the composition of which was evenly distributed among the partners, functioned for the most part in virtual fashion and acted as a guide rather than a director, leaving the local project managers to decide the direction of their parts of the project. An overall high level management board with executive authority might, in retrospect, have been more appropriate and might have distributed the tasks more evenly if that were feasible.

SUMMARY AND RECOMMENDATIONS

The EMERSION project successfully developed and implemented an industry-oriented education model for software education in China, established a staff team in HIT which has been trained in the learning and teaching methods of the model, and set up international research teams which has led to significant collaborative research among the partners. The project won a high reputation and received wide favourable publicity in Ireland, the United Kingdom and China, and particularly with the Chinese Government (central and provincial), the 35 Chinese National Pilot Schools of Software and the Chinese software industry.

A fully documented industrially-focused education model was developed. Many aspects of this model merit further research and development. The ethos of the project was strongly influenced by the industry oriented educational ethos of

DIT and UW. This could be further developed and evaluated to help strengthen actively collaborative contacts between industry and academic institutions in Europe. While industry sources have agreed that the work placement element of undergraduate courses might be very important, it could be open to substantial improvement in its organisation and monitoring, and further research into appropriate structures and methodologies within the institutions and the industries would be of value. The final year project is a vital element in an undergraduate degree programme in computer science/computing/software engineering. The project helps the student to link the various subject strands and methodologies she/he has encountered on her/his studies into a coherent unit. This however is not sufficient. The project and resulting thesis should also display a significant degree of creativity which ensures that the final result is greater than the sum of the parts. Research into this theme in a number of countries, would be a worthwhile extension of the EMERSION project and would enrich and enhance the education model developed. The participation of postgraduate and undergraduate students from different countries in collaborative projects on such topics could be most valuable. It would also be of interest to educational institutions and industry in both the EU and China.

Clearly, the collaboration between DIT, UW and HIT has proved very worthwhile with mutual development and mutual benefits. The series of CEISIE symposia continues to develop this network further.

Thus the EMERSION project offers a good example of positive mutually beneficial collaboration between China and Europe, together with useful insights into creating links globally between higher education and industry in the widest sense. It offers many useful experiences, lessons and examples for the partners involved but also for others across the world.

ACKNOWLEDGMENT

The EMERSION project was funded under the EU Asia-Link programme, 2003-2006.

REFERENCES

Carroll, D., Lawless, D., Hussey, M., Gordon, D., O'Leary, C., Mtenzi, F., & Collins, M. (2006, November). *Assuring quality in Chinese IT education*. Paper presented at the Asia-Pacific Education Research Association Conference, Hong Kong, China.

Chinese Government Report. (2001). *File No. 2001(6)*. Beijing, China: Ministry of Education.

EMERSION project management team. (2004). *EMERSION annual report to EU 2003/04*. Dublin, Ireland: Dublin Institute of Technology School of Computing.

EMERSION project management team. (2005). *EMERSION annual report to EU 2004/05*. Dublin, Ireland: Dublin Institute of Technology School of Computing.

EMERSION project management team. (2006). *EMERSION annual report to EU 2005/06*. Dublin, Ireland: Dublin Institute of Technology School of Computing.

Lawless, D., Gordon, D., O'Leary, C., & Collins, M. (2004b, September). *Determining key skills for IT graduates in the emerging knowledge-based economy*. Paper presented at the Inaugural Conference of the All Ireland Society for Higher Education (AISHE), Dublin, Ireland.

Lawless, D., Gordon, D., O'Leary, C., Mtenzi, F., Xu, X., & Bechkoum, K. (2005, April). *Establishing undergraduate research communities*. Paper presented at the Computers and Learning 2005 Conference, Bristol, United Kingdom.

Lawless, D., Wu, B., Carroll, D., Gordon, D., Hussey, M., & O'Leary, C. … Xu, X. (Eds.). (2007). *An industry-oriented model for software education in China: Adapting an Irish model to Chinese conditions*. Dublin, Ireland: Blackhall.

Lawless, D., Wu, B., Xu, X., Yuan, C., & Bechkoum, K. (2004a, September). *Requirements for an industry-oriented IT education model to support the emerging knowledge economy in China*. Paper presented at the 2nd International Conference on Knowledge Economy and Development of Science and Technology, Beijing, China.

O'Leary, C., Lawless, D., Gordon, D., Carroll, D., Mtenzi, F., & Collins, M. (2006b). *3D alignment in the adaptive software engineering curriculum*. Paper presented at the 36th Annual American Association for Engineering Education/Institute of Electrical and Electronic Engineering Frontiers in Education Conference. San Diego, CA.

O'Leary, C., Lawless, D., Gordon, D., Haifeng, L., & Bechkoum, K. (2006a). Developing a software engineering curriculum for the emerging software industry in China. In *Proceedings of the 19th Conference on Software Engineering Education and Training (CSEE&T 2006)* (pp. 115-122). Washington, DC: Institute of Electrical and Electronic Engineering.

Proceedings of the 2nd China-Europe International Symposium on Software Industry-Oriented Education. (2005). *Journal of Harbin Institute of Technology (New Series), 12* (Supplement). Harbin, China: Harbin Institute of Technology.

Proceedings of the 4th China-Europe International Symposium on Software Industry-Oriented Education. (2007). *Acta Scientiarum Naturalium, 46*(2). Guang Zhou, China

Proceedings of the 6th China-Europe International Symposium on Software Industry Oriented Education. (2010). *Computer Education, 9*(117). Xi'an, China.

Wu, B., & Bourrières, J.-P. (Eds.). (2010). Educate adaptive talents for IT applications in enterprises and interoperability. In *Proceedings of 5th China-Europe International Symposium on Software Industry Oriented Education*. Talence, France: University of Bordeaux.

Wu, B., MacNamee, B., Xu, X., & Guo, W. (Eds.). (2007). *Proceedings of the 3rd China-Europe International Symposium on Software Industry-Oriented Education*. Dublin, Ireland.

KEY TERMS AND DEFINITIONS

Academic Quality Assurance: The procedures adapted from Irish, United Kingdom and earlier Chinese practices and implemented in China to ensure the quality and standards of the teaching/learning on the industry-oriented software programme in China, so that the graduates would be of world class.

Curriculum Development: The array of critical reviews and adaptations to the Irish educational model and to teaching/learning activities relating to the various syllabuses, to successfully implement the curriculum in China.

Europe-China Co-Operation: A joint activity of European and Chinese colleagues, in this case applying an Irish industry-oriented education model in China, coping with the cultural and language differences in a constructive, mutually beneficial manner.

Human Resource Development: A key range of activities of the Europe-China co-operation to educate and train the staff of the co-operating institutions in the academic, organizational, cultural and behavioural flexibilities required to appropriately adapt and implement an Irish educational model in China.

Industry Oriented Graduates: Graduates of a higher education in which they have been exposed to typical technical, behavioural and environmental conditions and challenges of the software industry, and who are capable of functioning in that industry as productive software engineers.

Industry-Oriented Software Education Model: A higher education programme in software engineering with a curriculum and module syllabuses that cover the fundamental theory and contain considerable amount of practical implementation work, including projects on real-life industry problems, internship(s) in software industries, involvement of industry engineers in lecturing or supervising, etc., with a view to producing graduates who can readily and rapidly move into industry as productive and creative software engineers.

Knowledge Economy: The developing worldwide economy which will strongly rest on knowledge and intelligent analysis and synthesis of knowledge through computer systems to assist in the management of human affairs, and in which the role of software developers and engineers will be highly significant.

Chapter 3
Co-Operation Models for Industries and Software Education Institutions

Yanqing Wang
Harbin Institute of Technology, China

ABSTRACT

In order to underpin software industry-oriented education and make it more practical, a co-operation model for industries and software education institutes is described and discussed in this chapter. Based on the popular engineering education theory conceive, design, implement, operate (CDIO) associated with MIT and other universities (Crawley, 2001), and the value chain theory described by Porter (1996), an industry-institute-interoperation (I-I-Io) model was developed with five evolutionary stages - isolated, oriented, interacting, interoperating, and converging. The implementation of this co-operation model between institute and industry within the National Pilot School of Software at Harbin Institute of Technology, while still evolving, has already shown considerable vitality in the development of software engineering education.

INTRODUCTION

Participants' Motivation for Co-Operation

The four participants involved in the industry-institute co-operation to be discussed in this chapter

DOI: 10.4018/978-1-60960-797-5.ch003

- industry, institute, government and students - are all key stakeholders of the educational process.

Industry has a vital interest in recruiting skilled and capable graduate software engineers, and can and should play an invaluable role in computing education. The institute has the responsibility to provide the best and most appropriate education possible for students to prepare them for their careers, producing graduates with the knowledge and skills required by industry and helping to underpin software industry success. The government serves to provide coordination between industry and institute in software industry-oriented education (SIOE) within the wider interests of society as a whole. Finally, students are at the heart of the educational process and are significant beneficiaries of SIOE.

Industry: Business Value

From the industrial standpoint, business value is the predominant consideration for the enterprises involved. The advantages can be detailed in the four following areas, at least:

- *Human Resources*: Software industry oriented engineering education enables the institute to produce graduates who are highly-qualified, professional and with knowledge and skills that make them readily integrated into industry. Unfortunately, in China and many other countries, the shortage of such highly skilled and productive graduates remains a pressing problem for most enterprises.
- *Technique*: When many students with advanced software skills and techniques enter an enterprise on undergraduate internship, the limitations in their industrial development experience can be remedied to some extent. Even though internship students receive limited practical industrial experience, the new techniques and theories they have learned in their institutes can help solve technical problems in the company or, at least, provide some new insights and approaches of considerable value to working engineers.
- *Finance*: Employing internship students can save money for enterprise because the salary required is generally lower than that of full-time employees. The lower cost can

relieve some financial pressure within an enterprise.
- *Quality assurance*: High-quality students/ graduates can become high quality employees developing high-quality products that can save considerably on the testing and maintenance phases of products and so help enhance the prestige and market of the enterprise.

Institute: Prestige Value

The main driving motivations for the institute to participate in industry co-operation are summarized as follows.

- *Improving its national and international ranking*: A college can gain greater prestige when it produces more highly skilled and productive graduates for industry.
- *Improving software engineering education*: If the widely-perceived gap between engineering education and engineering practice is bridged, the value of engineering science would be enhanced and the industry raised to a higher level of success and prosperity.
- *Correcting poor practices*: Some institutes, even some key Chinese universities, have to face the embarrassing criticism of their applied software engineering education, that the graduates they produce are *unfit for a higher post but unwilling to take a lower one.*
- *Relieving employment pressure*: When the majority of graduates can find favorable employment, the pressure on institutes to help ensure the employment of their graduates can be relieved.

Government: Achieving Value

In almost all countries, the government plays a significant role in education. It supports developments in strategic, political and financial ways.

It also regulates the behavior of the institutes to seek to avoid imbalances in the production of graduates among the disciplines.

Education is a most important issue in every country. A successful institute-industry co-operation tends to improve the government's approval rating among the population. When institutes produce more suitably qualified graduates and industry gets more competitive and productive employees, the government's popularity is enhanced.

Students: Added Self-Value

Education is primarily a student-centered process. Although the detailed motivations of each stakeholder vary, government, institute and industry have a unity of purpose in education to develop sufficient numbers of skilled graduates in appropriate disciplines. Institutes offer educational and training programs to students, aiming to produce excellent professionals after graduation. Industry employs excellent graduates as its human resources. The government seeks to guide the education process towards this optimal outcome.

A major motivation for students involved in education is to achieve added self-value. From the viewpoint of the value chain, students have added value when they graduate from a key career discipline of the institute. At that stage they have acquired considerable knowledge, mastered many skills, and improved their productive and competitive capabilities as needed by industry. It is envisaged and intended that co-operative institute-industry education will amplify the added value effect for students by a more advanced and effective process. The benefits to students can include the following (Lawless et al., 2007).

- The opportunity to gain experience of the working methods, procedures and structures of commercial/industrial environments, and, through this experience, develop commercial software systems using the skills and competencies acquired in the academic setting

- Acquiring new technical, business and advanced communication skills appropriate to a professional environment, while improving self-confidence and enhancing essential workplace skills, such as teamwork, professional relationships and communications, which would benefit them throughout their careers and future employments

- The opportunity to explore career options by providing an opportunity to relate their academic studies as well as their interests and specific strengths to real-world career choices

- Development of a degree of maturity of thought and conception regarding the application and applicability of computer-based systems in a commercial environment and enhancement of their employability by future employers and their career prospects generally

CONCEIVE, DESIGN, IMPLEMENT, OPERATE (CDIO) SYLLABUS - HIGHLIGHTS AND DEFICIENCIES

In developing the co-operation model it was agreed by the school team to base the model on the advanced engineering education theory, conceive, design, implement, operate (CDIO), developed by a consortium of prestigious engineering universities - Linköping University (Sweden), Chalmers University of Technology (Sweden), Royal Institute of Technology (Sweden) and Massachusetts Institute of Technology (USA) (Crawley, 2001).

The CDIO Model for Engineering Education

CDIO is an innovative educational framework for producing the next generation of engineers. It provides students with an education stressing engineering fundamentals set in the context of conceiving, designing, implementing and operating real-world systems and products.

There are two high level objectives within contemporary engineering education which are in apparent conflict, educating students in an increasingly broad range of technologies while simultaneously developing the student's personal, interpersonal and system building skills (Crawley, 2001). The specific objectives of the CDIO syllabus are to create a rational, complete, universal, and generalizable set of goals for undergraduate engineering education.

The CDIO syllabus is *rational*, in that it reflects the modern practice of engineering. It is *complete*, in that it presents enough detail for the planning of curricula, the defining of learning outcomes and their assessment. It is *universal*, in that it has deliberately been written to be applicable to all engineering disciplines. It is *generalizable*, in that it has been structured in a manner to be easily adapted by programs at all schools of engineering. Furthermore, its goal is to create a topical listing that is comprehensive of other acknowledged principal source documents, and is thoroughly peer-reviewed by experts in the field.

In order to make its rationale clearer, the approach was to base the syllabus on the essential functions of engineering: *graduating engineers should be able to conceive-design-implement-operate (CDIO) complex value-added engineering systems in a modern team-based environment.*

Specific Highlights of CDIO

As stated by the authors of the CDIO syllabus, graduating engineers should appreciate the engineering *process*, be able to contribute to the development of engineering *products*, and do so while working in engineering *organizations*. Implicit in this is the additional expectation that, as university graduates, engineering graduates should be developing and maturing as whole, mature, and thoughtful individuals (Crawley, 2001).

The four high level expectations map directly on the highest, first level organization of the CDIO syllabus, as illustrated in Figure 1. Examining the mapping of the first level syllabus items to these four expectations, a mature individual interested in technical endeavours should possess a set of *Personal and Professional Skills*, which are central to the practice of engineering. In order to develop complex value-added engineering systems, students must have mastered the fundamentals of the appropriate *Technical Knowledge and Reasoning*. In order to work in a modern team-based environment, students must have developed the *Interpersonal Skills* of teamwork and communications. Finally, in order to actually be able to create and operate products and systems, a student must understand something of *conceiving, designing, implementing, and operating systems in the enterprise and societal contexts* (Crawley, 2002).

Figure 1. Building blocks of knowledge, skills and attitudes necessary to conceive, design, implement, and operate (CDIO) systems in the enterprise and societal contexts

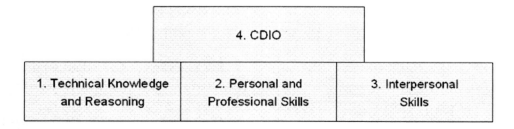

Limitations of CDIO for This Work

The CDIO approach has some identifiable limitations relating to the work under consideration in this chapter, and these need attention in this development.

Firstly, CDIO is mainly a syllabus template. Under the guidelines of CDIO, one can create a syllabus which is a rational, complete, universal, and generalizable set of goals for undergraduate engineering education, but some modifications are needed to adapt it to the specific circumstances of this work. In this sense therefore, CDIO is viewed as a framework to build up syllabuses for specific courses. Secondly, the concept of the process is not strong in CDIO. The word *process* is mentioned in a CDIO-related document. However, since it is still at an initial research stage, process management has not yet been explored in the CDIO system. Lastly, CDIO is not industry-involved, even though the CDIO objectives include the idea that graduating engineers should appreciate engineering processes and be able to contribute to the development of engineering products, while working in engineering organizations. Although the term *organization* is mentioned here, the concept of industry is not strongly emphasized. Thus, in the CDIO system, the relationship between institute and industry has not been addressed, let alone institute-industry co-operation.

In summary, the CDIO system is suitable for curriculum and syllabus development in engineering education. It does not seriously consider activities beyond the institute. Although CDIO has many highlights in engineering education, it merely presents references to software industry-oriented education research and practice. It does not sufficiently match the needs of research in institute-industry interoperation. Eventually, after the institute industry co-operation has been firmly established and successfully optimized, the CDIO system can be developed and expanded to incorporate this important aspect.

VALUE CHAIN ANALYSIS OF CO-OPERATION

The *value chain*, also known as *value chain analysis*, is a concept of business management that was first described and popularized by Porter (1996).

Enterprise Value Chain

A value chain is a chain of activities of a firm operating in a specific industry. The business unit is the appropriate level for construction of a value chain, rather than the divisional level or corporate level. Products pass through all activities of the chain in order and at each activity the product gains some value. The chain of activities gives the products more added value than the sum of added values of the individual activities. It is important not to mix the concept of the value chain with the costs occurring throughout the activities. A diamond cutter can be used as an example of the difference. The cutting activity may have a low cost, but the activity adds much value to the end product since a rough diamond is significantly less valuable than a cut diamond. Typically, the value chain described and the documentation of the processes, as well as the assessment and auditing of adherence to the process routines are at the core of the quality assurance and certification of the business.

The value chain categorizes the generic value-adding activities of an organization. The primary activities include inbound logistics, operations (production), outbound logistics, marketing and sales (demand), and services (maintenance). The support activities include administrative infrastructure management, human resource management, technology (R&D), and procurement. The costs and value drivers are identified for each value activity in Figure 2.

Value chain analysis can offer very useful insights to the study of institute-industry co-operation. The possible benefits of value chain analysis includes

Figure 2. Basic value chain, after Porter (1996)

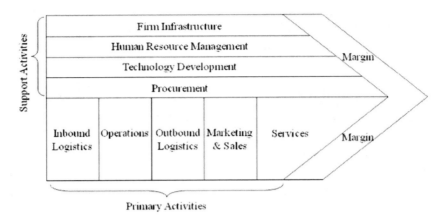

- phase partitioning, to distinguish primary and support activities
- interaction and communication between different partitions
- a competitiveness tool.

In order to develop co-operation with industry, every institute should partition its phases, distinguish primary and support activities and make the communication between partitions clear and fluent.

Institute Value Chain

Based on Porter's value chain analysis, the institute value chain is analyzed as follows, using Figure 3. As shown in this figure, the primary activities of an institute include

- dormitory, food and healthcare
- lecturing and laboratory teaching/learning
- practical training and work placement
- job finding
- workplace visit, interviews, feedback, etc.

Figure 3. Institute value chain

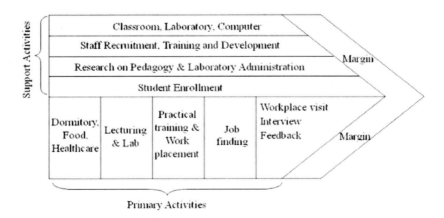

As well as these, a range of support activities play an indispensable role. Classrooms, laboratories and computers belong to the hard infrastructure. Employment and training of staff are human resource management activities. In the institute, the research on pedagogy and laboratory administration is a type of technology development. Finally, enrolment of new students is an activity similar to procurement. According to Porter's value chain analysis, it is concluded that while primary activities in education should be emphasized, the support activities may not be ignored.

Co-Operation Value Chain

The co-operation (between institute and industry) value chain is more like an industrial value chain since educational institutes and industrial enterprises are co-operating. To help better understand the co-operation value chain within the model, the roles of the four principal stakeholders in engineering education are elaborated here, that is, those of the student, the institute, the industry and the government.

The motivations of the four stakeholders have been discussed briefly in a previous section. Figure 4 shows the outline co-operation value chain model. The middle (secondary) school (drawn in dotted lines), involving institute-industry interoperation, is introduced to assist in describing the development of the overall model in the following sections. Also, since the function of government is relatively weak or indirect, it is not depicted in Figure 4.

Among the four roles, the student has a special position. Undoubtedly, students are assumed to be active and willing participants in the education process. But they play their roles to an extent like material on a production line since they cannot strongly change the education services or the required learning outcomes. The middle school students enter the institute as the input material to the higher education process; the skilled graduates emerge from the institute to join an enterprise as an output product of that process. Therefore, if we temporarily ignore the activity, inventiveness and creativity of the students in their education, the detailed co-operation value chain model can be developed theoretically, as shown in Figure 5.

From the developing value chain analysis outlined in Figures 4 and 5, the following comments and deductions can be made.

- The student should be at the centre of the model, in accordance with the essence of education, because otherwise it is impossible to have a successful educational process. However, in Figures 4 and 5, the student is not yet depicted in the central position within the model.

- The government function should be expressed clearly and fully. Either in western or eastern countries, the functionality of government in higher education is almost always relatively vague. Nevertheless, the government has the paramount control through the allocation of resources, especially finance; the educational management and decision-makers then basically exert the authority of the government. The more the public understands that the gov-

Figure 4. Outline co-operation value chain

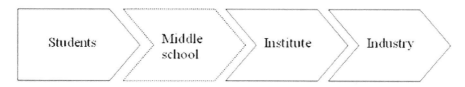

Figure 5. Detailed co-operation value chain

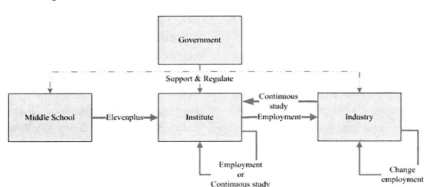

ernment is the actual game controller, the more pressure the government will feel, and the more responsibility government should take for the development, success and failings of education.

- There is vital need for institute-industry co-operation. Disregarding the functionality of middle school in Figures 4 and 5, it is clear that:
  ○ Skilled graduates are both the output of the institute and the input of industry
  ○ Some graduates work at institutes
  ○ Some employees change their employment in industry
  ○ Some employees continue their study in institutes.

The relationship of institute and industry is close and they do not function completely separately. The more qualified graduates from the institute get satisfactory jobs in industry, the less human resource pressure exists in industry. Without co-operation between the two parties, successful engineering education would not be readily achieved in the short term.

EVOLUTION OF THE INSTITUTE INDUSTRY INTERACTION (I-I-I) MODEL

Two Similar Institute-Industry Interactions

In order to express the ideas being developed more clearly, two similar or related types of interaction need to be envisaged – institute-industry-interaction (abbreviated to *I-I-Ia*) and institute-industry-interoperation (abbreviated to *I-I-Io*). They are both modes or degrees of co-operation between industry and institute but there are qualitative differences between them.

I-I-Ia means that institute and industry begin to interact with each other's activities. For example, when an institute assigns some students to visit an enterprise, the enterprise agrees and arranges necessary reception and guidance for them. At this stage, the institute and industry have a shallow relationship and each manages their own business largely independently.

With *I-I-Io* both industry and institute become actively and positively involved in most of the educational activities. Since *I-I-Io* is viewed as the most thoroughgoing co-operation between industry and institute, it is the optimum situation for synergistic co-operation of benefit to both. In the following description, co-operation according to the *I-I-Io* model is implied.

Evolution of Enterprise's Human-Resource Outlook

In the traditional enterprise, the development of human resources operates on an *inner loop* mechanism, in which the development of the skills and competencies of staff mainly depends on such approaches as intra-enterprise training, *transfer, help and tutoring, learning by doing*, and such processes. However, in a modern enterprise, besides *inner loop* mechanisms, *external loop* mechanisms are also adopted, with which enterprises positively join in the education process of institutes and assist in further educating qualified graduates to meet their needs.

Simple Institute-Industry-Co-Operation Model

The development of institute-industry co-operation has passed through many phases over time.

In earlier times when institute and industry had few areas of co-operation or none, the processes that teachers used to educate and train students in the institute was separate and distinct from the methods used by managers to inculcate and train their young engineers in industry. Not until students had graduated did they have a chance to learn about and understand industry in any detailed, practical way, as indicated in Figure 6(a). In that situation, industry did not participate in the education process of the university, while the institute did not understand the full employee requirement of industry. Therefore, engineering education and engineering practice tended to be seriously isolated from each other. Graduates often had little or no practical competency or skill when they got a position. Before the employees could create value for an enterprise, it would generally take a year or more for the enterprise to provide them with training in a range of relevant professional skills.

With the increasing focus to engineering education globally, the interaction between institute and industry has drawn more and more attention and effort by both of these stakeholders. Increasingly, some teachers join companies and become part-time (or even full-time) managers, while some managers from industry serve as part-time (or even full-time) lecturers in some institutes. Furthermore, many engineers re-enter institutes and pursue higher educational degrees, while many students come to enterprises for internship so as to better understand the requirements of the enterprises and the deficiencies in their own skills and capabilities, as indicated in Figure 6 (b). In effect, the evolution of engineering education is

Figure 6. Comparison between with and without institute-industry co-operation

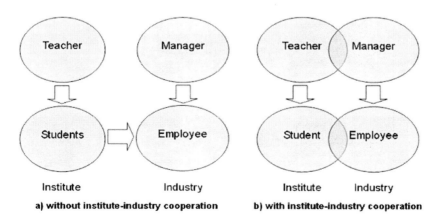

a) without institute-industry cooperation   b) with institute-industry cooperation

turning a new page in its development of vital complementary skills and competencies.

The Institute-Industry-Interoperation Model and Its Five Stages

This description of institute-industry co-operation and its development can be analysed in still finer detail as an evolving process.

As many educators and entrepreneurs have pressed their concerns as to the knowledge, skills and experience required by graduate engineers, the processes of institute-industry interoperation have been undergoing several stages of development. These may be described as *i.* isolated, *ii.* oriented, iii. interacting, *iv.* interoperating and *v.* converging stages.

Compared to the previous model of institute industry co-operation, the institute-industry-interoperation model tends to be increasingly focused on such aspects as co-operative education and sustainable development.

i. Isolated or Indirect Stage

In this original stage, there is no co-operation between institute and industry, as described earlier and indicated in Figure 7. Enterprise finds its human resources from the job market, while the institute educates students according to its own syllabuses and curricula, developed internally without direct industry input. The general job market provides the main link between the educa-

tion system and the job. The low efficiency and educational resource waste in this approach have been repeatedly emphasised.

ii. Oriented or Customized Stage

The main reason the oriented stage emerged was that more and more universities (especially in the United States) began to recognize the severity of the problems of their graduates in adapting to industry and of industry in absorbing those well-educated graduates, and launched an evolutionary solution. At that time, the institute began to make necessary adjustments relating to specialty skills and curriculum changes in order to meet requirements emerging in the human resource market. In this way the educational efficiency for producing applied and skilled graduates improved by some measure as shown in Figure 8.

iii. Interacting Stage

With the further evolution of higher education and the increasing competitiveness of global industry, the need for further evolution in the *I-I-Io* model became apparent. For example, such leading Chinese universities as Zhejiang University, Tsinghua University and Shantou University began to lead the theoretical development of engineering education in China. Furthermore, in 2001, the Chinese Ministry of Education called for the establishment of thirty five pilot schools of software with a pronounced industry orientation, which showed

Figure 7. Isolated stage of I-I-Io model

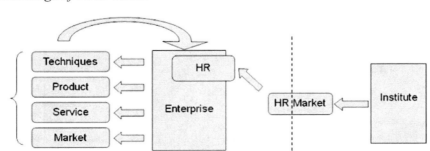

Figure 8. Oriented stage of I-I-Io model

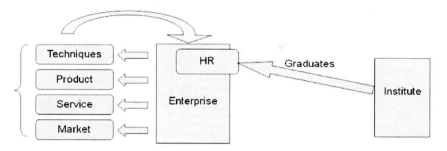

the high concerns about software engineering education at the national level in China.

In this new stage, institutes set about educating students with skills and competencies sought by industry. Institutes began to assign students to do practical training and internship in industry. Enterprises began to emphasize the propagation of their prestige and engineering approaches and even to be involved in pedagogical processes in the institutes. The successful experience of the schools of software in China shows that considerable improvement in efficiency and effectiveness has been achieved, as indicated in Figure 9.

iv. Interoperating Stage

Nevertheless, the level and mode of co-operation between institute and industry, while achieving some preliminary progress, were still limited. The achievements were still a long way from the destination of producing more qualified applicable and skilled graduates who could meet the requirements of industry. It was concluded that to realize this higher ideal, the institute-industry interoperation must enter a still more advanced stage, i.e. the interoperating stage, as indicated in Figure 10.

In this stage, it is envisaged that bridges be developed between institute and enterprise in areas such as human resources, research and development, quality assurance and others. The enterprise would locate subsections of its human resource department, R&D department, quality assurance department and others in the institute. At the same time the institute would establish work placement bases in the enterprise for its students to become involved in research and development and other processes, and, along the way, learn the details of the requirements of the human resource department. Such bridges between institutes and enterprises are being designed to help each stakeholder correct the mis-matches between engineering education and engineering practice.

Figure 9. Interacting stage of I-I-Io model

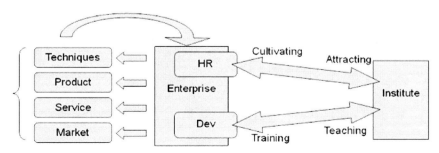

Figure 10. Interoperating stage of I-I-Io model

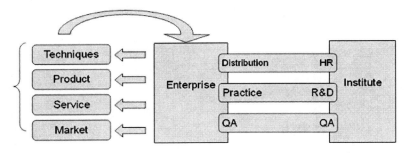

v. Converging Stage

Beyond the interoperating stage, it is possible to envisage that ultimately institute-industry co-operation could enter a converging stage, where enterprise and institute both situate engineering education in a still more strategic position and co-operatively engage in an expanding range of areas of mutual interest and benefit, and of benefit to students and graduates, as suggested in Figure 11. Although the two sides have different purposes, one for-profit and the other not-for-profit, producing more qualified graduates with the most appropriate skills and competencies would meet their different objectives. Provided the particular purposes of one or the other do not take precedence, a converging stage might be practical.

However, there is often a serious difference between the ideal and the actuality. The detailed operational methods and procedures for a converging stage have not been designed or agreed yet.

With the successful progression of the previous stages, the approaches to converging education may become clearer and more feasible.

TWO EXCLUDED CASES OF THE I-I-Io MODEL

In this section two actual cases of institute-industry collaborations, one an institute-run enterprise and the other an enterprise-run institute, are examined for lessons and insights. Although they both have features of both institute and enterprise, as will be explained, they are not compatible with the evolutionary *I-I-Io* model developed so far in this chapter.

Institute-Run Enterprise

An institute-run enterprise is a type of economic entity of which the university may be the exclusive

Figure 11. Convergence stage of I-I-Io model

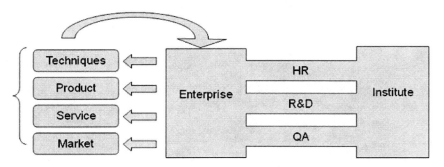

owner or the main investor through providing techniques, funds and buildings, and whose main business is the production of modern techniques and products. Such institute-run enterprises are generally an attachment to the institute or university. In China, for example, in the 1990s, some famous Chinese institute-run enterprises, such as *Peking University Founder Group, TsingHua Tongfang, TsingHua Unisplendour, Shanghai Fudan Forward Science and Technology* and *Create Group of Xi'an Jiaotong University*, showed strong development trends in high technology. These institute-run enterprises played the role of incubator enterprises (Fouts & Chan, 1997).

However, with the development of these institute-run enterprises, problems relating to policy gradually emerged.

- *Orientation drift and unclear ethos of the institute-run enterprise.* Education, research and serving society are the three primary functions of higher education, while the function of the enterprise is to generate profit. Sometimes the management in institute-run enterprises can become confused and allow the orientation to drift too far from the educational to the business function.
- *Unclear or even incorrect positioning of institute-run enterprises.* Most of the institute-run enterprises function neither as enterprises nor as institutes. Particularly since the creators often have double roles, academic and business, they cannot devote all their energies to enterprise management. Unfortunately, a successful academic is not necessarily a good manager or businessman but it is particularly difficult to carry both roles successfully.

From the standpoint of co-operation between institute and industry, the institute-run enterprise does have an apparent advantage, but this advantage tends to be merely geographical. It is indeed much easier for the students in the institute to find work placement or a job in an institute-run enterprise than in an outside company. But, given the acknowledged inherent deficiencies of institute-run enterprises, this advantage relatively insignificant.

The possibly short life-cycles of institute-run enterprises tend to ensure that they are not cases of the *I-I-Io* model. Co-operation between the institute and an institute-run enterprise does not appear to offer a long-term strategy, though many scholars are seeking strategies to solve the related problems (Hao, 2005; Si, 2004).

Enterprise-Run Institute

An enterprise-run institute consists of an educational organization created by one or more enterprises.

In recent years, with the rapid development of the Internet economy, the human resource market has become so large and profitable that some enterprises have established occupational training as a profit-making business enterprise. Sometimes this kind of organization flies the educational flag and emerges as educational institute. Unfortunately, because of the essence of enterprise, the enterprise-run institute cannot fully assume the responsibility of education.

From the standpoint of co-operation between institute and industry, an enterprise-run institute usually plays the role of a practical training base. It is not compatible with the synergistic *I-I-Io* model described above. The practical training provided can increase students' understanding of theoretical knowledge and improve their motivation to study. The students can also acquire practical skills and knowledge in a working community of professionals. Thus, while the enterprise-run institute makes some contribution to education, it remains far from a comprehensive and effective approach to engineering education.

CASE STUDY IN I-I-Io: NATIONAL PILOT SCHOOL OF SOFTWARE AT HIT

The School of Software at Harbin Institute of Technology (SoS@HIT) is approved by the Ministry of Education and the State Planning and Development Committee, and is one of the thirty five National Pilot Schools of Software in China. SoS@HIT makes full use of the comprehensive institute resources and rests on the advanced achievements and prestige of the computing discipline within HIT. Taking the *Internationalization, Industrialization, High Quality and Rapid Response* as the school ethos and following the principle of *High-jumping off, High-level and High-standard*, SoS@HIT emphasizes and builds on strong international cooperation. With the target of meeting international standards and industrial needs, the school endeavours to establish a world-class teaching atmosphere, employing an industry-oriented faculty team and fostering excellent software skills and competencies among its students (School of Software at Harbin Institute of Technology, 2010).

Since 2002, the experiences of SoS@HIT have proved very successful. One of its highlights, *Industrialization,* has been particularly successful and is regarded in China as a landmark example of co-operation between institute and industry. In the entire co-operation process, both the institute and industry engage in a range of activities to underpin the co-operation model.

Institute's Activities

i. Entrepreneurs' Forum

The entrepreneur's forum is a key element of *I-I-Io* in the SoS@HIT and its activities and its contribution to I-I-Io have been significant (Xu, 2006). Within the forum, managing directors from industry are invited to give speeches to the students to improve their knowledge and understanding of the software industry. This activity has proved successful in reducing the gap in ideas and practice between institute and industry.

ii. Students' Visits to Enterprises

The students' visits to industry also play an important role in the *I-I-Io* process. Each year, some excellent students of SoS@HIT are organized to make visits to some famous software companies in China. After viewing real work placements, receiving presentations from company spokespersons, and discussing issues arising with technical or managerial staff, the students get a sense of the companies and their cultures. When they return to the school, they give a comprehensive review and impressions of what they had seen and heard to the other students.

iii. Summit Forum for Co-Operation Between Institute and Enterprises

Each year, a symposium forum on the co-operation between the institute and the enterprises is sponsored by SoS@HIT and held in a city where many software companies are located. At the symposium, educators from institutes and managers from industry sit together and have extensive free discussions about the co-operation and issues involved in developing the necessary skills and competencies in the graduates. Since 2003, this symposium has been held six times, and its progress has been marked by a steady improvement in the co-operation between industry and the institute with both sides compromising, penetrating and understanding each other's system with the common purpose of educating better qualified software engineers for industry.

iv. Joint Laboratory

In order to educate top-level software graduates for industry, SoS@HIT has established joint laboratories with leading Chinese software enterprises such as Kingsoft Corporation. In each joint laboratory, work stations and equipment are provided by SoS@HIT, while an integrated development environment with necessary software toolkits are provided by the enterprise. The enterprise arranges seminars on special topics or provides related guidance for lecturers and students in SoS@HIT. The main function of each joint laboratory is education and practice in software development.

v. Practical Training

Practical training has proven to be an effective way to foster students' understanding of theoretical knowledge and its applications, as well as encouraging their motivation to study (Li, 2003; Rompelman & Vries, 2002; Trevisan, 2004). Following other institutes' successful experiences in this regard, from 2007, most of Year 2 students in SoS@HIT are sent to contractor bases to undertake practical training before they enter the following academic year. The duration of this training is about four weeks. In the process, students work and study together in the software companies and finish one or more small real-life projects so as to develop their understanding of the entire process of software development. Through the training period students gain an appreciation of how to apply theoretical knowledge to practical applications and, after they return to the institute, tend to be able to recognize their own deficiencies and so redirect the focus of their studies.

As of 2010, SoS@HIT has established stable relationships with practical training bases in companies such as China National Software & Service Corporation in Beijing (http://www.css.com.cn/eng/index.htm) and Neusoft Corporation in Dalian (http://www.neusoft.com).

vi. Internship

In order to meet the requirements of the Chinese and international IT industry for appropriately qualified software graduates, SoS@HIT has made significant strides in internship base management since 2002. Nowadays, its contractor internship bases are located in Harbin, Beijing, Shenzhen, Zhuhai, Jinan, Qingdao, Weihai and elsewhere. The majority of the top twenty Chinese IT enterprises are its partners in this work. These bases provide excellent conditions for software practice in industry settings and form a strong backbone for the education and training of high-level high-quality graduates of SoS@HIT.

The detailed internship strategy in SoS@HIT is a *3+1* model for undergraduates. This means that students study on-campus for the first 3 years and then undertake the major internship in a software enterprise for about ten months of the last year. The remaining 2 months are reserved for the preparation and presentation of the graduating dissertation. The students are allowed to select a dissertation topic similar to the project work they may have done in the internship in the enterprise. SoS@HIT learned this approach to internship from Dublin Institute of Technology, with the difference is that in DIT, the internship is undertaken in the last semester of Year 3 rather than in Year 4.

Through these internship bases, industries and SoS@HIT have built up a lively and stable co-operative relationship, while the co-operating enterprises have an excellent opportunity to select able employees from the graduates.

Industry's Activities

i. Campus Propaganda by Human Resource Sections

Prior to or during the graduation season each year, many top-level Chinese software enterprises come to the HIT campus to carry out recruitment activities. Most of them are the co-operative partners of SoS@HIT. They are welcomed to the campus and the institute organizes related activities such as seminars, speeches, interviews and even written examinations.

ii. Lectures by Development Sections from Industry

SoS@HIT invites managers or senior engineers in enterprises (usually from development sections) to give lectures to its students on the company's activities. Because of multiple development experiences and good understanding of project management, the lecturer-managers frequently leave very good impressions and insights with the students.

iii. Setting up Development Sub-Section in the Institute

To further deepen the co-operation with industry in the near future, SoS@HIT is planning to invite some software enterprises to set up development sub-sections in the institute.

Case Analysis

The experiences of SoS@HIT indicate the great value to students, to the institute and to the industries of the different forms of co-operation between the institute and industry.

i. The Co-Operation by SoS@ HIT is Indispensible

From point of view of industrial and institutional needs, the co-operation is very necessary. Most of the top IT enterprises in China are actively in-

volved in the co-operation processes with SoS@ HIT. The Chinese Ministry of Education supports SoS@HIT in many ways. The great majority of students and graduates of SoS@HIT place a high value on the co-operation and its importance to their careers.

ii. The Co-Operation by SoS@ HIT is Successful

Over some years' of operation, the co-operation schemes organized by SoS@HIT have been very successful in producing graduating classes of highly employable graduates with an increasing number embarking on postgraduate study internationally. Table 1 gives the statistics for the SoS@HIT graduating classes and the percentages obtaining employment in industry in China, those proceeding to a master's qualification and those obtaining postgraduate placements internationally from 2006 to 2009.

From these data, the average *success* percentage (including employment, continuing study in China and overseas) is approximately 94%, and the annual overall success percentage has been rising throughout the period.

iii. The Co-Operation by SoS@ HIT Can Be Improved

Comparing the current conditions of the institute-industry co-operation of SoS@HIT with the evolutionary *I-I-Io* model defined above, it would be

Table 1. Placement of graduates from 2006 to 2009

Year of graduation	Contracted employee	Continuing study (master's degree)	Continuing study (overseas)	Total
2006	62%	21%	3%	85%
2007	59%	28%	7%	94%
2008	60%	29%	7%	96%
2009	59%	33%	6%	97%
Total	60%	28%	7%	94%

accurate to state that it stands mostly at the third stage (interacting stage) and only partly arches into the fourth stage (interoperating stage). To implement the highest ideal of I-I-Io, there is still much work to be done by both the institute and industry, and the institute is working hard to achieve the necessary improvements.

REFERENCES

Crawley, E. F. (2001). *The Conceive, Design, Implement, Operate (CDIO) syllabus: A statement of goals for undergraduate engineering education.* MIT CDIO (Report No.1). Boston, MA: Massachusetts Institute of Technology.

Crawley, E. F. (2002). *Creating the Conceive, Design, Implement, Operate (CDIO) syllabus: A universal template for engineering education.* Paper presented at the 32nd American Society for Engineering Education/Institute of Electrical and Electronic Engineering (ASEE/IEEE) Frontier in Education Conference, Boston, MA.

Fouts, J. T., & Chan, J. C. K. (1997). The development of work-study and school enterprises in China's schools. *Journal of Curriculum Studies, 29*(1), 31–46. doi:10.1080/002202797184189

Hao, Y. (2005). *A study of institutional alternative for hi-tech industry development of China's universities.* Unpublished doctoral dissertation, Huazhong University of Science and Technology, China. (in Chinese).

Lawless, D., Wu, B., Carroll, D., Gordon, D., Hussey, M., & O'Leary, C. ...Xu, X. (Eds.). (2007). *An industry oriented model for software education in China: Adapting an Irish model to Chinese conditions.* Dublin, Ireland: Blackhall.

Li, J. (2003). Exploration and practice in the construction of practical training bases in higher vocational education. [in Chinese]. *Vocational and Technical Education, 24*(22), 19–21.

Porter, M. E. (1996). What is strategy? *Harvard Business Review,* (November-December): 61–78.

Rompelman, O., & Vries, J. D. (2002). Practical training and internships in engineering education: Educational goals and assessment. *European Journal of Engineering Education, 27*(2), 173–180. doi:10.1080/03043790210129621

School of Software at Harbin Institute of Technology. (2009). *White Paper on software industry oriented education.* Harbin, China: Harbin Institute of Technology. (in Chinese).

Si, S. Z. (2004). Discussion on the role orientation and development model of school-running enterprise in our country. [in Chinese]. *Technology and Innovation Management, 25*(4), 53–55.

Trevisan, M. S. (2004). Practical training in evaluation: A review of the literature. *The American Journal of Evaluation, 25*(2), 255–272.

Xu, X. (2006). The approach and practice of software industry-oriented education in China. *Proceedings of the 2nd China-Europe International Symposium on Software Industry-Oriented Education.* [new series]. *Journal of Harbin Institute of Technology, 12,* 1–3.

KEY TERMS AND DEFINITIONS

CDIO: An advanced engineering education theory that stresses engineering fundamentals in the context of conceiving, designing, implementing and operating real-world systems and products.

Convergence Education: A possible ideal advanced form of institute-industry co-operation, where both sides situate engineering education in a strategic position and engage in an expanding range of co-operations of mutual benefit, and of benefit to students and graduates, without the interests of one side or the other taking undue precedence.

Institute Industry Interaction (I-I-Ia): An arrangement in which institute and industry interact at a shallow level with each managing their activities largely independently.

Institute Industry Interoperation (I-I-Io): An arrangement in which industry and institute become actively and constructively involved together in many educational activities, based on thoroughgoing co-operation and seeking synergistic benefit to both.

Value Chain: A series or chain of activities within a firm operating in a specific industry.

Chapter 4
UB1-HIT Dual Master's Programme:
A Double Complementary International Collaboration Approach

David Chen
IMS-University of Bordeaux 1, France

Bruno Vallespir
IMS-University of Bordeaux 1, France

Jean-Paul Bourrières
IMS-University of Bordeaux 1, France

Thècle Alix
IMS-University of Bordeaux 1, France

ABSTRACT

This chapter presents a double complementary international collaboration approach between the University of Bordeaux 1 (UB1) and Harbin Institute of Technology (HIT). Within this framework, the higher education collaboration (dual Master's degree programme) is supported by research collaboration that has existed for more than 15 years. Furthermore this collaboration is based on the complementarities of competencies of the two sides: production system engineering (UB1) and software system engineering (HIT). After a brief introduction on the background and overview, the complementarities between UB1 and HIT are assessed. Then a formal model of the curriculum of the dual UB1-HIT Master's programme is shown in detail. A unified case study on manufacturing resource planning (MRPII) learning is presented. Preliminary results of the Master's programme are discussed on the basis of an investigation carried out on the first two cohorts of students.

DOI: 10.4018/978-1-60960-797-5.ch004

BACKGROUND AND OVERVIEW

Research relationships between the University of Bordeaux 1 (UB1, France) and Harbin Institute of Technology (HIT, China) exist for several years and both parties have established strong and long-term relationships with their industries over some 30 years. In the research domain on computer integrated manufacturing and production system engineering and integration, the co-operation between the University of Bordeaux 1 (IMS-LAPS: Laboratory for the Integration of Materials into Systems-Automation and Production Science Department) and China started in 1993. Several Europe-China projects coordinated by UB1 have been carried out (1993-1995; 1996-1997; 1998-2002) in this domain, involving more than 7 major Chinese universities such as Tsinghua University, Xi'an Jiaotong University, Harbin Institute of Technology, Huazhong University of Sciences and Technologies, and others. More recently, the cooperation between the University of Bordeaux 1 and Harbin Institute of Technology has been strengthened to develop enterprise interoperability research activities in the Interop Network of Excellence (2004-2007) programme under the auspices of the European 6th Framework Programme for Research & Development (FP6) (European Commission, 2003b).

There is a long and strong cooperation between UB1 and HIT in research on other topics as well, including enterprise system modelling, engineering and integration. However co-operation in higher hducation was not so well-developed in the past. Consequently, it was logical to extend the existing co-operation from the research base to incorporate higher education.

Therefore, in September 2006 UB1 and HIT launched a dual master's degree programme on enterprise software and production systems. This programme relies on the know-how of HIT in computer sciences and enterprise software applications, and of UB1 in enterprise modelling, integration and interoperability research.

This joint international programme aims to train future *system architects* of production systems, with the ability to model, analyze, design and implement solutions covering organization, management, and computer science in order to improve performance of both manufacturing and service enterprises. It also aims to develop the capabilities of students to develop and grow in an international working environment particularly in China or France but also in most other countries where the themes covered by the programme are now and will continue to be vital.

The programme is organized over two years. The first year's courses are given in HIT and are concerned with industrial oriented computer sciences. The second year's courses are given in UB1 and dedicated to production management and engineering. The first two cohorts of the master's programme have successfully completed their studies and their industry internships in China and France and have obtained the Master's Degree of the University of Bordeaux 1 and the Master's Degree of Harbin Institute of Technology in September 2008 and 2009.

Table 1 gives an overview on the organization of the two year programme. All courses are presented in English, including examinations and internship defense. One characteristic is that the industry internship can be carried out in China, or in France or in any third country in the world.

The internship placements are mainly in companies, large as well as small/medium enterprises (SMEs), which have industrial co-operation projects with China, but not necessarily limited to that. Besides IT-oriented work, the internships are situated in the manufacturing industry sector as well as that of the services, typically as a responsible person in charge of industrial management (production, quality, and maintenance), a person in charge of design, development and implementation of software applications, a consultant, or a project leader.

Table 1. Organisation of the dual master's programme

Year 1		
Teaching/training	Semester	Location
Project	First	Harbin or Bordeaux
Internship	First	World
Courses	Second	Harbin
Detail: • Project (135h / 9 ECTS - European Credits Transfer System), • Training in enterprise (305h / 21 ECTS), • Algorithm and System Design and Analysis (90h / 6 ECTS), • Database Design and Application (analysis and design) (94h / 6 ECTS), • Software Architecture and Quality (93h/6 ECTS), • Project Management and Software development (92h / 6 ECTS), • Object-Oriented Technology and UML (86h / 6 ECTS).		
Year 2		
Teaching/training	Semester	Location
Courses	Third	Bordeaux
Training in company	Fourth	World
Detail: • Modelling of industrial systems (135h / 9 ECTS), • Production management (135h / 9 ECTS), • Industry performance measurement (45h / 3 ECTS), • Industry systems integration (90 h / 6 ECTS), • Option (45h / 3 ECTS), • Training in enterprise (450h / 30 ECTS).		

COMPLEMENTARITIES UNDERPINNING THE COLLABORATION

Software Engineering and Production System Engineering

As mentioned above, this collaboration is based on the complementary strengths of UB1 (production system engineering) and HIT (software system engineering).

Considering an enterprise from the general point of view as a system providing goods and services or, from the narrower point of view of its information system, it is clear that both of these approaches relate to the fundamental philosophy of engineering. In both cases the purpose is to design an overall architecture for the system, consistent and relevant to a predefined mission.

Models and simulations have a central role in both approaches.

Production system engineers view the enterprise as a system having a purpose related to a strategy. Within this purpose and strategy, performances are defined and enable the evaluation of how well the enterprise runs.

The necessity for communication and co-operation between sections within a company or between companies within a network has led to the important concept of integration. Today, the numerous forms of co-operation and the versatility they require brings into prominence the concept of interoperability that can be broadly understood as a loose integration.

Because of the complexity of the enterprise, it is always considered to relate to a *reference* (a conceptual model or reference architecture). With respect to this reference, the engineering methodologies used are supported by modelling languages and frameworks (enterprise modelling), the role of which is to enable the understanding of the structure and behavior of the enterprise. The existing diversity of languages and software supports leads to the need to analyze them in detail, in order to compare them and potentially use them together. In this perspective, a pure syntactical approach is not enough, and therefore current scientific developments in this field are related to semantics and deal with meta-models and ontology.

Furthermore, the consideration of the human-being as a component of the enterprise must always be remembered. For this reason the relation of the models with decision-making (of design and/or of management) is an important issue, whatever the approach used.

From a software engineering point of view, the need for integration can be matched through the provision and the implementation of software tools, mainly enterprise resource planning (ERP) tools. This domain then focuses on IT solutions analysis, implementation projects, IT solution performance analysis, and the identification of the usability domain and the limitation of classical methods. The ways in which the functions of the information system are integrated using such IT tools is globally understood today. Organizational challenges are also quite well known. The main outstanding issues relate to supporting the processes of the enterprise by consistently integrating the several IT solutions that have functionalities that generally cover more than is required. In this context, the capability to match the models of the enterprise (the requirements) with the models emerging from the IT solutions (the so-called space of solutions) becomes crucial. Finally, a continuing core problem is ensuring a permanent alignment of the information system and its various implemented IT solutions with the strategy of the company. Because the economic environment is dynamic, this leads, of necessity, to a policy of continuous engineering.

In summary, the two domains relate both to the design, integration and control of systems under performance conditions. In order to match the dynamic requirements and take changing constraints into account, it is necessary to continually improve the understanding of the interactions between the various models and to gather and integrate the various points of view such as organization, software, etc. In this drive to keep on improving performances, the exploitation of the complementarities between software engineering and production systems engineering is a thoroughly necessary requirement.

Enterprise Interoperability as an Emerging Topic Related to These Complementarities

Enterprise interoperability is a topic currently emerging at the confluence of software engineering and production systems engineering. It is a topic of considerable and growing scientific and technical research, fundamentally because of the considerations presented above.

Worldwide, the competitiveness of enterprises, including SMEs, will strongly depend in the future, on their ability to develop and implement massively and rapidly networked dynamic organisations. New technologies for interoperability within and between enterprises will have to emerge to radically solve the recurrent difficulties encountered - largely due to the lack of conceptual approaches - to structure and interlink enterprises' systems (information, production, decision) (European Commission, 2003b).

Today, research on interoperability of enterprise applications does not exist as such. As a result of the IST Thematic Network IDEAS (Baan, 2003), the roadmap for interoperability research emphasises the need for integrating three key thematic components, shown in Figure 1:

- software architectures and enabling technologies to provide implementation solutions
- enterprise modelling to define interoperability requirements and support solution implementation
- ontology, to identify interoperability semantics in the enterprise.

Interoperability is seen as the ability of a system or product to work with other systems or products without special effort on the part of the user/customer (Baan, 2003).

The ISO 16100 standard (2002) defines manufacturing software interoperability as the ability to share and exchange information using common syntax and semantics to meet an application-specific functional relationship through the use of a common interface. The interoperability in enterprise applications can more simply be defined as the ability of enterprise software and applications to interact usefully. The interoperability is considered to be achieved if the interaction can, at least, take place at the three levels: data, application and business enterprise through the architecture of the enterprise model and taking semantics into account, as shown in Figure 2.

At the beginning of the 2000s, research in the interoperability domain in Europe was badly structured, fragmented, and sometimes overlapping unnecessarily. There was no unified consistent vision and no co-ordination between various European research centres, university laboratories and other bodies. Not only was this the case with the pure research, but it was true in the training and education areas as well. To improve this situation, two important initiatives were launched by the European Commission: Interop Network of Excellence and Athena Integrated Project (European Commission, 2003a; 2003b).

The Interop Network of Excellence and the Athena Integrated Project

Interop NoE was a Network of Excellence (47 organizations, 15 countries) supported by the European Commission for a three-year period (2003-2006) (European Commission, 2003b). This Network of Excellence aimed to extract value from the sustainable integration of these thematic components and to develop new industrially significant knowledge. Interop's role was to create the conditions of a technological breakthrough to avoid enterprise investment being simply pulled by the incremental evolution of the IT becoming commercially available.

Figure 1. Three key thematic components and their integration (Baan, 2003; European Commission, 2003b)

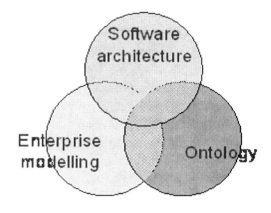

Figure 2. The three levels of interoperability (European Commission, 2003a)

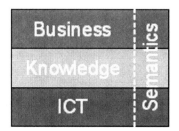

Consequently, Interop's joint programme of activities aimed to:

- integrate the knowledge in ontology, enterprise modelling, and architectures to give sustainable sense to interoperability
- structure the European research community and influence organisations' programmes to achieve critical research mass
- animate the community and spread industrially significant research knowledge outside the network.

In more detail, the joint research activities were composed of the following work packages:

- enterprise modelling and unified enterprise modelling language (UEML): unifying for interoperability and integration
- ontologies for interoperability
- domain architecture and platforms
- domain interoperabiliy
- synchronization of models for interoperability
- model driven interoperability
- model morphisms
- semantic enrichment of enterprise modelling, architectures and platforms
- business/IT alignment
- methods, requirements and method engineering for interoperability
- interoperability challenges of trust, confidence/ security
- services/take-up towards SMEs.

Athena (Advanced Technologies for Interoperability of Heterogeneous Enterprise Networks and their Applications) was also an Integrated Project supported by the European Commission for the three-year period (2003-2006) (European Commission, 2003a).

Its objective was to be the most comprehensive and systematic European research initiative in the field of enterprise application interoperability, removing barriers to the exchange of information within and between organizations. It would perform research and apply results in numerous industrial sectors, cultivating and promoting the *networked* business culture. Research and development work was carried out hand in hand with activities conceived to give sustainability and community relevance to the work done. Research was guided by business requirements defined by a broad range of industrial sectors and integrated into piloting and training. Athena would be a source of technical innovations leading to prototypes, technical specifications, guidelines and best practices, trailblazing new knowledge in this field. It would mobilize a critical mass of interoperability stakeholders and lay the foundation for a permanent, world-class hub for interoperability.

Projects running within Athena were organized in three action lines in which the activities would take place. The research and development activities were carried out in action line A. Action line B would take care of the community building while action line C would host all management activities (European Commission, 2003a).

Concerning the R&D action line, six projects were initially defined as follows:

- enterprise modelling in the context of collaborative enterprises (A1)
- cross-organisational business processes (A2)
- knowledge support and semantic mediation solutions (A3)
- interoperability framework and services for networked enterprises (A4)
- planned and customisable service-oriented architectures (A5)
- model-driven and adaptive interoperability architectures (A6).

Relations between the three action lines are shown Figure 3.

Interop NoE and Athena IP have strongly influenced and contributed to research and develop-

Figure 3. Interaction of Athena Action Lines

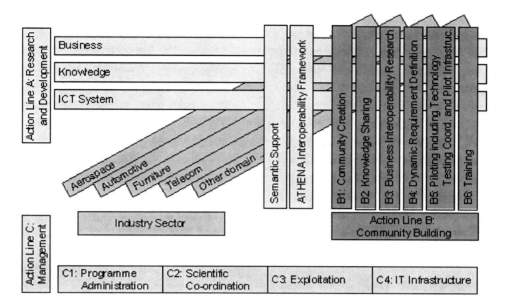

ment on enterprise interoperability in Europe and beyond. Harbin Institute of Technology was also been invited to participate in Interop NoE meetings and in the creation of the Interop Virtual Laboratory which is considered one of the important achievements of this Network of Excellence.

The Interop Virtual Laboratory (Interop-VLab)

Interop-VLab, a sustainable European scientific organization, is the continuation of the Interop Network of Excellence. It aims at federating and integrating current and future research laboratories, both academic and industrial, in order to fulfil objectives that a participating organization would not be able to achieve alone. It is supported by local institutions to promote interoperability in local industry and public administration. Interop-VLab's mission includes the following:

- **Promoting the enterprise interoperability domain and acting as a reference**: establishing a sustainable organization, at

European level, to facilitate and integrate high level research in the domain of enterprise interoperability and be a reference for scientific and industrial, private and public organisations

- **Contributing to the European Research Area**: contributing to solving one of the main issues of the European Research Area - the high fragmentation of scientific initiatives - by synergistically mobilizing European research capacities, enabling the achievement of critical mass by aggregating resources to match major future research challenges that would not be possible by individual organisations
- **Developing education and professional training**: promoting and supporting initiatives of European higher education institutions in the domain
- **Promoting innovation in industry and public services**: facing the industrial challenge of creating networks and synergies, Interop-VLab aims to promote and support applied research initiatives addressing in-

novation and the reinforcement of interoperability between enterprises, at European, national and local levels; this approach will also help to create synergy between European, national and local research programmes.

Harbin Institute of Technology is the leading partner of the China Pole of Interop-VLab. The China Pole is constituted of ten important Chinese universities spread across China. Besides research related projects, an Interop master's degree programme involving Interop-VLab members including HIT and UB1 was also planned.

FORMAL MODEL OF THE UB1-HIT DUAL MASTER'S DEGREE CURRICULUM

This section presents the details of the dual UB1-HIT master's degree curriculum. Because this programme is built on two separate disciplines and carried out in two locations in two different countries, the main challenge to its success would be the development of a deep mutual understanding of the curriculum implemented in each location and a close collaboration between the two teams, to avoid unnecessary redundancies and emphasizes synergistic complementarities. To meet this objective, a detailed and explicit representation of the curricula was necessary.

Usually university training curricula are presented in a textual form, often using tables. In general, inter-relationships between various courses and lectures tend not to be identified and/or explicitly described and considered. Sometimes this can create difficulties for students in fully understanding the relationships between component courses and their logic, and consequently in mastering the overall knowledge that they need to acquire (Alix et al., 2009).

Based on the feedback from the students after three years running on an experimental basis, it is necessary to present the master's degree programme overall curriculum in a more formal and explicit way so that both students and teachers on both sides can have a clear and unambiguous understanding of the contents of the programme and of their roles within it. Therefore, the purpose of this section is to present the formal model of the UB1-HIT dual master's programme curriculum. Unified Modelling Language (UML) was chosen to model the lectures delivered in the two years and the possible relationships between the series of lectures in the two years. Complementarities and potential future improvements are also discussed below.

Model of Year 1 Curriculum in HIT

This section describes and model of the Year 1 curriculum carried out at Harbin Institute of Technology School of Software in China. The objective of the Year 1 training is focused on software engineering, information systems analysis and design, programming techniques and IT project management.

This curriculum is mainly organized in three modules as shown in Figure 4: Language; Science and Methodology; IT Technique.

In the Language module, there are two courses, English and French.

- English: Because of all the courses of this joint master's programme are in English, a command of English is very important. The objective is to give the students the ability to read and write reports/papers in English, and to communicate with professors fluently, orally and aurally, in English.
- French: This course aims to teach the Chinese students daily French, which can help them to adapt to French daily life when they arrive in France.

The Science and Methodology module aims to teach students how to carry out scientific research,

Figure 4. UML model of year 1 curriculum at HIT

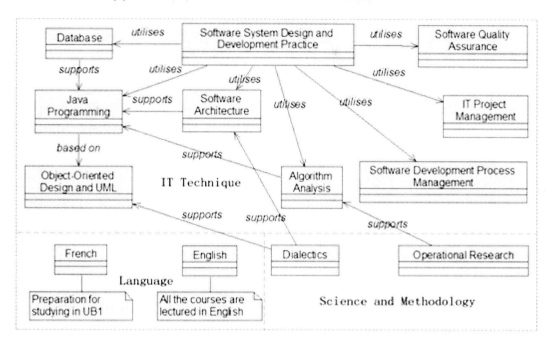

how to analyse the objects in the universe and the relationships among them. This module contains two courses, dialectics and operational research.

- dialectics: This course is to teach students the resolution of disagreement through rational discussion and ultimately the search for truth.
- operational research: This shows how to use mathematical modelling, statistics, and algorithms to develop optimal solutions to solve complex problems, improve decision-making, and make process efficiencies, to finally achieve a management goal.

The IT Technique module is the main part of the first year study. This centres on software engineering. It offers a series of IT technique courses, such as databases, Java programming, etc., as well as a series of software management courses, such as software quality assurance, IT project management, etc.. In addition, there is a practical course

in this module, in order to put both IT and project management knowledge into practice.

- IT: this set of modules aims to teach students the skills of design and implementation of IT solutions for different kinds of firm. The modules are as follows.
  - databases: this module focuses on how to use a relational database, including, designing a proper entity relationship model (ERM), creating correct data view based on ERM, querying data by structured query language (SQL), defining store procedure for a database, etc.
  - algorithm analysis: this module is an important part of broader computational complexity theory, providing theoretical estimates for the resources needed by any algorithm to solve a given computational problem: it shows how to analyze an algorithm, how to determine the amount of re-

sources (such as time and storage) necessary to execute it, and finally achieve the goal of optimising the program.

○ software architecture: this module shows how to analyze, design and simulate the structure or structures of the system - the software components, the externally visible properties of those components, and the relationships between them.

○ Java programming: this module introduces one of the most popular programming languages: after completing this module, students should have the ability to implement an executable application and learn other programming languages by themselves.

○ object-oriented design and UML: unified modelling language (UML) is a standardized general-purpose modelling language in the field of software engineering: it includes a set of graphical notation techniques to create visual models of software-intensive systems; after this course, students should have the ability to use UML to design a proper software system model.

• Management: This set of modules contains lectures on the methodology of IT project management. The courses involve the following modules.

○ software quality assurance (SQA): this topic covers the software engineering processes and methods used to monitor and ensure quality: it encompasses the entire software development process - software design, coding, source code control, code reviews, change management, configuration management, and release management.

○ IT project management: this topic shows how to lay out the plan for an IT project, and how to realize, and anticipate and avoid the risks of failure of the IT project development: after this course, students should be able to use the methodology learned to reduce the cost of the IT project and to make the project efficient and as successful as possible.

○ software development process management: this module gives more details about SQA and IT project management in the development phase of a project.

• Practical work: This module gives students a chance to put their knowledge into practice. Students are required to manage a full IT project by themselves, from requirement analysis, system model design to software implementation, test, and then software deployment: after completing this module, students will have an overall understanding of software engineering.

Model of Year 2 Curriculum in UB1

This section presents the model of the Year 2 curriculum at the University of Bordeaux 1 in France. The objective of this training is focused on enterprise system engineering, and in particular, enterprise modelling, production management, enterprise integration and interoperability.

The curriculum of year 2 is organised in five modules, as shown in Figure 5: MSI (industrial system modelling); ESI (industrial system management); MPI (industrial system performance); PRI (industrial system integration); OPT (option - bibliographical research work).

The MSI module is mainly concerned with enterprise modelling and design. It starts with a lecture on system theory, laying down the fundamental concepts of the systemic view of the enterprise. Then enterprise modelling focuses on

Figure 5. UML model of year 2 curriculum at University of Bordeaux

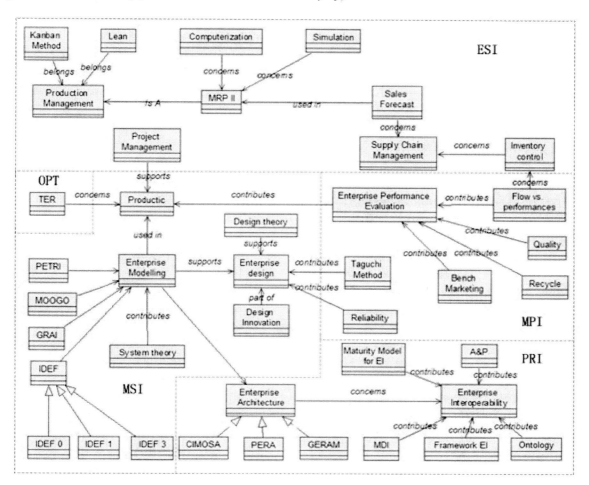

GRAI (graphs of interlinked results and activities) and IDEF (integration definition) methodologies (IDEF0 function modelling, IDEF1 information modelling and IDEF3 process modelling). The MOOGO (method for object-oriented business process optimization) process modelling tool developed by the Fraunhofer Institute for Production Systems and Design Technology (IPK) of Berlin and Petri net formal modelling are complementary to GRAI and IDEF. Productic (production science) is a lecture presenting the general problems and state-of-the-art of enterprise engineering. In parallel, design theory and innovation are presented to allow understanding of the basic concepts and principles of enterprise system design.

The ESI module focuses on production planning and control techniques with the emphasis on the MRPII method. MRPII teaching is mainly organised around an extended case study (details are given below), including (a) paper exercises, (b) game based simulation, (c) computerisation using *Prélude* software (Chen & Vallespir, 2009). Sales forecasting and inventory management methods (for example, the order point method) support both manufacturing resource planning (MRPII) implementation and supply chain management which is also another important lecture in this module. In addition, other recent methods, such as KANBAN based on JIT (just in time) and lean manufacturing, allow complementing MRPII. In parallel, project management techniques such as the PERT (programme evaluation and review technique) method are also presented.

The MPI module covers enterprise performance evaluation. Besides the Taguchi method and the reliability approach which can be related to design issues in the earlier MSI module (as shown Figure 5), a large part of the teaching is focused on quality concepts and methods. Benchmarking is also considered an important approach to improving the performance and quality of the enterprise systems and products. Another lecture is concerned with problems and solutions for recycling which is becoming more important in modern industrialised societies. Finally a game based on simulation shows how to link the flow (physical, information) in an enterprise to the performance (quality, delay), and how to act on the flow to improve the performance.

The PRI module is about enterprise integration and interoperability. Here, enterprise integration is approached principally through the use of enterprise architecture and framework modelling approaches, such as CIMOSA (computer integrated manufacturing open system architecture), PERA (Purdue enterprise reference architecture) and GERAM (generalised enterprise reference architecture and methodology). In parallel, basic concepts, framework and metrics for enterprise interoperability are also presented, because these are becoming significant new trends replacing traditional integration oriented projects. It is also noteworthy that teaching in this module is largely based on e-learning on the one hand and on the other, on seminars presented by well-known European experts in MDI (model driven interoperability), A&P (architecture & platform) for interoperability, and ontology for interoperability.

Finally the OPT module was originally designed to be a slot for optional courses. For the time being it has only one option (bibliographical research work). The students are asked to choose a subject proposed by professors and perform a bibliographical research on this. This work is done by groups of two students. Each group must write a report, present the work and answer questions in front of a jury. This work is an initiation to research work and aims at developing the capability of students to carry out bibliographical research.

Complementarities and Possible Improvements

Relationships between the courses in years 1 and 2 are tentatively identified as indicated in Figure 6. Several types of relationships are defined as follows:

- *is a* relationship: for example the IT project management lecture given in year 1 is a particular type of project management (general) studied in year 2
- *part of* relationship: the software quality assurance lecture in year 1 is part of more general quality course in year 2
- *support* relationship: this means that one course is used as a preparation or a means for another one, such as for example software oriented design and UML that are used to develop MDI and implement A&P in year 2. Enterprise modelling techniques can also be used to model user's requirements at higher level abstraction in software system design, for example, control and information management (CIM) level in the model drive architecture (MDA) framework.

Several complementarities can be identified.

- At the global level, courses on computer science are complemented by training on enterprise and production systems. This allows HIT students to acquire supplementary knowledge to be better able to develop

Figure 6. Links between the courses of the two years

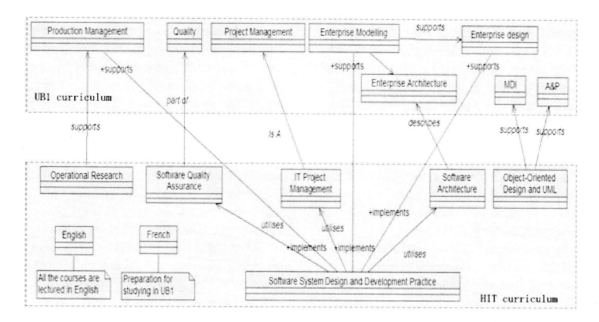

production system oriented software such as enterprise resource planning (ERP), customer relationship management (CRM), supply chain management (SCM) and others. On the other hand, UB1 students who are more familiar with industrial systems are empowered with software development skills.

- At a more detailed level and from the modelling point of view, enterprise modelling (mainly at conceptual level focusing on global system modelling) is complementary to IT oriented modelling. This is also true from the architecture perspective where enterprise architecture needs to be detailed in IT architecture and IT architecture must also be consistent with enterprise architecture.

- Both Years 1 and 2 deal with design issues. Design related lectures in year 2 (design innovation, design theory, Taguchi, reliability, etc.) provide generic design concepts and principles complementary to software design techniques learned in year 1.

At the course level, several potential improvements are envisaged as follows:

- Better coordination on the project management courses of the two years is needed. A consistent framework is necessary to position each lecture to show links and complementarities.

- More explicit relations between IT architecture and enterprise architecture must be defined, and, in particular, the alignment between business/IT, and the consistent elaboration of IT architectures in relation to enterprise architecture.

A UNIFIED MRPII TRAINING CASE STUDY

Professional training in universities on MRPII-based production planning and control techniques as well as its implementation is one of the key issues in most of the production related master's degree programmes in France. Quite often, MRPII-based education and training do not reach a satisfactory level in university curricula. There are several reasons for this. One is the lack of production and industry concepts and experience among most master's degree level students. Another reason relates to the high conceptual character of production planning and management methods, requiring mastery of many abstract ideas, definitions and terms. The third reason is that the lectures, exercises and practical work on computers usually deal with different discrete examples, case studies and illustrations. A unified common case study allowing students to learn, understand, analyse and practise MRPII-based production planning techniques is still elusive.

In this section, an innovative and experimental MRPII training project is presented. This project was first implemented in the master's degree programme (in engineering, direction and performance of industrial systems (IPPSI)) at the University of Bordeaux 1 during academic year 2008-2009, and has been partly used on an experimental basis in the dual UB1-HIT master's programme. The characteristic of this project is to combine an MRPII game, enterprise modelling (the GRAI methodology) and software implementation within a single common case study. The objective of the project is to provide the students with a unified and consistent case study to learn MRPII-based production planning, from the fundamental concepts, through paper exercises and manual game simulation to the implementation of an MRPII-based software system. After the presentation of the principles and broad organisation of the project, we will show the various phases the students follow to learn MRPII-based production planning and control in a gradual and systematic manner. The experiences of the students obtained through formal feedback and possible improvements in the approach will also be discussed.

Description of the Case

Turbix (Centre International de la Pédagogie d'Entreprise (CIPE), 2008b) is a small company that manufactures reduction gears referenced from R1 to R8 (8 finished products). The reduction gears are composed of two types of parts, E1-E8 manufactured in the company, and P1-P5 purchased externally. The E1-E8 parts are manufactured using two types of raw materials, M1 and M2. Figure 7 shows the structure of R3.

Turbix is organised in two workshops, the machine shop to manufacture the E parts and the assembly shop to manufacture the finished products (R). Masteel and Fournix are two suppliers providing raw materials M and purchased parts P, respectively. The overall organisation and physical flow is shown in Figure 8.

Because of different customer lead times, R1 and R2 are produced according to sales forecasts established beforehand. R3-R8 are manufactured upon firm customer orders. E1-E8 and P1-P5 are manufactured and purchased according to the needs for R1-R8 production. M1 and M2 are purchased according to the needs for E1-E8 production.

Figure 7. Example: R3 product structure (Centre International de la Pédagogie d'Entreprise (CIPE), 2008a)

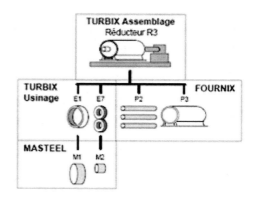

Figure 8. Organisation and physical flow of Turbix (Centre International de la Pédagogie d'Entreprise (CIPE), 2008a)

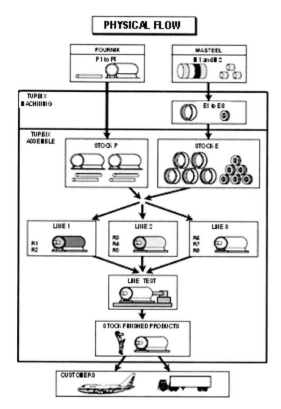

On the basis of this physical organisation, the architecture of the production management implemented in Turbix is presented Figure 9.

First Component: The Manufacturing Resource Planning (MRPII) Game

The objective of the MRPII game (Centre International de la Pédagogie d'Entreprise (CIPE), 2008b) is to allow a group of participants to discover for themselves how the MRPII method works and what are the steps one must follow to implement MRPII software in a company. Participants using this game can plan the production and purchasing orders using the MRPII technique, and simulate the execution of planned orders through various functions of the company - commercial

service, manufacturing service, inventory/stocks, purchasing service. etc. During the simulation, each participant takes a precisely defined role/responsibility.

In detail, the game allows students

- to understand the structure and functioning of the existing production system
- to plan the master production schedule (MPS) for the finished products and draw up the material requirement planning (MRP) for parts E and P
- to calculate load and perform load levelling
- and finally to simulate the functioning of the production system over a period of two months, all consistent with the management architecture in Figure 9.

Second Component: The GRAI Methodology

The GRAI methodology (Vallespir & Doumeingts, 2006) was developed at the Department for Automation and Production Science/Graphs of Interlinked Results and Activities (LAPS/GRAI) of the Laboratory for the Integration of Materials in Systems (IMS) at the University of Bordeaux 1. This methodology sets out to model, analyse and design the decision-making sub-systems of

Figure 9. Turbix management architecture

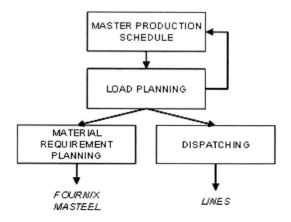

a production management system. The method consists of

- a conceptual reference model defining the set of fundamental concepts
- modelling formalisms, and
- a structured approach.

The GRAI methodology is used in the project to model and analyse the existing production system of Turbix, to detect its potential inconsistencies and to design a new improved system.

Third Component: The Prélude Production MRPII Software

Prélude Production is an MRPII compliant software developed for professional training and teaching purpose (Centre International de la Pédagogie d'Entreprise (CIPE), 2008a). Its user-friendly interface allows students to learn how to manipulate MRPII software in a gradual way. This software is used in the project to computerise the production planning and management activities in Turbix Company. After the implementation of Prélude Production in the company, it is used to plan and control the daily production activities. It is also used together with the game to perform a simulation. Figure 10 shows the main functions of the Prélude Production software.

The Programme and the Implementation of the Project

In this section, we present the programme for the project and its organisation and implementation. The project is carried out by the students over several months. Two groups of students are

Figure 10. Main functions of Prélude Production software (Centre International de la Pédagogie d'Entreprise (CIPE), 2008a)

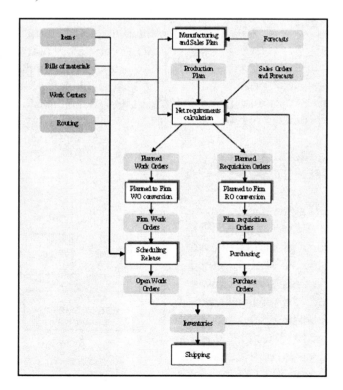

formed, each group of about 10 students. Figure 11 gives the overall logic of the project.

Initialisation Phase

To start the project, the objective, the organisation and time table, as well as the expected results at the end of each phase are presented to the two groups of students.

Playing the Game

The next phase aims to show the students how to carry out the planning and simulation without the MRPII software tool. The objective is to allow students to develop a better understanding the basic concepts and techniques of the MRPII calculation, and, at the same time, a thorough understanding of the existing Turbix system.

The game is played over one day and a half. At the beginning the students use the traditional inventory management technique (order point method) to manage the Turbix system for a one month (January) period. Then they are asked to migrate to the MRPII technique. Manual MRPII calculation is done to plan all the orders needed for the finished products (R1-R8), and parts (E1-E8) and (P1-P5). Load calculations on the four lines in the assembly workshop (the L1-L3 assembly lines, and the L4 test line) are carried out in order to validate the master production schedule (MPS). The MRPII simulation is launched on a day-by-day basis for the duration of the next month (February), for managing the production activities (purchasing, manufacturing and assembly) and the management activities (order release, production follow-up, inventory, orders close-up, etc.).

Existing System Analysis

After the MRPII game, the students are asked to analyze the functioning of the existing production system based on their knowledge and experience gained during the game. The GRAI method,

using GRAI grid and nets, is used to model the decision-making structure of the existing project management (PM) system. Based on the model of the existing system, GRAI rules can be applied to detect possible inconsistencies. If inconsistencies are found (for example, a bad decision horizon or faulty period values), the students will propose necessary corrections to the existing system in order to improve its functioning.

Simulation of Improved System

After the analysis and possible redesign of the production system in Turbix, the students then play the game again. The game simulation is done on the new system, having implemented the set of suggested corrections and modifications to the existing system. For example, one of the possible suggestions that might be proposed by the students is to adjust the value of the planning horizon in the

Figure 11. Overall logic of the project

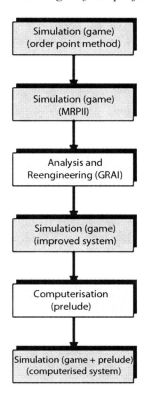

MPS and the MRP levels to allow an improved co-ordination between them.

Implementation of Prélude Production Software

During this phase, the students are asked to computerise the production planning and control activities in Turbix using Prélude Production software. For this task, the students are divided into small groups (2 students per group per computer). Firstly, the students need to make a compilation of all the relevant technical data (bill of materials, routings, items and workstations) and put them in an appropriate form to be entered in the computer. Then a small scenario (using a number of sales forecasts and firm orders) is given to students to allow them to test the Prélude Production implemented for Turbix. This tends to be a very interesting task because the students need to find errors they may have made during the data collection.

MRPII Software Based Simulation

After the validation of these test results, the simulation can begin. During the simulation, the students are asked to perform the same activities they did during the game but this time using the MRPII software.

This phase allows students to compare the two simulations, the game simulation without computer aid and the simulation with the MRPII software (Prélude Production).

DISCUSSION AND REMARKS

The experimentation carried out among students of the master's class in 2008 showed strongly the student interest and feasibility of the project. The main added values of the project were found to be the following:

- The project allowed the students not only to learn MRPII concepts and techniques, but also to practise the MRPII-based production control in a concrete and unique case study. The students could evaluate and compare the problems, difficulties and benefits at the different stages of the project using the same case.
- The game played before the computerisation stage allowed the students to take an active part in the activities of the enterprise as if they were actors in the company, thus putting them in a situation similar to that in the real enterprise
- The use of the GRAI method before computerisation allowed the detection of possible inconsistencies in the system. The benefits are to show the usefulness of enterprise modelling to improve company performance, and to computerise a re-engineered system after the correction of inconsistencies.
- The project showed that computerisation of production management is not only a matter of software. Before introducing an MRPII package in a company, it is necessary to analyse and re-engineer the existing system to make it consistent, to have the appropriate technical data, to define the most suitable parameters for the software, etc..

This project has contributed to improving MRPII-based production management training courses in French universities by providing a unified case study framework which covers the various types of exercises (understanding fundamental concepts, paper-based MRPII planning and manual simulation, enterprise modelling/analysis and re-engineering, computerisation, MRPII software-based simulation). One of the improvements planned for the near future is the reinforcement of the use of the GRAI methodology in the second phase of the project. It will also be necessary to investigate ways of increasing the time horizon of the simulation (from two months, possibly to 6 months or preferably one year). The extension of the time horizon will allow simulation of a long term production plan and the incorporation of some strategic production management decisions.

PRELIMINARY ACHIEVEMENTS AND ASSESSMENT

This section describes the results of the two first cohorts of students on the master's programme, and the feedback received from them. The students are asked to give a personal overview and overall appreciation on the content of the programme as well as the difficulties encountered in studying and comprehending each year and the benefits expected at the end of the programme. Finally the students who have earned all the European Credit Transfer System (ECTS) credits at the end of the second year of the programme and are eligible for the dual master's degrees, are asked for a professional perspective/discussion on the advantages of the programme and degree.

The first cohort of students, class 2008, had thirteen students, twelve Chinese and one French. The second cohort, class 2009, had fourteen students in year 2, ten Chinese and four French. The third cohort, class 2010, has fifteen students in its year 1, ten Chinese and five French. The relatively low number of French students, although growing, is probably because the predisposition to go abroad for study is weak in France and the students who go aboard tend to be pioneers.

The employment opportunities for the graduates are in both manufacturing and service companies. Graduates can become managers and more specifically production, quality, or maintenance managers, R&D engineers and managers, consultants, project coordinators and managers in the general domain of implementing enterprise software applications (such as ERP, SCM, PLM and many others) in large companies and in

SMEs. If, as would seem likely, the internship is a springboard to employment, another employment opportunity is in research teams and projects in academic institutions. Indeed, in 2008 eight students did their final internship in an academic or research laboratory, three in France and five in other European countries. In 2009, ten students have chosen research internships, five in French laboratories and five in other European ones.

Survey of the Opinions of the Students

In December 2008, a questionnaire was sent to all the students of class 2008 and class 2009. The objective was to obtain an evaluation of the programme, taking into account the student's difficulties, the facilities and their expectations before, during and after the programme, and to obtain feedback on the professional experience gained after the two periods of internship by the two cohorts. A simplified view of the questionnaire used is presented below.

Questionnaire Used

1. Position, name and address of the company or university?
2. Position of the internship activity (daily job) in the company?
3. Competencies before year 1, before year 2 and at the end of year 2
4. Difficulties met and facilities provided during the first and the second year of the programme?
5. Advantages and disadvantages offered/ encountered in relation to the double competency, EM (enterprise modelling) and IT (information technology), of the programme?
6. Thoughts about the continuity between Harbin and Bordeaux
7. In your daily job do you use the double competency (if not, which one do you use),

advantages offered by IT / EM knowledge in your job?

8. Differences and similarities between the form and operation of the internship in Harbin and in Bordeaux?

9. Is the double competency an advantage in finding a job or PhD position?

Seven students of class 2008 replied, two of them employed in private companies, three PhD students, and two looking for a job or further training opportunities. Twelve students of class 2009 replied.

Results from Class 2008

(a) **Competencies**: Most students (5) had low or only a fundamental level of software programming skills, and some students (2) had no software domain knowledge but principally mathematics or control theory and engineering respectively before the programme year 1. At the end of the first year, almost all the students (6) had achieved competency in software engineering, especially software architecture, software development, Java and databases. At the end of two years, most students believed they had acquired (i) knowledge about enterprise modelling and production management, (ii) knowledge about enterprise modelling methods like GRAI and IDEF, (iii) deep understanding of SCM, quality assurance and performance measurement, and (iv) knowledge through the bibliographic research work in academic fields like ontology and interoperability. After the full programme, most of the students agreed that they had made progress in the English and French languages.

(b) **Difficulties and facilities**: During the first year of the programme, most problems came from language misunderstanding which made some courses difficult to assimilate. Three students thought that the courses were heavy even though they had a good studying environment (2 of them

lacked knowledge and experience in software engineering). In the second year of the programme, 4 out of the 7 students who responded thought that topics such as interoperability and service oriented architecture were too conceptual and difficult to comprehend. With insufficient background knowledge of practical enterprise cases, models that are abstract and connections between these models are hard to understand.

(c) **Double competency statement**: Students have acquired knowledge of software development and enterprise modelling by the end of the two years. They have good knowledge of how IT works in the enterprise and also a good understanding of business processes which can help them to find the right technology when they design an enterprise management system. In their daily jobs five students out of the seven use this double competency. IT knowledge is used directly and regularly by persons in employment in companies while the PhD students use IT to implement programs to prove, analyze and show their research results. For those in employment, enterprise management knowledge supports their understanding of the framework and architecture of the issues they work on and supports the design of solutions in their daily work.

(d) **Teaching specificities**: The teaching in the IT domain tends to be considered more theoretical while the teaching in the EM domain is considered more practical because of the game-based simulations and exercises that can be seen as playing realistic roles. The enterprise games are also considered a useful tool to explore a particular context and have special values because most these games tend to be team-oriented. In Harbin the internship takes place at the same time as the course. Consequently, students have a complete project in which they use IT technology to carry it out. An advantage, according to the students, is that they can go deeper into detail through asking for information from the teachers but that sometime this becomes too closely detailed to form a proper overall view. In Bordeaux, the internship has a specific period and the subject in question is sometimes disconnected from the course even if that subject deals with management. This requires more individual initiative and creativity because the students can feel alone in confronting their problems even if they can ask their teacher. But it is considered a strong advantage that the students are totally immersed in the company.

Results from Class 2009

(a) **Competencies**: At the beginning of year 1, 9 of these students had competencies in software engineering: operating system, data structure, databases, IT project management, software quality assurance and some popular development languages such as Java, C++ and.NET. One student had specialized in automatic control and another had knowledge linked to mechanical engineering and production management. Thus the competencies were much more diverse than in the previous cohort. Before year 2, most of the students (9) had improved their programming skills as software engineers. By then they had more experience in programming and project management, and knowledge of advanced databases, algorithm, software architecture and so on. They had also improved communication skills, with a good level of French and fluent English. The other two students had acquired knowledge of programming using Java, database design, and IT project management. At the end of semester 4, all the students had gained knowledge in enterprise computing and engineering, including production management, enterprise modelling, and quality management.

(b) **Difficulties, facilities**: Like the previous cohort, the first difficulty cited is language. The second arises from the fact that students are not au fait with the production environment and so concepts relative to an enterprise are difficult to comprehend, the concept of interoperability for example is understood, but the finer details are not, and while the model-driven architecture and

enterprise modelling methods are readily learned, the lack of experience makes their use far from obvious. All the students complained about the schedule of the course, with too many courses planned in too short a period and too many different types of knowledge to be learned in different areas/domains.

(c) **Double competency statement**: Despite difficulties, students agreed that they had acquired a double competency. Not only did they know how to do programming but also understood how an enterprise works using IT technologies. The background of one domain was felt to be a great help when working in the other. The dual competency provides more choices for a future career. Even if it is not easy to re-orient one's mind from the software view to the enterprise view, they were confident that they would be able to bring these views together in the future.

(d) **Teaching specificities**: In Bordeaux, there are more games-based training exercises as opposed to the programming practicals in Harbin. As regards the internship, they did not find major differences between Harbin and Bordeaux. In the first year, the goal was to develop software systems, and students worked directly from the analysis, and then designed the system and wrote the code. In the second year, students needed to read the materials about the production system to gain a holistic understanding of the subject.

Remarks

The dual master's degee programme represents a good challenge for all the responding students because of the challenging multidisciplinary and cross-domain training during the two years. The students also became very aware of the interests and needs of companies which are very close to the topics and subjects dealt with in the programme.

Needs Expressed During the Internship (So-Called, M2)

This section provides the analysis of the internship of year 2 of class 2008, because internships of class 2009 are only in progress. As mentioned earlier, in 2008 five students did their internship in private companies. One internship topic concerned pure management issues, while all the others combined IT problems and the use of enterprise modelling methods to analyze and model enterprise systems.

Topic Relative to Management Only

A well known large company in the domain of material construction had proposed a study on pricing strategy because the market is becoming more and more competitive, and the pricing strategy must be adjusted to take into account product turnover, life cycle phase and other dynamic variables. This study focused on the analysis and comparison of the commonly used pricing strategies: premium pricing, value pricing, cost/plus pricing, competitive pricing and penetration pricing. The internship project led to the proof that the value strategy was the best strategy for new products and high-end products, but that for all other products, the competitive strategy was shown to be the best one. This conclusion has enabled the company to improve customer loyalty, keep market share and make expected profit (Jia, 2008).

Internship Studies Involving Combined Topics

One study led to the analysis of the possibilities of applying data mining techniques in cross-selling to increase the overall sales of a company specialising in material construction. The study elaborated a process methodology based on data mining software, and described the way to build mining models to do cross-selling analysis. The student described how to write associative prediction queries, integrate these queries into a Web

cross-selling application and then discussed the architecture of a web application with data mining predictions (Li, 2008).

Another subject proposed by the same company concerned the exchange of data between servers of 120 commercial agencies which constitute the company. The objectives of the company were to (i) find a solution which could monitor the servers, (ii) analyse their performance, and (iii) predict potential problems and inform the system administrator in advance. Furthermore the company needed software to help the administrator do his daily work, in verifying the backup machine and the working situation of the servers, and other tasks. The mission of the student was to choose a correct solution to satisfy the company's needs and then design and implement the architecture on the existing system (Yang, 2008).

A third combined topics study related to a small company specializing in internet search engines. The main challenge of the company was to offer to internet users the relevant information about an enterprise, a product or a service. For this task the search engine limits the referencing to the web site of the enterprise in order to have consistent and precise information. Blog, personal page and forum pages are avoided. The student participated fully in the whole project, from the requirement analysis phase to the development phase, including learning and using specific languages, technologies, etc. The student acted as an actor in the project but also as project manager during the development phase (Wang, 2008).

The fourth internship was carried out in a large French worldwide company, in the Oracle project pole. The student worked on the ERP technology taking into account the requirements of a specific customer that is a public sector administration. The company maintains the Oracle IT system for the administration. The student worked on the purchase order process from the demand, to the invoice payments, including the orders and receipts. This allowed him to study the complete acquisition workflow, and introduce some new concepts of finance and accounting, and new concepts and ontology in the financial area (Fausser, 2008).

Analysis of the Topics by the Private Companies Involved

Information on projects carried out by the students during their internships in private companies was collected through the report they gave at the end of year 2 of their programme. Three subjects out of the five were proposed by one enterprise. This indicates the difficulty of finding industrial internship in France, mainly due to the language barrier. French companies find the double competency of the student very interesting but most are not prepared to integrate students who do not speak French into their company. A second important conclusion is that most of the topics (4 out of 5) required a double competency, and in those cases the students successfully applied IT techniques to improve the performance of those companies.

CONCLUSION

This chapter presents an international collaboration between the University of Bordeaux 1 and Harbin Institute of Technology. This collaboration is characterised by the fact that it is based on:

- a long-term strategy of both institutions (UB1 and HIT) to develop sustainable co-operation in the domain of interoperability which is considered a priority subject on both sides
- the two competencies, in UB1, enterprise modelling and interoperability, and production system sciences, and in HIT, computer sciences and software engineering, are complementary in the development of R&D and in this education programme
- the combination of research activities and education/training allow benefits to flow

from the latest advances in research in enterprise software application interoperability (such as the European Union R&D projects, Athena, Interop, and others).

This collaboration model has considerable potential to be duplicated and extended to other universities and other countries.

The formal UML model to represent the joint master's programme curriculum allows explicit identification of all elementary lectures and the possible relationships between the lectures and modules. We believe that this formal modelling approach can help students to better understand the training curriculum and lead to an improved quality of education. Furthermore it also allows the teachers involved to check the overall consistency of the curriculum, to better coordinate and organise their lectures, to avoid unnecessary redundancies and overlapping coverage, introduce possible contractions and bring out synergies and complementarities.

The feedback on the students' experience of the dual master's degree programme shows that it responds to real business needs and concerns. Even with the language barrier, more companies are becoming interested in students with the double competency. For the students, even though the programme is difficult to assimilate during the two years because of its breadth and density, they are satisfied at the end because they have come to understand the crucial impact of IT on enterprise performance.

ACKNOWLEDGMENT

The authors thank Zhiying Tu and Zhenzhen Jia (University of Bordeaux 1) for their contribution to this chapter.

REFERENCES

Alix, T., Jia, Z., & Chen, D. (2009). Return on experience of a joint master programme on enterprise software and production systems. In B. Wu & J.-P. Bourrières (Eds.), *Educate adaptive talents for IT applications in enterprises and interoperability. Proceedings of 5th China-Europe International Symposium on Software Industry Oriented Education* (pp. 27-36). Talence, France: University of Bordeaux.

Baan, A. Z. (2003, March). *IDEAS roadmap for e-business interoperability: Interoperability development for enterprise application and software – roadmaps (IST-2001-37368)*. Paper presented at the e-Government Interoperability Workshop, Brussels, Belgium.

Centre International de la Pédagogie d'Enterprise (CIPE). (2008b). *Jeu de la GPAO* (gestation de la production assistée par ordinateur). Retrieved October 30, 2010, from http://www.cipe.fr

Centre International de la Pédagogie d'Entreprise (CIPE). (2008a). *Manufacturing resourses planning software package*. Retrieved October 30, 2010, from http://www.cipe.fr

Chen, D., & Vallespir, B. (2009). MRPII learning project based on a unified common case-study: Simulation, reengineering and computerization. In B. Wu & J.-P. Bourrières (Eds.), *Educate adaptive talents for IT applications in enterprises and interoperability. Proceedings of 5th China-Europe International Symposium on Software Industry Oriented Education* (pp. 233-240). Bordeaux, France: University of Bordeaux.

Chen, D., Vallespir, B., & Bourrières, J.-P. (2007). Research and education in software engineering and production systems: A double complementary perspectives. In B. Wu, B. MacNamee, X. Xu, & W. Guo (Eds.), *Proceedings of the 3rd China-Europe International Symposium on Software Industry-Oriented Education* (pp. 145-150). Dublin, Ireland: Blackhall.

Chen, D., Vallespir, B., Tu, Z., & Bourrières, J. P. (2010, May). *Towards a formal model of UB1-HIT joint master curriculum*. Paper presented at the 6th China-Europe International Symposium on Software Industry Oriented Education, Xi'an, China.

European Commission. (2003a). *ATHENA - Advanced Technologies for Interoperability of Heterogeneous Enterprise Networks and their Applications: Integrated project proposal. European 6th Framework Programme for Research & Development (FP6-2002-IST-1)*. Brussels, Belgium: European Commission.

European Commission. (2003b). *INTEROP - interoperability research for networked enterprises, applications and software, network of excellence, proposal part B. European 6th Framework Programme for Research & Development*. Brussels, Belgium: European Commission.

Fausser, J. (2008). *Maintenance of Oracle e-business suite V11 (Internal report of Internship of M2)*. Talence, France: University of Bordeaux.

International Organization for Standardization (ISO DIS 16100). (2000). *Manufacturing software capability profiling - part 1: Framework for interoperability* (ISO TC/184/SC5, ICS 25.040.01).

Jia, Z. (2008). *Pricing strategy for Point P based on analysis and comparison of commonly used pricing strategy (Internal report of Internship of M2)*. Talence, France: University of Bordeaux.

Li, Z. (2008). *Data mining applied in cross-selling (Internal report of Internship of M2)*. Talence, France: University of Bordeaux.

Vallespir, B., & Doumeingts, G. (2006). *The GRAI (graphs of interlinked results and activities) method*. Talence, University of Bordeaux 1: Interop Network of Excellence Project tutorial.

Wang, Y. (2008). *Improvement and extension of professional search engine (Internal report of Internship of M2)*. Talence, France: University of Bordeaux.

Yang, W. (2008). *Monitoring work situation of servers in Saint-Gobain Point P (Internal report of Internship of M2)*. Talence, France: University of Bordeaux.

KEY TERMS AND DEFINITIONS

Dual Master's Degree: A master's degree programme involving at least two different universities / institutions from two different countries, and allowing students to obtain two degrees from the two institutions.

Enterprise Modelling: Representing the enterprise in terms of its structure, organisation and operations according various points of views (technical, economic, social and human).

Interoperability: A property referring to the ability of diverse systems and organizations to work together (inter-operate). The term is often used in a technical systems engineering sense, or alternatively in a broad sense, taking into account social, political and organizational factors that impact system performance.

Production Management: A set of techniques for planning, implementing and controlling industrial production processes to ensure smooth and efficient operation. Production management techniques are used in both manufacturing and service industries.

Software Engineering: A profession dedicated to designing, implementing, and modifying software so that it is of higher quality, more affordable, maintainable and rapid to build.

Section 3
Curriculum Issues

Chapter 5
A Holistic Approach to Software Engineering Education

Tugrul Esendal
De Montfort University, UK

Simon Rogerson
De Montfort University, UK

ABSTRACT

This chapter introduces a final-year software engineering module that brings elements of software quality, professionalism, and ethics into one coherent teaching/learning unit.

The rationale for the module is simple. The evolution of Information Technology has led to software being pervasive in today's society. Everyone is either a direct user of software or a recipient of its services. This puts the spotlight on software engineers to deliver fit-for-purpose software that ensures beneficial outcomes for all. However, this is not so easy to do, as evidenced by the many software disasters of varying severity.

There is, consequently, a demand for professionalism of the highest order, which in turn demands a new approach to software engineering education. It is the authors' contention that a unified study of software quality, professionalism, and ethics is the right approach, and such a holistic approach is a crucial component in getting the best out of software engineering education.

These ideas were developed and refined in a compulsory 30-credit module for software engineering and computer science students. The module employs a number of novel techniques in delivery and assessment, as well as a number of online learning tools. These provide an exemplar environment of new educational experiences for those preparing for a career in software engineering. Also included in this chapter are summarised feedback ideas received from students and the experiences of the tutors delivering the module. This leads to a series of recommendations for future developments, which will be of interest to all involved in software engineering education.

DOI: 10.4018/978-1-60960-797-5.ch005

INTRODUCTION

Ubiquity of Software

How ubiquitous software has become! Not long ago, data processing departments were the exclusive users of software. They had large and expensive computer systems on which to run their applications, which were managed by teams of information technology professionals. Many people did not even know what a computer looked like.

The arrival of personal computing changed all this. First, the desktop computer brought information technology into the home; and then, the laptop computer made it an integral part of our everyday lives. In parallel with that, the availability of processor chips put computing power into everyday objects, from cars to mobile phones, turning analogue devices into digital ones.

Nowadays, many objects rely on software to deliver their services. For example, most music is recorded, disseminated, and listened to on digital equipment. In hospitals, specialised digital devices monitor patients and help doctors to diagnose ailments. Aeroplanes can now fly without pilots on board. The common denominator in all of these examples is software. National and regional governments are another example. They have various crucial responsibilities to their communities and need complex computing systems to meet those responsibilities. At the other end of the spectrum, small organisations, with no in-house software capabilities, use off-the-shelf commercial software applications to process the data that underlie their businesses.

Software Complexity and Developer Responsibilities

The complexity of the service provided is necessarily reflected in the complexity of the software itself. Word processing is, in principle, a relatively simple application; but, its complexity grows when graphics and *what you see is what you get*

formatting capabilities are added. A system that connects crime fighting agencies or one that takes astronauts into space is far from simple. Moreover, any software that may have health or safety implications (such as that in a nuclear power plant), or one on which people rely for their well-being (like that managing social security payments), must be absolutely reliable, no matter how complex it is.

This places non-negotiable responsibilities on all software engineers, in two areas:

1. Software quality, to use the *best* tools and techniques to deliver the *best* possible products
2. Professionalism and ethics, to ensure awareness of all stakeholders in the deployment of software and to safeguard their rights.

Software Disasters

The logical chain is straightforward: as our reliance on software grows, so does the demand for *good* software, which, in turn, requires *good* software engineers, the responsibility for which falls on educational institutions and specialist training organisations.

However, over the last decade, there has been a catalogue of system failures throughout the business world that evidences the fact that software development is not always being approached in a holistic way. Many examples can be found readily on the Internet, in response to the search keywords *software disaster*. They are of varying degrees of severity. Four significant examples are summarised below:

1. The launch of Airbus A380 was delayed by a year or more in 2006 because of software incompatibility problems. The wiring in one part of the aircraft did not match the wiring in another because the two parts were built by different partners using different versions of their communications standards

(http://www.zdnet.com.au/top-10-worst-it-disasters-of-all-time-339284034.htm).

2. The United Kingdom Child Support Agency's computer system overpaid 1.9 million people and underpaid around 700,000 in 2004, because it was decided to introduce a large and complex IT system at the same time as the agency was being restructured, and this resulted in enormous operational difficulties and errors (http://code-hacker.wetpaint.com/page/Worst+Software+Blunders).

3. Up to half a million British citizens did not get their new passports in 1999 because the agency had to bring in a new computer system after a change in the legislation that required all children under 16 to have a passport when going abroad, and this was done without sufficiently testing it and without training the staff (http://www.zdnet.com.au/top-10-worst-it-disasters-of-all-time-339284034.htm).

4. In 2000, the customers of an Internet company that supplied groceries and petrol could find substantial discounts by bidding for them online. The software system for groceries worked well but there were problems with the petrol system. Customers had to pay for the petrol online, wait for a card to arrive in the mail, and then find a local petrol station that would honour the discount on the card. The conclusion was that the hassle was not worth the savings and customers abandoned the scheme (http://www.pcworld.com/article/125772-4/the_25_worst_tech_products_of_all_time.html).

What was the underlying problem in each case, and, indeed, was there a common thread? The overall assessment of the situation in each case was that the main problem was an imbalance between the product and its deployment. In other words, the focus on the product and its technology, often including the project that delivered the product, was not matched by an awareness or due consideration of the stakeholders involved in the process of deploying the product. As a result of such mismatches, the wider implications of software deployment are often overlooked. And, unfortunately, it is these overlooked implications that often result in those software disasters that cause users and/or recipients to suffer.

Something needs to be done. A holistic approach to the production of software requires the involvement of holistic *rounded* software professionals. Our primary argument in this chapter is that an unbalanced and, consequently, non-holistic approach to educating software engineers cannot produce the *rounded* computer professionals the industry needs and society deserves.

Towards a Solution

To support this argument, a final-year module, entitled *Software Quality, Professionalism and Ethics*, is presented as a constructive step towards a solution. The module was jointly developed and team-taught by the authors, and in it the ideas summarised above were developed and refined.

The premise for the module is simple. The role of any software engineering course in higher education must be to promote the understanding of the causal relationship between bad/good practice and bad/good systems in software. In order to achieve this, three broad aspects need to be addressed: the technology (software quality), its application (professionalism) and the overall underpinning integrity (ethics).

Traditionally, these three aspects have been considered in isolation and have often been delivered by tutors from disparate faculties, with little or no interaction and/or collaboration between the staff. This approach does not reflect the practical reality of modern software development, implementation and use. Such an educationally isolationist approach is, therefore, inappropriate for students to understand the various influences on and wider implications of modern software deployment.

When software development and deployment is placed in its broader perspective, it has to take into account product quality, its impact on users, potential benefits and risks to the recipients of its output, and the responsibilities of the developers to these and other stakeholders, together with their interrelationships. We would argue that, without these considerations, software development will be, at best, inappropriate and, at worst, disastrous. It is essential, therefore, that software engineering students, graduating from programmes that claim to prepare them for the world of professional software development, are educated in this broader perspective of their work.

The module presented here adopts a strategy for facilitating a holistic approach to systems development, to address this gap in the educational provision.

BACKGROUND

The Software Quality, Professionalism and Ethics module is a compulsory final-year component on the honours B.Sc. course in Software Engineering at De Montfort University, delivered by the Faculty of Technology.

De Montfort University is a leading post-1992 institution for professional, creative and vocational education, underpinned by research excellence. The University's history is founded in the technical and trade education of the late 19th Century. The name comes from Simon De Montfort, Earl of Leicester, who is widely credited with establishing the first parliament in 1265. The university has approximately 20,500 students and 3,240 members of staff and, in addition, special collaborative arrangements with more than 80 universities and colleges in over 25 countries.

The Faculty of Technology is one of the larger faculties of the university, offering a wide range of courses in Media, Engineering, Business Computing, Technical Computing, Games, Forensics and Security, at both undergraduate and postgraduate levels. The Faculty's research excellence was recognised in the 2008 United Kingdom Research Assessment Exercise. The Faculty also maintained its previous position of excellence in the 2009 National Student Survey, with students showing high levels of satisfaction with their courses.

The Software Engineering course is available in either of two modes: 3-year full-time or, optionally, 4-year sandwich, which includes a 12-month industrial placement between years 2 and 3. The course covers a range of technical topics, including programming, object orientation, algorithms, and databases.

The overall aim is to give students the opportunity to stretch themselves intellectually in meeting the challenges of building complex software systems that perform reliably.

The metamorphosis illustrated in Table 1 provides an overall meta-structure for the desired development of a professional software engineer. At each stage, the student adopts a particular role. Each role has a distinctive, tutor-defined expectation of what should be achieved.

The Larva stage ideally includes one year of relevant employment in industry. In our experience, this gives students the maturity to appreciate fully the wider implications of their discipline and allows them to participate constructively in discussions. The recommendation, therefore, is always for the sandwich version of the course.

The Software Quality, Professionalism and Ethics module was perceived as part of the Pupa stage of development, where students are in their final stage of transition from learner to practitioner. The module is meant to help them with that transition.

MODULE DESIGN

When designing the module, the decision was taken that it should be facilitating, empowering, experiential, and reflective.

Table 1. Development of a software engineer

Stage	Role	Expectation
Egg *1st year*	Collector of facts	Assemble the fundamental building blocks of chosen discipline; needs to be explicitly guided
Larva *2nd year*	Absorber of knowledge	Experience software development, project management and other related subjects; still being guided but less so; ideally does industrial placement
Pupa *Final year*	Reflector on the wider implications of the discipline	Form holistic views of software quality, professionalism and ethics; encouraged to become active and autonomous learner
Adult *Young professional*	Practitioner and disseminator of good practice	Confidence in acquired knowledge, supported by honed skills and sensitivity of wider issues; a *rounded* professional and a life-long learner

It was clear from the outset that, in order to apply these concepts successfully, the academic had to act as a tutor, rather than as a lecturer. The distinction here is in the degree of interaction with students, not the dictionary definition of the words. Put simply, a lecturer is essentially non-interactive, whereas a tutor is.

Also, as pointed out by Knowles (1978), for students to develop into autonomous learners, they must be given ownership of their learning. An important component of this process is the encouragement to participate in discussions.

The module was designed to be interactive with the academic given the role of tutor, to guide the student towards maturing into a rounded practitioner. The module defines *rounded practitioner* as a graduate who understands the obligations that he/she has as a software engineer and responds positively to them. These obligations are categorised according to the headings of the Association for Computing Machinery/Institute of Electrical and Electronic Engineering Computer Society (ACM/IEEECS) Software Engineering Code of Ethics and Professional Responsibility.

The tutor-student relationship within this maturation process was further deemed to require facilitation and empowerment. In other words, the students should be given increasing responsibility for their own learning.

The need for this empowerment further demanded the reconsideration of both the structure and delivery of the module itself. The outcome was that

- lectures would be renamed *large group sessions* or *seminars* and would focus primarily on guidance, stimulation, and challenge (as in a tutorial), rather than on unidirectional dissemination of information (as in a lecture)
- the syllabus and its delivery would encourage, whenever possible, tutor-student and inter-student interaction, drawing on their respective experiences
- students would be encouraged to question issues relating to module content and develop their own stance, using their academic knowledge and practical experience in a reflective manner.

It was also identified as essential that the students should have, as specific learning objectives:

- undertaking rigorous pieces of investigation into software quality, professionalism and ethics
- demonstrating an ability to articulate an argument and communicate that in a professional manner to a wide audience
- critical evaluation of the roles that software developers play, by analysing the relationship between software (or IT) and society
- defining the different personal factors that impact upon the performance of young computing professionals.

In order to encourage reflection, it was decided to dedicate the last fifteen minutes of each weekly group session, termed the *quiet time*, to the recording of thoughts and conclusions, particularly those relating to the students' industrial experiences, linked to the topics covered. To facilitate this, students were issued with workbooks at the start of the year. The workbook is designed to give space to each week's reflection. The intention is that these spaces would be filled in on a weekly basis. This is done partly to help students to put the topics just presented and discussed into context and partly as a step towards their preparation for the subsequent activities.

SYLLABUS

In order to deliver these objectives, the module content was designed around five overlapping and interrelated elements: quality measurement, quality assurance, conduct, professionalism and social impact. These five elements were then covered by a syllabus that contained the following topics:

- quality framework, measurement techniques and tools
- capability maturity model (Humphrey, 1989), ISO (International Organization for Standardization) 9126 for software quality (ISO, 2001), and networked European software and services initiative (NESSI) (at www.nessi-europe.org)
- defining professionalism - taxonomy of ICT professions
- professional conduct - individual, team, company, governing body, policy makers
- licensing and self-regulation - normative frameworks
- social impact audit - stakeholders, issues, remedies, link to quality.

The module structure was developed to also provide the necessary linkages between software quality, professionalism and ethics, to illustrate that nothing exists or functions in isolation. For example, when discussing reliability as a quality characteristic, students are given notice that they will be discussing, in the coming weeks, issues relating to tight deadlines encroaching on testing time and how to balance such conflicting requirements. Similarly, when discussing social impact audits later in the year, they are referred back to the ISO 9126 quality keywords to see which ones need to be emphasised in each context.

LEARNING TOOLS

The topics mentioned above are underpinned by five learning tools:

- self-awareness inventories, for *student, know thyself* type added value
- CHEMCO rich case study, from which issues for consideration, exercises, and assignments are drawn
- skills framework for the information age (SFIA) to appreciate the current range of IT-related roles
- experiential learning via industrial stories (ELVIS), an interactive system that enables students to incorporate their industrial placement experiences into their learning, and culminating in a student-led seminar
- virtual learning environment (VLE), to encourage blended learning.

Each of these tools is summarised below.

Self-Awareness Inventories

At the start of the academic year, students are subjected to two self-evaluation exercises:

1. learning styles inventory (Honey & Mumford, 1992)
2. self-perception inventory (Belbin, 1981).

Learning styles inventory (LSI) is used to make students aware of their preferred approach to learning. The inventory consists of 80 statements. Students either agree or disagree with each one. Based on their responses, students can then identify their own particular preferences, as being activist, reflector, theorist or pragmatist. These are not fixed personality characteristics but acquired preferences that can be adapted in response to changing circumstances. Therefore, students are encouraged to strengthen their under-preferred styles, in order to become better at learning from a wider range of experiences.

Similarly, self-perception inventory (SPI) is used to give students insight into their behavioural tendencies in a team environment. The inventory works by measuring how strongly an individual expresses traits from eight different team roles, which are chairman, shaper, plant, monitor/evaluator, company worker, resource investigator, team worker, and finisher/completer. Each role has typical features, together with positive qualities and allowable weaknesses. The aim is to use these preferred team roles to form balanced teams.

We acknowledge that the reliability of LSI has been seriously questioned (Freedman & Stumpf, 1978) and that the construct validity remains questionable (Allinson & Hayes, 1988). However, the LSI is used primarily to make students more aware of their own approach to studying and its weaknesses do not prevent this. It is also thought that tutors gaining an awareness of student learning styles may facilitate the development of more focused teaching strategies.

SPI is not without its critics either. It has been said (Aritzeta et al., 2007) that, while some of the roles seem to represent distinct analytical constructs, others are less well defined and are not easily differentiated. Other sources (Broucek & Randall, 1996; Fisher et al., 2001) claim that observational and analytical approaches yield five roles, and not eight. Their conclusion, backed up by earlier research (Barrick & Mount, 1991), is that this big five approach is a more stable con-

struct. These issues will be reviewed for the next version of the module.

CHEMCO Rich Case Study

CHEMCO is a (fictitious) manufacturer of various chemical substances. It has a website, which outlines its various departments and their operations, including the IT/data processing department.

The CHEMCO case study is used throughout the module, to help students' consideration of various aspects of practice in a simulated real-world context. The CHEMCO home page is at http://www.ccsr.cse.dmu.ac.uk/staff/Srog/teaching/info3402/Chemco2/index.htm.

SFIA

The skills framework for the information age (SFIA) provides a common reference model for the identification of the skills needed to develop effective information systems making use of information and communications technologies. It is a two-dimensional framework, consisting of areas of work on one axis and levels of responsibility on the other. Each entry is accompanied by a brief description.

The SFIA Foundation maintains an informative website. The home page is at http://www.sfia.org.uk/cgi-bin/wms.pl/46

The module uses SFIA to draw students' attention to

- the range of skills needed by the IT industry
- where their previous employment fits onto the big picture
- help in planning their future career.

ELVIS

ELVIS (experiential learning via industrial stories) is a custom-built online tool to help students share their experiences, drawn from either employment or academic studies (Esendal & Rogerson, 2008).

The mechanism that ELVIS uses for capturing and sharing experiences is the production of short, work-based stories, related to topics covered in the module. A story is simply a narrative that makes a point. The production of these stories is closely linked to the reflection during group sessions. At the start of each quiet time, students are prompted to consider if the topics discussed relate to their own experiences and, if so, to record them with a view to publishing them as ELVIS stories.

ELVIS allows students to enter their stories into a store and tag them. Once published, the stories are available to the whole group. They can be selected via tags, viewed and printed. However, ELVIS is not a wiki because only the author is allowed to edit content. The ELVIS framework and its story page, with a sample story, can be found at http://www.cse.dmu.ac.uk/~the/SIOE.htm.

Those students who do not have relevant work-based experience are advised to search for news items on events and organisations, as reported in the press. Recommended publications are Silicon, Computer Weekly, Computing, The Guardian, IT News, IT World and Public Technology.

The culmination of ELVIS activities is the student-led workshop at the end of the year. The purpose of this is for students to bring together their ideas and reflections formulated during the year and discuss them in an open forum.

Virtual Learning Environment (VLE)

The university's resident virtual learning environment is Blackboard. It was made an integral part of the module in several ways:

- as a store for learning materials (e.g. lecture notes, sample academic papers, case studies, assignment details),
- as a grade reporting system, and
- as a communications medium (e.g. discussion board, announcements and email).

This was done because it is widely accepted that VLEs, in *blended* environments, offer new opportunities for students to gain valuable first-hand experience in using technology for collaboration, and to have access to a much greater range of resources in support of their subject learning. Evidence also suggests that a collaborative approach to learning, supported by instructional technology, could potentially lead to deeper understanding and new knowledge creation (Lehtinen et al., 1999; Mäkitalo et al., 2001).

Another factor is that Blackboard can facilitate the evaluation of actual student engagement with the module. For example, tutors can monitor the usage of the discussion board or access to the learning materials.

Further evaluation of learning and student engagement is also provided by Blackboard, in the form of statistical evidence relating to student feedback and module marks. Use of the Blackboard email system provided additional opportunity for both staff and students to contribute to evaluation and feedback.

The discussion board facility also proved to be very useful. Threads were initially set up by the tutors but, very quickly, students started creating their own.

A wide range of issues were discussed. For example, software testing as experienced during the placement year, balancing quality and costs, and cutting corners to meet deadlines were all popular topics. Issues relating to module management were also discussed, e.g. learning strategies, module content, and the effectiveness of e-learning versus face-to-face learning were all busy topics.

Ethical issues were particularly popular, prompted by the examples and exercises in the group sessions, and often leading to heated debates. For example, a number of students stated that they would get the job done, no matter what, whereas others disagreed with this, saying that too many ethical considerations were being ignored.

Occasionally, tutors archived threads. This was done when, for example, the thread had dried up or the topic had little relevance to the module or the focus needed to be shifted to other threads. In one case, a thread was archived because the content was getting abusive. This incident led to the creation of the module code of conduct, which is an example of the ongoing improvement process.

There would also appear to be a potentially rich research opportunity here.

Message postings to the discussion board can be analysed, using, for example, the Garrison et al. (2001) model, to determine the variety of contributions made by individual students. The model itself was developed by Archer et al. (2001) as a framework for understanding how such a community of inquiry functions. As such, the model illustrates the interaction of the three essential elements: social presence, teaching presence, and cognitive presence.

The discussion board data could be used to evaluate whether or not the discussion area promotes *higher order* or *deep* learning, concentrating on the cognitive presence aspect. Cognitive presence is defined as the extent to which learners are able to construct and confirm meaning through sustained reflection and discourse in a critical community of inquiry (Garrison et al., 2000) and, therefore, reflects higher-order knowledge acquisition and application related to critical thinking.

In order to evaluate cognitive presence, messages can be coded as being either a *triggering* event (the initiation phase of inquiry), *exploration* (a divergent phase), *integration* (constructing shared meaning) or *resolution* (resolving the issues or problem posed in the first phase). These categories of message posting can then be mapped to the Belbin types, to discover, for example, whether or not there is any correlation between the perceived group type of the student and actual types of messages posted by that student.

DELIVERY

Delivery was done co-operatively, by the two tutors in group sessions, according to the following principles:

- specific topics by the designated expert, the other interjecting when appropriate
- interactive and practical
- a mixture of theory, derived from both classic and current literature, and practice, with exercises drawn from on-going and current news items and students' and tutors' own experiences.

These group sessions comprised subject content presentations, whole group discussions, surveys, tests, break-out group exercises, and a formal debate, the topic for which was the registration of software engineers to practice. Group sessions were monitored for attendance and marks were awarded for both face-to-face and online participation.

The material was delivered in 28 weeks of contact time. A copy of the weekly learning plan, showing how the various activities fit together, is given in the Appendix.

ASSESSMENT

In relation to assessment, the overall aim was to make each assessment component a learning opportunity and care was taken to combine practical activities (e.g. software maintenance) with academic activities (e.g. writing a paper).

There was no written examination. Assessment was through three distinctly different assignments, the types of which the students had not encountered previously. The order of assignments and their types were designed to take students from the familiar to the unfamiliar and, on the way, help them to become autonomous learners.

Table 2. Assessment activities and marking scheme

Activity	Methodology	Weighting	Tools/Resources
1. Software maintenance assignment	Group work & submission	20% for upgraded product & maintenance report	Visual Basic or Java in labs, with time-tabled support
2. Social impact analysis assignment	Group work but individual submission	20% for final report to Board of CHEMCO	SoDIS package in labs, with time-tabled support
3. Academic paper writing assignment	Individual work & submission	30% for mini-paper	• Library • Internet • Personal experiences
4. Involvement in the module	Individual work & submission • ELVIS stories (15%) • Contributions to the online discussion board (2%) • Attendance at large group sessions (13%)	30% in total	• ELVIS Online • Blackboard

Marks are allocated according to the activities in Table 2.

Given the novel nature of this assessment strategy, the following explanatory details may be useful.

1st Assignment: Software Maintenance

This exercise gets students started on their journey with something familiar but not too familiar. Maintenance was something they had not done before, although they had developed many applications during their studies.

Two separate effort estimation packages are made available, both having the same functionality, and in very similar states of incompleteness, but written in different languages by consultants commissioned by CHEMCO (i.e. final-year students from previous years). The languages are Visual Basic.NET and Java.

The students form themselves into consultancy groups of two or three members each, and, depending on their expertise and preferences, choose one of the packages. Their task is to learn about the underlying estimating technique, analyse their chosen system for errors and weaknesses, and make the necessary changes, with the overall aim of bringing the software up to a required standard.

The work is supported by weekly *software clinics*, during which the groups discuss their progress with the tutors. Each consultancy group submits the upgraded version of their package, a maintenance report that outlines what was done and by which member, and a review of the final product's quality characteristics.

2nd Assignment: Qualitative Risk Assessment

For this assignment, students first learn to use a custom-built package, called software development impact statement (SoDIS), and then, in pairs (or threes), undertake a SoDIS analysis for the proposed PRO-CHEM system for CHEMCO. The CHEMCO website is their primary source of information. SoDIS project auditor software is available from http://www.softimp.com.au/sodis.

Each student produces a report, of no more than four content pages, for the CHEMCO Board of Directors, outlining their findings. They are expected to highlight all issues they feel should be brought to the attention of the Board, for which they exercise judgement. For example, they may decide not to do a detailed analysis for all stakeholders or they may decide that some of the requirements would not yield any significant issues.

The report must be fit for purpose and written in a way that Board members can understand. The challenge is to make technical topics understandable to non-technical members of the Board.

3ʳᵈ Assignment: Academic Mini-Paper

This work gives students the opportunity to explore in greater detail a particular aspect of the syllabus that is of particular interest to them. They can choose a single theme (quality or professionalism or ethics) or a combination of two themes (quality and professionalism, or quality and ethics, or professionalism and ethics) or a combination of all three themes (quality and professionalism and ethics).

The sample titles given in Table 3 are made available.

The assignment is in two parts. In part 3a, students have to research the existing body of knowledge and identify four papers from reputable academic journals and conference proceeding, relating to their area of choice. The students are given a few indicative journal names to get them started. They are also warned that searching for papers and choosing a title is an iterative process and will take time to complete.

Each paper is reviewed in 250 words, focusing on the main message of the paper and why it is worthy of being chosen. The title of the mini-paper is derived from these reviews. Marks are given for the quality and relevance of papers chosen, the quality of the reviews done, the relevance of

proposed title to the papers reviewed, and the quality and novelty of title and associated arguments.

An *assignment clinic* gives students advice and support for part 3b. They can modify their title at this stage.

In part 3b, students write a mini-paper of 1000-1200 words, with feedback from part 3a to help them. The mini-paper must be properly referenced (e.g. the four original papers, plus, typically, five more papers). In writing the mini-paper, students must demonstrate critical reflection, logical reasoning and original thinking. The paper must be logically coherent and grammatically correct.

Marks are given for critical reflection, original thinking, logical reasoning, style and grammar, and references. Sample submissions are posted on Blackboard, by agreement with the author.

DISCUSSION

The above presentation attempts to make clear

- how the module provides an overall learning environment that allows individual students to decide how and when to access the information store in order to increase their knowledge and experience
- the assessment strategy that enables students to determine their individual learning pathways, to achieve the specified learning outcomes
- the novel approach in which students are given the opportunity to build upon their

Table 3. Sample mini-paper titles

Area	Sample title
Q – quality	*The effectiveness of the Capability Maturity Model Integrated (CMMI) in seeking guaranteed perfection*
P – professional practice	*Professionalism is more than complying with the BCS code of practice*
Q&E – relevance of ethics to quality assurance	*The ethical dilemma of delivering lower quality on time and within budget*
Q&P&E – cross-section of all three	*Metrics as a utilitarian approach to professionalism*

own experience and knowledge to address software development in a new light

- the overall approach of experiential learning, with the tutors acting as guides through complex and multi-faceted issues and problems.

These ideas and techniques were developed over a four-year period. In its most recent year of delivery, the module ran with a cohort of 146 students, achieving the best results across all final-year modules. The external examiner noted and commented favourably on what the module was trying to achieve. In this respect alone, the module can be deemed to be a success. However, how did the students feel about it, and equally importantly, what did the tutors think?

As regards the students' perspective, in addition to informal feedback during the year, students were also asked to evaluate formally their learning experience at the end, using Blackboard. Generally the student responses were mixed. Some wanted less debate in the lectures because the felt they did not learn from that. Others appreciated the opportunity to contribute freely during lectures. Initially students found the general openness of the assessment process and the lack of a formal examination difficult, but gradually came to be happy with them. Given this initially widespread unease, the decision was taken to tighten the wording and requirements of the 1st assignment, to ease the students towards openness in their subsequent assignments and the module in general. Interestingly, the students were generally positive that this module prepared them for the world of work. A few students were not convinced that they learned anything in the module that would get them a job, and some, interestingly, suggested that while they now knew their responsibilities would their co-workers or employers listen to them.

From the tutors' perspective, there were three main issues relating to the students' engagement with the module:

- Some students in the cohort, following their previous school and university experience, tended to expect to be taught and told what to do and when to do it, rather than taking greater personal responsibility for their own learning. They failed to grasp the value of how the module exposed them to different learning opportunities and tools to assist in engaging a diversity of students.
- Some were slow to respond to the new regime of co-operation and open discussion, due to shyness or fear of looking silly stoping them making public their thoughts and experiences.
- Some confused *reflection* with *note taking*, in that, when asked to reflect on the day's topic, they ended up writing what was discussed, not what they thought about it or how they related to it or where it might take them.

CONCLUSION

The module strategy enables motivated students to shine. They make presentations, argue their point, take part in a formal debate, and visibly benefit from the experience. It is not unusual for such students to end up wanting to do more activities. In fact, on several occasions students asked why these topics are not covered in earlier years. This encouraging finding at the Pupa stage might suggest that there is value in investigating similar approaches at the Egg and Larva stages.

Others, not necessarily unmotivated but quiet, hide in the group, minimise their interaction, and do the best they can through listening to others and making online contributions. But, it is their choice, which is part of taking ownership, of maturity, and of exploiting opportunities.

Attendances tend to be always high in the group sessions and students always make sure that they sign the register to get their attendance marks. Of course, attendance does not mean engagement, but it is a step in the right direction.

In conclusion, concentrating on technical issues alone limits a university's ability to produce *rounded* IT professionals. The module described in this chapter is, we believe, a definite step towards damage limitation and helps to give students the confidence to cope with wider workplace issues.

ACKNOWLEDGMENT

The development of the module describe was partly supported by a research informed university teaching award during the academic year 2007-2008.

REFERENCES

Archer, W., Garrison, D. R., Anderson, T., & Rourke, L. (2001, March). *A framework for analyzing critical thinking in computer conferences.* Paper presented at the European Conference on Computer-Supported Collaborative Learning (Euro-CSCL 2001), Maastricht, Netherlands.

Aritzeta, A., Swailes, S., & Senior, B. (2007). Belbin's team role model: Development, validity and applications for team building. *Journal of Management Studies, 44*(1), 96–118. doi:10.1111/j.1467-6486.2007.00666.x

Barrick, M. R., & Mount, M. K. (1991). The big five personality dimensions and job performance: A meta-analysis. *Personnel Psychology, 44*, 1–26. doi:10.1111/j.1744-6570.1991.tb00688.x

Belbin, R. M. (1981). *Management teams: Why they succeed or fail.* London, United Kingdom: Heinemann.

Broucek, W., & Randall, G. (1996). An assessment of the construct validity of the Belbin self-perception inventory and observer's assessment from the perspective of the five-factor model. *Journal of Occupational and Organizational Psychology, 69*(4), 389–405.

Esendal, T., & Rogerson, S. (2008, July). *Using technology to incorporate students' work-based experiences into a blended-learning environment.* Paper presented at the International Conference on Information Communication Technologies in Education (ICICTE 2008), Corfu, Greece.

Fisher, S., Hunter, T., & MacRosson, W. (2001). A validation study of Belbin's team roles. *European Journal of Work and Organizational Psychology, 10*(2), 121–144. doi:10.1080/13594320143000591

Garrison, D. R., Anderson, T., & Archer, W. (2000). Critical inquiry in a text-based environment: Computer conferencing in higher education. *The Internet and Higher Education, 2*(2-3), 1–19.

Garrison, D. R., Anderson, T., & Archer, W. (2001). Critical thinking and computer conferencing: a model and tool to assess cognitive presence. *American Journal of Distance Education, 15*(1), 7–23. doi:10.1080/08923640109527071

Honey, P., & Mumford, A. (1992). *The manual of learning styles* (3rd ed.). Maidenhead, United Kingdom: Honey.

International Organization for Standardization/International Electrotechnical Commission. (2001). *Software engineering - product quality - part 1: Quality model.* (ISO/IEC 9126-1).

Knowles, M. S. (1978). *The adult learner: A neglected species* (2nd ed.). Houston, TX: Gulf.

Lehtinen, E., Hakkarainen, K., Lipponen, L., Rahikainen, M., & Muukkonen, H. (1999). *Computer supported collaborative learning: A review of research and development. The J. H. G. I. Giesderbs Reports on Education, 10.* Nijmegen, The Netherlands: University of Nijmegen, Department of Educational Sciences.

Mäkitalo, K., Salo, P., Häkkinen, P., & Järvelä, S. (2001, March). *Analysing the mechanism of common ground in collaborative Web-based interaction.* Paper presented at the European Conference on Computer-Supported Collaborative Learning (Euro CSCL 2001), Maastricht, The Netherlands.

Watts, H. (1989). *Managing the software process.* Reading, MA: Addison Wesley.

KEY TERMS AND DEFINITIONS

Blended Learning: The combination of face-to-face classroom based learning and computer-mediated learning where students and tutors come together to improve the quality of the learning experience which is independent, sustainable and useful.

ICT Ethics: To integrate ICT and human values in such a way that ICT advances and protects human values, rather than doing damage to them, thus promoting the formulation and justification of policies for the ethical use of ICT and the carefully considered, transparent and justified actions leading to acceptable ICT outcomes.

Professionalism: Conduct consistent with the tenets of the given profession as demonstrated by acceptable behaviour such as honesty, integrity, fairness, competence, ethical action and public service.

SoDIS: The software development impact statement process, a way to improve the quality of project scoping, stakeholder identification and analysis, linked with requirements or tasks analysis, project management and risk assessment processes.

Software Engineers: Those professionals involved in the planning, management, development, implementation and maintenance of software.

Software Quality: The measures of how well software is designed and how well the software conforms to that design taking into account different stakeholder perspectives.

Stakeholders: Those, whose situation, experience and/or opportunity are directly or indirectly affected by the development or delivery of the software in question.

APPENDIX

Weekly Learning Plan

Week	Group Seminar 2 hours	Lab 1 hour	Assignment	Attendance Mark (cumulative)
1	Introduction; learning culture; resources.	no session	Assignment 1 handed out	0.0
2	Introduction to ELVIS; publishing stories	no session		0.5 (0.5)
3	Intro to SW Quality; quality characteristics; metrics	no session		0.5 (1.0)
4	Project Management	Software Maintenance Clinic (in consultancy groups)		0.5 (1.5)
5	Risk Management		Ass 1a: Pre-maintenance report (5%)	0.5 (2.0)
6	Software Quality Techniques			0.5 (2.5)
7	Design metrics Assignment 1 clinic			0.5 (3.0)
8	Implementation metrics			0.5 (3.5)
9	Product metrics			0.5 (4.0)
10	Maintenance metrics		Ass1b: Product & report (15%)	0.5 (4.5)
11	Mission critical software vs Commercial software	no session		0.5 (5.0)
12	Quality, professionalism and ethics. Assignment 3 briefing.	no session	Publish ELVIS stories Part1 by 15 Dec	0.0 (5.0)
16	Nature of software development; success and failure; stakeholders.	no session		0.5 (5.5)
17	Risk – Traditional approach	SoDIS Project Auditor Exercise (in lab groups)		0.5 (6.0)
18	Risk – Social perspective			0.5 (6.5)
19	Obligations & responsibilities; professional relationships		Ass 3a: Background & Title (10%)	0.5 (7.0)
20	Code of conduct			0.5 (7.5)
21	People			0.5 (8.0)
22	Code of Practice			0.5 (8.5)
23	Clinic for assignment 3		Publish ELVIS stories Part2 by 2 Mar	0.0 (8.5)
24	No session.		Ass 2 Sodis Report (20%)	-
25	Licensing and self regulation debate preparation	no session		1.0 (9.5)
26	Licensing and self regulation debate.	no session		1.5 (11.0)
27	Student-led workshop (collect student notebooks)	no session	Hand in notebooks Publish stories Part3 by 1 Apr	2.0 (13.0)
28			Ass 3b: Mini Paper (20%)	

All materials for each week's group seminar are available on Blackboard.

Chapter 6
Industry Oriented Curriculum and Syllabus Creation for Software Engineering Series Courses in the School of Software

Yushan Sun
Harbin Institute of Technology at Wehei, China

ABSTRACT

The overall curricula, with individual syllabuses and teaching modalities, were created for a coherent series of industry-oriented software engineering courses within general computer science degree programmes. This series was created as a systematic, disciplined, and quantifiable approach to the development, operation and maintenance of software, based on Institute of Electrical and Electronic Engineering and Association for Computing Machinery documentation as wewll as insights from many universities around the world (Joint Task Force on Computing Curricula, 2004). It combines computer science foundations with engineering, organization, teamwork, communication, and project management issues. Practical project and team-oriented exercises are included, and a significant industry-related project is an integral element within the series.

In the creation of the syllabuses, the pedagogical theory known as the elaboration theory of instruction was used to carefully select the topics to be taught in class. In the classroom presentation, a bottom-up approach was adopted, in which practical and industry examples are used as the first means of introducing concepts, and then an interactive teaching method is used. Students were required to complete a large number of practical design assignments and projects. By this active and inclusive method, the students tended to engage actively and creatively in the course.

DOI: 10.4018/978-1-60960-797-5.ch006

INTRODUCTION

Defined as the application of a systematic, disciplined and quantifiable approach to the development, operation and maintenance of software, software engineering education has attracted considerable attention from the Institute of Electrical and Electronic Engineering and the Association for Computing Machinery as well as from many universities around the world (Joint Task Force on Computing Curricula, 2004). Documentation from these sources that include guiding principles, suggests that in software education it is necessary to combine computer science foundations with engineering, organization, teamwork, communication and project management topics. Practical project and team-oriented exercises are needed to complete a significant project when studying such a course.

As software projects have become more complex, the burden of software engineering education in computer related departments has become considerably heavier. Different universities have adopted different approaches, with some teaching the course along the traditional lines offering a single course named software engineering, with others offering a range of software engineering-related courses. The problem with the former approach is that a single course cannot adequately cover so much rich material, and the problem with the second approach is that the courses tend to be designed separately so that some unnecessary overlaps can occur and the interrelationships between them are not fully elucidated. Also, since students are required just to earn sufficient credits to graduate, key modules may often be skipped by many students.

In many traditional departments of computer science, software engineering is the only required course within the software engineering discipline for the students whose major is not software engineering. Often, this course deals mainly with software engineering theory and principles. Many universities offer this subject as a single course, with teaching mainly focused on the theory. Students spend some 40 classroom hours learning software engineering theory with a small number of basic exercises. Without the reinforcement of practical work, students tend to forget the theories learned from this class soon afterwards.

CREATING AN INDUSTRY-ORIENTED CURRICULUM FOR SOFTWARE ENGINEERING SERIES COURSES IN THE SCHOOL OF SOFTWARE

However, in the School of Software within Harbin Institute of Technology (HIT) at Wehei, where students take software engineering as their major subject, a practical industry-oriented teaching ethos is implemented with a view to students achieving a seamless transition to the software industry upon graduation. Not only is attention paid to the theory but still more is paid to the practice. To deal with the problems mentioned above, when drafting the overall curriculum, the overlaps, interfaces and interrelationships between the series courses in the curriculum are thoroughly considered and each course carefully designed to have a number of large-scale and hands-on projects for the students to complete (Fenwick & Kurtz, 2005; Reichlmayr, 2006). The overall scheme of the series of sub-courses is shown in Figure 1.

In this scheme, a single course in software engineering is not considered enough, but rather, the software engineering course is designed as a group of sub-courses to include software engineering, object oriented design, software architecture and design patterns, as well as software quality assurance and testing (Petkovic et al., 2006; Zuser et al., 2006). All are required courses. This group of courses is then followed by two optional application courses.NET and J2EE, of which the students select one. Both courses emphasize not only programming skills but also design issues, including software architectures and design patterns.

Figure 1. Series of sub-courses in software engineering education

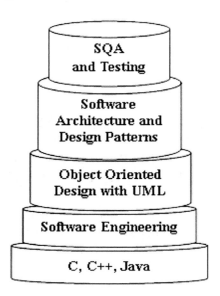

The contents of each course are described in the next section of this chapter, and in the following section, the inter-connections between them are discussed. In the final two sections, teaching-related issues and the expectations of students are further explored.

The Sub-Courses: Teaching Objectives and Contents

A. Software Engineering

The objective of this course is for students to learn the principles of software engineering in the context of contemporary specification, design, coding, testing, evaluation, and maintenance methodologies.

The course content includes the following topics:

- managing software projects (project management concepts, software process and project metrics, software project planning, risk analysis and management, project

scheduling and tracking, software quality assurance and software configuration management)
- conventional methods for software engineering (systems engineering, analysis concepts and principles, analysis modeling, design concepts and principles, architectural design, user interface design, component-level design, software testing techniques, software testing strategies, technical metrics for software)
- object-oriented software engineering concepts (object-oriented concepts and principles, object-oriented analysis, object-oriented design)
- project assignments.

One software engineering project is required and this is done in teams. Each team designs a separate software project, including requirement specifications, system analysis and program design, using conventional procedural design methods. In addition, a certain amount of detailed design is also required.

B. Object Oriented Software Design and UML

The objective of this course is for students to acquire a working knowledge of the foundations of object-oriented design and analysis. Content includes development of conceptual models of the problem domain of a software product, development of software models of the software solution to the problem as clarified during analysis, and constructing programs that implement the design models. The purpose of this course is to have students learn to think in terms of objects, so that they can identify the objects in a system and assign responsibilities to system components. After completing the course, students are expected to be able to analyze problems and develop conceptual models, generate designs from the models developed, and implement the design using an object-oriented language such as C++ or Java. The Unified Modeling Language (UML) is used to develop object models.

One project is assigned to the students who are required to complete it in teams. The project requirement must include objected-oriented analysis, object-oriented design, detailed design and coding.

C. Software Architecture and Design Patterns

The objective of this course is that the students learn the increasingly important features of high-level software architecture and detailed design using software design patterns, within the broad field of modern software engineering. In a comprehensive and creative course, the students are expected to master the outlines and principles of how to create a high quality software system. Specifically they are expected to understand the commonly used (as well as some rare) software design patterns and software architectures, master the main principles, grasp the advantages and disadvantages of each, know the types of situation in which to use each one and learn and understand the interconnections between the different aspects of software development.

The contents of this course include Java interface, Java abstract class and inheritance, factory method pattern, adapter pattern, strategy pattern, chain of responsibility pattern, bridge pattern, singleton pattern, facade pattern, visitor pattern, state pattern, memento pattern, command pattern, design patterns in J2EE.

For the software architecture section of this sub-course, the following elements are included:

- call and return software architecture with object oriented applications
- dataflow software architecture
- Java implementation of dataflow software architecture
- event driven software architecture

- Java implementation of event driven software architecture
- client-server software architecture
- P2P software architecture
- grid computing software architecture
- layered software architecture
- information shared software architecture
- SOA software architecture.

At least four small program projects are assigned to be completed by each student individually by using design patterns and two more substantial projects to be completed in teams using appropriate software architectures.

D. Software Quality Assurance and Testing

The objectives of the software quality assurance and testing course are for the student to be able to understand the quality framework for the software development process in the traditional structured environments as well as in unstructured environments and, with tips, techniques and other alternative approaches, be capable of implementing a continuous quality improvement approach and promoting effective testing methods.

This is a required course, covering modern quality assurance principles and best practice. It provides the student with a detailed overview of basic software testing techniques, software life cycle testing review, and client/server and Internet testing methodologies. It also introduces testing in the maintenance environment and modern testing tools.

The contents of this course are as follows:

- software quality assurance framework (software quality assurance, quality, software configuration management, statistical software quality assurance, software reliability, mistake-proofing for software, software quality assurance plan, the ISO

9000 quality standards, capability maturity model)

- overview of testing techniques (software testing fundamentals, test case design, black-box testing, white-box testing, gray-box testing, manual vs. dynamic testing, static vs. dynamic testing, taxonomy of software testing techniques)
- life cycle testing review (life cycle testing overview, verifying the requirements phase, verifying the logical design phase, verifying the physical design phase, verifying the program unite design phase, verifying the coding phase)
- client/server and internet testing methodology (development methodology overview, information gathering (plan), test planning (plan), test case design (implement), test development (implement), test execution/ evaluation (implement/ check), prepare for the next spiral (act), conduct the system test, conduct acceptance testing)
- testing in the maintenance environment (overview of software maintenance, enhancement/defect requirements analysis, preliminary maintenance test planning (plan), enhancement prototype design (plan), completed maintenance test planning (plan), maintenance test case design (implement), maintenance test development (implement), maintenance test execution/evaluation (implement/check), prepare for the next test cycle (act), maintenance system testing, maintenance acceptance testing)
- object-oriented testing (overview, testing OOA and OOD models, object-oriented testing strategies, test case design for OO software, testing methods applicable at the class level, interclass test case design, metrics for the OO design model)
- modern testing tools (introduction to testing tools, methodology to evaluate testing tools, modern maintenance tools).

Students are required to complete a planning report on software quality assurance, a design report and the software architecture project (including the software testing).

Relationships Between the Sub-Courses

Within the School of Software, a systematic approach to software engineering education is adopted. There is a comprehensive curriculum that covers the software engineering series courses, ranging logically from programming languages C, C++, and Java, through software engineering, object-oriented design with UML, software architecture and design patterns, to software quality assurance and testing.

Software engineering is concerned with developing quality software, and so this basic course was designed to introduce the fundamental theory with a certain number of applications. For instance, the software development life cycle and the design procedure for a program are emphasized. Although it is not a course on specific techniques, it does provide some theoretical consideration of software testing and an introduction on software architectures to prepare for the later courses on object oriented design and UML. In particular, the course prepares the students to understand the software development life cycle with object-oriented design replacing the procedural design in the traditional approach. This is intended to assist students in designing effective and high quality software.

A substantial project, encompassing design and coding, is required in this course.

The next sub-course is that on software architecture and design patterns, which covers overall software architecture issues, including the main traditional software architectures, as well as many of the frequently used software design patterns. Trade-offs in the use of design patterns and software architectures when designing a program are considered here. In order to develop understanding of the justifications for and uses of the different patterns and architectures, the students are required to write a substantial amount of code in object-oriented languages (preferably in Java) and to finish some programs using the design patterns and software architectures learned.

The last sub-course in this series is software quality assurance and testing, which covers not only quality assurance theory but also some very important testing techniques. Software quality assurance and testing is an umbrella activity that applies at the each phase in the software development life cycle. As future software professionals, it is vital that students acquire a deep understanding of software testing and continuous quality improvement.

To give students opportunities to write large scale software tools for the business environment, the .NET and J2EE courses are then offered and students are required to select one of them. With a command of the material of the earlier courses, the students should be able to undertake these advanced courses.

For all the courses discussed above, the instructors follow the recognized English version textbooks (Gamma et al., 1995; Kuchana, 2004; Pressman, 2009; Shaw & Garlan, 1996). In addition, all of these courses are taught in English or in English and Chinese.

After completing this series of courses, and especially after they finish their periods of training in computer companies, the undergraduate students should be able to write large scale real-life business programs. With this significant amount of software development experience, including software design and programming, the students should have the equivalent of at least two years of programming experience.

APPLICATION OF THE ELABORATION THEORY OF INSTRUCTION IN DESIGNING THE SYLLABUS FOR SOFTWARE ARCHITECTURE AND TEACHING PRACTICE

As a course for the year 3 students in the School of Software, the course in software architecture and design patterns aims to provide students with sound concepts, principles, methods and best practice in these key disciplines of software engineering. The aim is to produce qualified software developers and possible software architects. Popular software design patterns and important software architectures are taught.

The course has the following characteristics.

- It is a new course in the software engineering area to cover topics in software design chosen from a wide range of material, with many concrete implementation techniques also covered.
- It is based on already existing and well-known structures and architectures, and thus has some abstract elements that are difficult to understand.
- It requires a large amount of design/coding practice.

After completing the course and the related practical assignments and projects, the student will possess an understanding of and familiarity with the structures of some well-known software design patterns and software architectures, as well as being able to use them relatively readily in future software design tasks and projects.

The syllabus for this course has undergone a number of enhancements in the light of experience. For the practicality of teaching the course, it became apparent that the material to be covered needed to be selected carefully. Instead of teaching students a wide range of concepts, design patterns and software architecture styles, as initially envisaged, it was decided that a reasonable percentage of the knowledge be presented and that students would thus be enabled to more deeply understand the material through intensive design/coding practice. In the following sections, the evolution of the philosophy and main considerations in creating the syllabus, teaching methods and teaching practice are presented.

Problems in Designing the Syllabus and the Approach Adopted

In creating the syllabus for this new course, surveys and research were carried out to decide on the scope. Initially, it was planned that, ideally, the course should include object-oriented design principles: reliability, security, scalability, customizability, modularity, extensibility, maintainability and customer experience, at least 23 software design patterns (Gamma et al., 1995), and over 10 well known software architectures.

However, considering that the allowed classroom presentation hours were limited to 36, the feasibility of including all of these topics and covering them adequately was questioned.

The traditional approach to designing a software engineering course tends to cover every well-formulated concept. However, this course is different in that the materials need a considerable amount of hands-on practice before students can understand them. The 36 teaching hours dictated a departure from the traditional approach. If all of the desired materials were put into the course, they could only be covered in a superficial way. Many students would not obtain the depth of understanding and the practical grasp of the topics required of professional software engineers. It was agreed by the School team that some topics would need in-depth teaching and that others would be treated in a more general way.

The syllabus design is based on the pedagogical theory known as the elaboration theory of instruction (Reigeluth & Darwazeh, 1982). For the purpose of selecting and organizing the content of a course, this theory advocates using an epitomizing method, rather than using a summarizing method (Stirewalt, 2004). Here, the summarizing method emphasizes coverage of as many topics as possible, while the epitomizing method emphasizes coverage of a reasonable number of fundamental concepts and their presentation at a concrete level that is more immediately meaningful to the students. For the subject of software architecture and design patterns which is a developing area that contains very many topics, a major concern is that the course should draw students' attention and arouse their interest. The approach is that students should learn this from concrete design experience, even beginning with a poor design but gradually improving the design by changing the structure to achieve the desired functionalities as well as desired properties such as extensibility, maintainability, etc. The key element in the approach is to allow students to develop their own ability in design.

Therefore, the syllabus was designed in such a way that it covers in considerable detail 10 design patterns from Gamma et al. (1995) and the 10 software architectures, and finally devotes 2 hours classroom teaching to outlining and summarizing all the other patterns and architectures.

Bottom-Up Approach in Teaching the Course

For the classroom teaching and the assignments and projects the following approach was used.

- An example is used as the first step in introducing the concepts. The instructors prepare the course materials carefully, using heuristic step-by-step examples to guide the students naturally from easy/clumsy designs to difficult/ elegant designs, so that students can absorb the necessity of introducing the required software design patterns. Thus, accurate and convincing examples are needed in teaching these topics.

- An iterative method is used in the classroom teaching. The instructor presents the subject matter in the first part of a class period (50 minutes) and then the students are expected to finish at least part of a design/coding assignment so that they can encounter the problems in the classroom where the instructor can have time to answer at least some of the questions that arise. The instructor then can use the final 10 minutes to summarize the main content of the class and the material so as to re-emphasize the knowledge covered in the class period.
- Classroom discussions are organised on topics assigned by the instructor. The topic is announced at the end of the class period and the discussion is carried out at the beginning of the next class period. A topic for such a discussion often arises from the assignments or other projects.
- There is an emphasis on hands-on software design/coding assignments/ projects.

There are 10 software design/coding assignments that students are required to complete. Students carry them out in teams. Each assignment consists of a design part and an implementation part. For instance, students may be asked to add a new class or new functionalities to an already well-designed and implemented program, and to provide the coding for this addition. For all the assignments, written reports are also required to accompany the source code.

A Case Study in Teaching the Course

This section describes an example of teaching a required strategy pattern to show the bottom-up teaching approach described above. This lecture begins by presenting students a design as shown in Figure 2 for sorting an integer array.

The students are then asked to discuss the advantages and disadvantages of this design and eventually arrive at the following disadvantages,

that when a new algorithm is added to the class, this whole class needs to be recompiled and when an algorithm is modified, this whole class also needs to be recompiled.

The question of how to improve the design then arises. Students are asked, and helped if necessary, to arrive at the possible solution of separating the client program from the algorithm part and thus encapsulating all the algorithms into a class called SortingAlgorithms, as shown in Figure 3.

Then the discussion continues on the advantages and disadvantages of this approach before arriving at the advantage of not requiring the client class to be recompiled when a new algorithm is added to the class of SortingAlgorithms. However this does have the disadvantage that when a new algorithm is added to the class, this SortingAlgorithms still needs to be recompiled, and when an algorithm is modified, SortingAlgorithms also needs to be recompiled. Next, the instructor asks the students whether or not any better solutions might exist and finally the solution of continuing to continue split the class SortingAlgorithms leads to the new design, shown in Figure 4.

At this point, it becomes apposite to introduce the strategy pattern which was originally defined (Gamma et al., 1995) as in Figure 5 below.

The class *Context* may pass all the needed data by the algorithm to the strategy class. This has the advantages that when a new algorithm is added to the class, class *Client* and *Context* do not have to be recompiled (provided the new algorithm is not needed in the *Client* and *Context*),

Figure 2. Class design for sorting an integer array

Sorting
+main() +bubbleSort (int[] numbers): int[] +heapSort (int[] numbers): int[] +insertionSort (int[] numbers): int[] +quickSort (int[] numbers): int[]

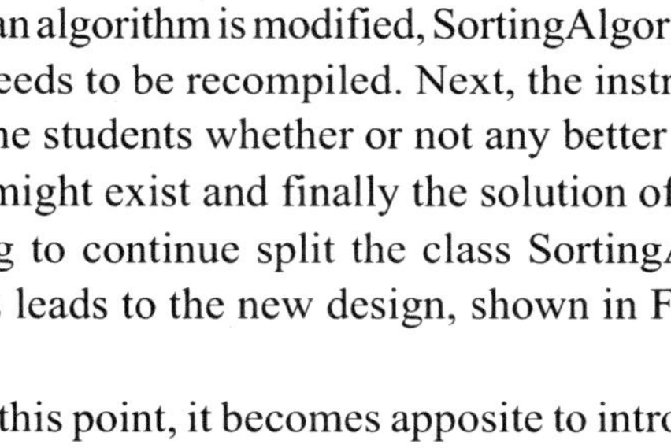

Figure 3. Class design for encapsulating the sorting algorithms into one class

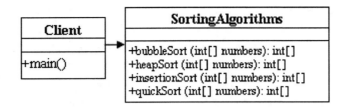

Figure 4. Class design for encapsulating each sorting algorithm into a separate subclass

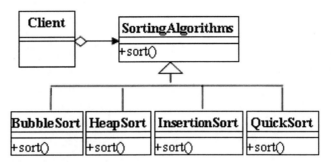

Figure 5. Class design for the strategy pattern

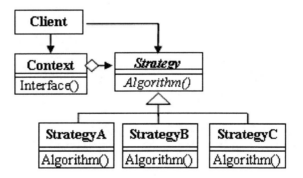

and when an algorithm is modified, if the parameters of the algorithm remain the same, class *Client* and *Context* do not have to be to be recompiled.

Then the students will see from the classroom discussion that a design has been arrived at based on the strategy pattern shown in Figure 6.

In the class design, the ClientGUI is a user interface for the users to select a sorting algorithm.

The second half of the class is then devoted to the students actually doing a software design

and the related coding assignment in class. The students are asked to run the sample program for the design derived earlier and then are assigned the task of adding another functionality to the program.

In this assignment each student is required to

- run the program StrategyGUI first to investigate how an integer array is sorted

Figure 6. Class design for the sorting program of an integer array in strategy pattern

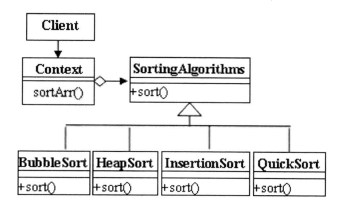

- add a class to implement SortAlgorithm to do a Bidirectional bubbleSort (naming this class BidirBubbleSort)
- in the StrategyGUI, modify the JcomboBox part to add an option to allow bidirectional bubbleSort.

Finally the students are asked to carry out the new design by adding a new functionality to the design derived earlier. They must first add a new class called BidirBubbleSort, and then write a certain amount of coding to implement the design. This design/coding assignment may or may not be completed in the class period, and any remaining part is completed by the students themselves outside of the classroom.

CONCLUSION

An overall industry-oriented curriculum and the related syllabuses have been created for the purpose of industry-oriented software education. In this chapter, as an example, the creation of a syllabus for the course in software architecture is discussed.

In the creation of the syllabus, the pedagogical theory known as the elaboration theory of instruction was used to carefully select the topics to be taught in class. In the classroom presentation, a bottom-up approach is adopted, in which examples are used as the first means of introducing the concepts, and then an interactive teaching method is used. Students are required to complete a large number of practical design assignments and projects. By this active and inclusive method, the students become interested and engage actively and creatively in the course, which is satisfactory for students and teachers.

ACKNOWLEDGMENT

This chapter was supported by the first Driver Project for Bilingual Teaching, and the project for Education Model and Practice in Raising International Software Talents by Collaboration of Universities and Enterprises, both from the Education Department of Shandong Province.

REFERENCES

Fenwick, J. B. Jr, & Kurtz, B. L. (2005). Intracurriculum software engineering education. *Association for Computing Machinery Special Interest Group on Computer Science Education (SIGCSE) Bulletin, 37*(1), 540–544.

Gamma, E., Helm, R., Johnson, R., & Vlissides, J. M. (1995). *Design patterns: Elements of reusable object-oriented software*. Boston, MA: Addison-Wesley Longman.

Joint Task Force on Computing Curricula. (2004). *Software engineering 2004: Curriculum guidelines for undergraduate degree programs in software engineering*. Washington, DC: Institute of Electrical and Electronic Engineering Computer Society, Association for Computing Machinery.

Kuchana, P. (2004). *Software architecture design patterns in Java*. New York, NY: Auerbach Publications. doi:10.1201/9780203496213

Petkovic, D., Thompson, G., & Todtenhoefer, R. (2006). Teaching practical software engineering and global software engineering: evaluation and comparison. In *Proceedings of 11ᵗʰ Annual Special Interest Group on Computer Science Education Conference on Innovation and Technology in Computer Science Education (ITiCSE)*. (pp. 294-298). New York, NY: Association for Computing Machinery.

Pressman, R. S. (2009). *Software engineering: A practitioner's approach* (7th ed.). Maidenhead, United Kingdom: McGraw-Hill.

Reichlmayr, T. J. (2006). Collaborating with industry-strategies for an undergraduate software engineering program. In the *Proceedings of the 3ʳᵈ International Summit on Software Engineering Education (SSEEIII)* (pp. 13-16). New York, NY: Association for Computing Machinery.

Reigeluth, C. M., & Darwazeh, A. (1982). The elaboration theory's procedure for designing instruction: A conceptual approach. *Journal of Instructional Development*, 5(3), 22–32. doi:10.1007/BF02905492

Shaw, M., & Garlan, D. (1996). *Software architecture: Perspective on an emerging discipline*. Upper Saddle River, NJ: Prentice Hall.

Stirewalt, R. E. K. (2004). Teaching software engineering bottom-up. In *Proceedings of the 2004 American Society for Engineering Education Annual Conference & Exposition*, Session Number 3532 (pp. 13755-13763). American Society for Engineering Education.

Zuser, W., Hetzl, J., Grechenig, T., & Bernhart, M. (2006). *Dimensions of software engineering course design*. IEEE Computer Society 28ᵗʰ International Conference on Software Engineering (pp. 667-672). Washington, DC: Institute of Electrical and Electronic Engineering.

KEY TERMS AND DEFINITIONS

Elaboration Theory of Instruction: In designing the syllabus for a course, this theory suggests that the material to be taught should be arranged for presentation starting with the simple and proceeding to the complex; this corresponds to the epitomizing teaching method, in which only a sufficient number of important basic important concepts are presented at a concrete level that is immediately meaningful to the students.

Industry-Oriented Teaching: An approach to teaching from an IT industry perspective to include not only the theory but also the practical aspects (such as hands-on projects specifically designed for the course, real-life projects from IT companies, software design/coding team projects from a university-enterprise co-operative laboratory or a period of internship in a software development team within a company) so that students may better understand the practical industrial application of materials covered in the classroom teaching.

Inter-Relationships Between the Series Courses: The logical links between two courses such as, for example, that one course should be completed as a prerequisite before the other is taught, or that unnecessary overlapping material from the second course be removed for better efficiency.

Practical Project: A software design/coding project from a university-enterprise joint laboratory, or an IT project directly from an IT related company.

Seamless: Transition to the Software Industry: To avoid the situation where companies need to train a new graduate employee from a traditional department of computer science for one or two years before she/he can become independently productive, an industry-oriented education seeks to produce graduates not only with program development skills, but also with higher software development training and ability, including system analysis, system design, system implementation and software maintenance and testing, so that when they enter a company, it is not necessary to train them for any appreciable period, other than for orientation to the work systems and environment.

Software Engineering Education: Education dedicated to teaching students the philosophy, methodology and methods to build high quality, reliable, extensible, maintainable software.

Chapter 7
Problems First

Gary Hill
University of Northampton, UK

Scott Turner
University of Northampton, UK

ABSTRACT

This chapter considers the need to focus initial programming education on problem-solving, in advance of programming syntax and software design methodology. The main vehicle for this approach is simple Lego based robots programmed in Java, followed by the programming of a graphical representation/ simulation to develop programming skills. Problem solving is not trivial (Beaumont & Fox, 2003) and is an important skill, central to computing and engineering.

An approach will be considered, illustrated with a series of problem-solving tasks that increase in complexity at each stage and give the students practice in attempting problem-solving approaches, as well as assisting them to learn from their mistakes. Some of the problems include ambiguities or are purposely ill-defined, to enable the student to resolve these as part of the process.

The benefits to students will be discussed including students' statements that this approach, using robots, provides a method to visually and physically see the outcome of a problem. In addition, students report that the method improves their satisfaction with the course.

The importance of linking the problem-solving robot activity and the programming assignment, whilst maintaining the visual nature of the problem, will be discussed, together with the comparison of this work with similar work reported by other authors relating to teaching programming using robots (Williams, 2003).

DOI: 10.4018/978-1-60960-797-5.ch007

INTRODUCTION

This chapter considers the teaching of programming and problem solving to undergraduate first year computing students, using robots and graphical programming to emulate the robot tasks.

Probably the most important skills a computer scientist or engineer must possess are those of problem solving. These skills are highlighted in numerous benchmark and guideline statements for engineering and computing (Adams et al., 2008). While it is appreciated that being a good problem solver involves knowledge and experience, there are other interventions, such as training and practice, that can improve process skills in engineering and computing undergraduates.

Mindstorm based robots have been used previously for teaching programming to computing and engineering students (Fagin, 2003; Lawhead et al., 2003; Price et al., 2003; Williams, 2003). Here we make use of them for problem-solving. Synergies can be achieved using robots to develop problem-solving skills and skills of pre-object programming (for example Culwin et al., 2006) and simulation of robots for teaching programming as a visual approach in the teaching of the widely used programming language Java.

The approach discussed here focuses upon the development of problem-solving skills first and not on learning a new programming language from the outset. Therefore, initially, any programming is kept simple with the minimum of commands, with *objects* unknowingly used, as these are later introduced/learned during the programming stage of the computing module. Work within the team (Turner & Hill, 2008) suggests that using Lego robots within the teaching of problem-solving and the resulting java GUI emulation has some benefits for the students. The students come on the courses with a range of experiences and abilities, but many of them have limited or no experience of programming. In other words, this is likely to be the first time they are exposed to programming or expected to program. It was felt within the

course team that giving the students a tool that is non-threatening and that would also provide early success in a physical and visual form (which, if it were to break, it would not matter), would be beneficial. Lego-based robots are initially used, followed by the same problems being repeated as a graphical representation/simulation to satisfy these same criteria.

Other authors have noted the suitability of robots for teaching programming. Lawhead et al. (2003) stated that robots provide entry level programming students with a physical model to visually demonstrate concepts, that the most important benefits of using robots in teaching introductory courses is the focus provided on learning language-independent truths about programming and programming techniques and that robots readily illustrate the idea of computation as interaction. This chapter advances the idea that developing problem-solving skills first, then embarking on programming, is beneficial. We explore this idea in detail by discussing the module where these ideas have been tested.

The module is structured into two parts, eight weeks (16 hours) spent on problem-solving, followed by sixteen weeks (32 hours) of graphical programming in Java. The underlying approach is that as the module develops the focus evolves from general concepts of problem-solving (e.g., brain-storming, functional decomposition) to solving problems based around robots which increase in difficulty (but not necessarily in complexity). The module is first assessed by a robot-based project, which then leads into developing the same problem via a graphical user interface in Java, which is finally assessed. The authors believe that the visual nature of the work and the linkage of the assignments aid the development of the necessary skills.

PROBLEM-SOLVING

Problem-solving is not trivial (Beaumont & Fox, 2003). In fact, if one considers the cognitive domain within Bloom's Taxonomy (Bloom, 1956), problem-solving involves the high-level skills of synthesis, evaluation, analysis and applications, and so it is, perhaps, not surprising that students often struggle in this area. A much discussed related area of computational thinking (Wing, 2006) has raised the profile of aspects such as problem-solving, by highlighting the importance of thinking like a computer scientist. By this it is meant that the thinking processes involved in being a computer scientist are more complicated than just being able to program, in that computational thinking is reformulating a seemingly difficult problem into one we know how to solve, perhaps by reduction, embedding, transformation, or simulation.

The module discussed in this chapter, during the problem-solving stage, involved two explicit but related problem-solving approaches. The first was based on the basic principles of analysis, design, testing design, implement and test. The second approach is similar, but includes brainstorming and therefore more suited to group working (University of Minnesota, 2003).

A series of problem-solving tasks, which increase in complexity, were provided to give the students practice in attempting these approaches and to learn from their mistakes. Some of the problems included ambiguities or were ill-defined, to enable the student to resolve these as part of the process. An example of this was to calculate the area of a rectangular room. What does this mean? Floor area or does it mean area of the floor, ceiling, and/or four walls?

Mindstorm (Lego, Denmark) robots formed the core of the problem-solving activities, based on six exercises; these were also designed to gradually increase in complexity, and one of them formed part of the assessment. The assessment included a task which involved the student producing routines to enable the robot to solve problems such as following a maze, putting a ball in a goal or moving rubbish into a containment area. The assessment task was also developed further in the programming assignment where the students were asked to repeat the same exercise but as a graphical emulation. During the problem-solving robotic tasks students were given a simple set of instructions to control the robot and templates for each exercise within which to fit these instructions, as shown in Figure 1. The emphasis during the problem-solving exercises was the analysis of the problem, not the generation of code.

Evaluation

Two questionnaires were used as part of the evaluation of the approach. The first was conducted at the beginning of the module, to consider the student's initial thoughts and concerns in relation to problem-solving. The second questionnaire was conducted after the practical robot exercises, to gauge their response to using robots for teaching and learning problem-solving.

The first question asked was, did they think that robotics-based problems help with developing problem-solving skills; all respondents said it did. When asked how it helped, the main two

Figure 1. Template for the wall-following routine and downloading the routine to the robot

types of comment (50%) suggested the approach provided a physical or visual representation of the problem or enabled the problem to be viewed in different ways as indicated in Figure 2.

Approximately 81% of the respondents said they did enjoy this approach and 19% said it was okay. When asked about the positive aspects of the approach, shown in Figure 2, 13% of the respondents did not provide any further comment. The physical representation of the problem and visualization accounted for 68% of the comments.

An interesting feature of the feedback concerns proposed areas for improvement, where 53% of respondents did not want to or did not include comments on how this approach could be improved. This, together with the high levels of satisfaction scores, can be taken, in part, as a positive indication that the approach is at least along the right lines. 13% of the comments discussed the physical arrangement of the robots (usually not enough sensors or the exercises not interesting). A further interesting point is that 13% of the comments said

the problems experienced could be attributed to the programming language.

Sample Task 1: Problem-Solving

Brief: Using the Mindstorm robots, produce a routine that moves a bomb (a drinks can) into a containment area and returns the robot back to behind the safety line.

Three levels of challenge were built into the task:

- **Basic: Level 1**: Build and program a robot that can take a bomb that is just in front of the robot into a containment area which is marked with a black line, and then move the robot back behind the safety line leaving the bomb in the containment area.
- **Moderate: Level 2**: Build and program a robot that can detect whether there is a bomb in the area or not, and if detected move the bomb into the containment area. If not, don't

Figure 2. Student's view on how the robot-based approach helped

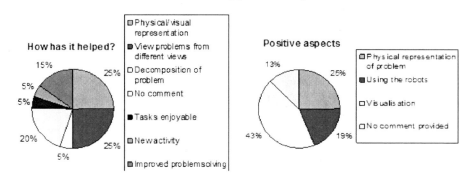

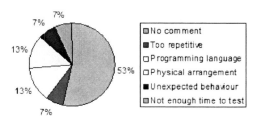

move to the containment area. If the bomb is present it will be in front of the robot.

- **Advanced: Level 3**: Build and program a robot that can find a bomb, regardless of where it is located, move it into the containment area, which is marked with a black line, and move the robot back to a safe distance as quickly as possible.

The majority of students submitted work that addressed the level 1 and 2 tasks, with a minority submitting work expressing innovative thinking on how to complete the level 3 task.

There is enough scope in this approach to have different levels of complexity/functionality within an assignment/task, thus offering a basic *pass* level for a particular task, but also the scope for those students that desire more of a challenge.

Graphical Programming

Graphical programming, using Java, forms the second section of the module (16 sessions of 2 hours duration each). The approach taken was to get the students producing graphical user interfaces (GUIs) at the earliest possible opportunity. A recommended course text (Bell & Parr, 2006), which uses Java as the programming language, was used to facilitate the GUI programming.

This section of the module was assessed by the production and documentation of a Java GUI application that emulated the robot problem introduced in the earlier problem-solving sessions. It was expected that the design would be based upon an *enhancement* of the previous robot routines produced in the earlier assignment. A requirement of one assignment was to write a test method runRobot() which was to be called and used to solve the maze (from the red (R) to the green (G) square) as in Figure 3. The assignment also specified that forward() and rotate() methods were to be called from within runRobot().

As in the problem-solving section the grades, feedback and engagement with the activity were consistently positive. The idea of linking the problem-solving and programming assignments,

Figure 3. Prototype GUI application from the programming exercise

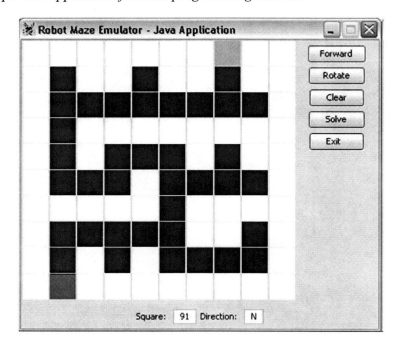

with the same task, was seen as a positive feature. One student made the explicit comment that they felt there was a good progression from problem-solving to programming. In addition, the students commented that they could take the ideas developed in one part of the module to the second part, thus evidencing clear transferability of skills.

Another interesting observation was that while the assignment explicitly stated that the Java GUI application should emulate the one shown in the assignment brief of Figure 3, an additional adaptation of this could be submitted to include extra functionality/complexity – for additional reward. It was pleasing to receive approximately 15% of the assignments wishing to incorporate such extra features, one of which is shown in Figure 4.

The module tutor found that the students not only find the programming of GUIs in Java challenging and interesting, but fun and exciting. The eureka moment is evident with each small problem solved and the increasing functionality of their GUI application. While the assignment itself is complex and may seem daunting to the students at the outset, they gradually become more excited by the revealing of each new aspect/concept of Java that is introduced to them - partly due to its application to their assignment. To explain the development of the programming section of the module it is useful to use one of the example tasks.

Sample Task 2: Graphical Programming

Brief: Produce a technical report and accompanying application using Java that will simulate a robot that can collect and move a block of rubbish (drinks can) into a containment area and return the robot behind a safety line.

Again three levels of challenge were built into the task.

- **Basic**: Create a simulation of a robot that can take a block of rubbish that starts just in front of the robot (R) into a containment area (B), which is marked with a black line, and then move the robot back behind the safety line (G) leaving the rubbish in the containment area.
- **Moderate**: Create a simulation of a robot that can detect whether there is a block of rubbish in the area or not, and if detected move it into the containment area. If not, do not move to the containment area. If the rubbish is present then it will be in front of the robot.
- **Advanced**: Create a simulation of a robot that can find a block of rubbish regardless of where it is located and move it into the containment area, which is marked with a black line, and move the robot back to a safe distance.

The Java GUI application must emulate the movement of a robot to collect an item of rubbish and move it to a containment area before returning to a safe area/distance. The user (not necessarily the designer) can be used to stop the robot to say it has reached the safe area/distance. Solutions that detect that a safe area or safe distance has been reached are likely to score more highly in terms of design. You could expect that the robot will meet obstacles such as solid boxes, and should be able to deal with these. It is expected that you may attempt to use and adapt previous robot routines produced as part of the earlier problem-solving assignment.

Attempt to emulate the application shown in Figure 5.

Approach to Task

Basic System Requirements:

- 10 x 10 grid of JButtons or Icons.
- 8 JButtons for Solve, *Clear*, *Room 1-3*, *Forward*, *Rotate* and *Exit*.
- The *Forward* JButton should move the robot forward one square for each press.

Figure 4. Student prototype GUI application showing additional functionality/complexity

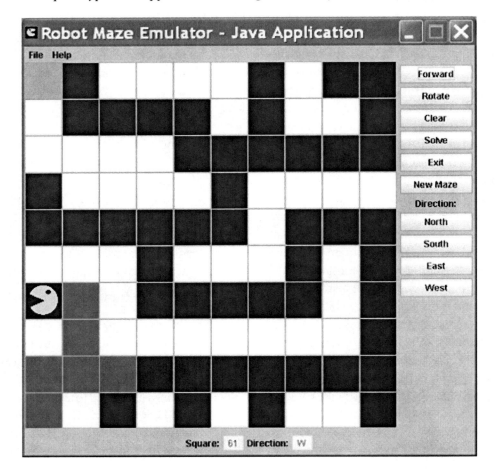

- The *Rotate* JButton should rotate the robot 45⁰ clockwise for each press.
- JLabels for *Square* and *Direction*. Use your own square identification method e.g 1 to 100. and N, NE, E etc.
- JTextFields for the current room option, *location*/*square* and *direction* of the robot.
- Create a JFrame application, which opens to the set size (in Figure 5).
- JFrame title set as *Robot Rubbish Finder Emulator - Java Application*.

Additional System Requirements (functionality & complexity)

- Application icon for the JFrame used, of your choice.
- The *Solve* JButton should show the robot (Y) moving from the green (G = safe) and returning, after detecting and moving the rubbish (■) from within the red (R = danger) area into blue (B =containment) zone (Figure 3).
- The *Clear* JButton should clear/reset the room to its start condition.
- Discuss and implement the option to choose a room and obstacle configuration.

Figure 5. Prototype application in opening state

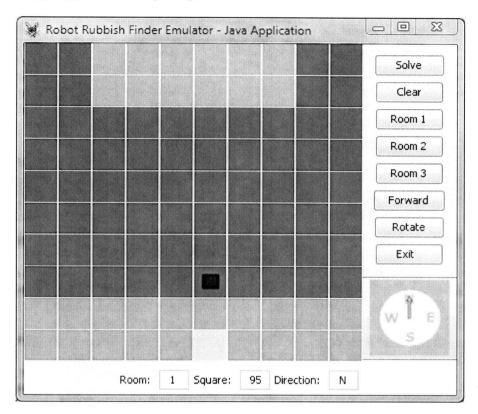

- The *Room 1-3* JButtons should display different room and obstacle configurations.
- A JMenuBar could be included with JMenus for the *File* and *Help*, which include JMenuItems of *Exit*, *Instructions* and *About*.
- Additional JButtons may be used to improve the applications usability e.g rotate 45°, 90°, clockwise and anticlockwise.
- Create a JFrame application, which is not resizable.
- Create a JFrame application, which centres itself on the monitor.
- Use of a robot image indicating the current position and direction of the robot.
- Use obstacle images, such as chair, table etc.

- Discuss the possibilities for incorporating intelligence/checks for whether moves are valid.
- Implement intelligence/checks for whether moves are valid.
- A runRobot() method should be used to solve the room. The runRobot() method should include forward() and rotate() methods (see below).

```
public void runRobot()
{
    forward();
    ...............
    rotate();
}
```

The applications must be demonstrated (see below). The source code file containing the main() method and the compiled byte code class files should be named as follows:

```
CRobotRubbish.java & CRobotRubbish.
class
```

Task Solution: Graphical Programming

The task is deliberately prescriptive and aimed, not just at re-using skills and techniques developed within the previous section/assignment, but enhancing them.

In addition to creating a graphical simulation/emulation in Java as in Figure 5, students were asked to incorporate obstacles into the problem. Students were also encouraged to consider/incorporate additional functionality/complexity e.g. intelligence checks for valid movement of the robot.

As with the problem-solving assignment, most of the students submitted work addressing the task at the Basic and Moderate levels with a small proportion (approximately 25%) of students incorporating innovative thinking on how to complete the Advanced level task outlined above.

Another aspect of the module that is liked by the students, is the incremental revealing/introduction of key programming concepts and skills alongside a GUI assignment. To illustrate this approach further, it is worth highlighting the topics covered in the 16 sessions, which are used for the incremental development. The list of these topics, given below, relates not only to the chapters from the course text (Bell & Parr, 2006) but to the increase in complexity and functionality that can be applied to the assignment:

1. Introduction
2. First Programs.
3. Using Graphics Methods.
4. Variables and Calculations
5. Methods and parameters
6. Using Objects (+ 19. Program style)
7. Decisions - If and Select
8. Repetition - While and For -
9. Writing classes (+ 10. Inheritance)
11. Calculations
12. Data Structures (array lists)
13. Arrays - one dimensional
14. Arrays - 2D
15. Strings
16. Assignment completion.

The first two sessions serve a number of purposes, to introduce the programming section of the module, Java and the chosen integrated development environment (IDE), the recommended course book (Bell and Parr, 2006) and finally the assignment. Before discussing Java, it is worth explaining that the assignment is available at (or before) the first session. Therefore students can be introduced to the assignment and the resulting expectations right from the start. In fact, the lecturer begins the first session with an explanation of how the two sections of the module seamlessly link together. Next the assignment is introduced, showing exactly what is expected of them and a prototype Java application is demonstrated. The students appear to be shocked by the complexity of the prototype application demonstrated. It is felt that this is because the application does look complicated and polished, but they are reassured that they will be able to produce a similar prototype application at the end of the 16 sessions.

The notes from the first session show the creation of JFrame applications, which include a JPanel, JButtons and JTextFields. Although linking all these components to the assignment in the first week would be too confusing, tending to overload the students, it can be seen that there is a surprising amount of progress they can make in their first session. The first two chapters are revisited, during the next few sessions, to demonstrate how much of the problem (GUI assignment) could be solved with just a little knowledge of Java.

The students see that their assignment will be a JFrame application; the square grid of the JButtons representing the area of operation that will be contained within a JPanel and they will need 8 JButtons and 3 JTextFields. During the early phase of this section of the work, it would be suggested to the students that time should be set aside in the timetabled practical sessions (and between sessions) to enable the creation of a Java class, as prescribed in the assignment brief (in this case CRobotRubbish.class), and add a JPanel and the 8 buttons to the frame. As a supplement, the use of meaningful object names would be introduced, suggesting that each button could be named, for example, jBSolve, jBClear, JBRoom1, etc., instead of button, button1, button 2, etc., as implied by the recommended course book. In addition, JTextFields would be introduced (Ses-

sions 1& 2) so that the students could add three JTextFields for the Room, Square and Direction. At an early stage (Session 4) the students can appreciate that the resulting application, shown in Figure 6, begins to take shape.

Another breakthrough for the students, in terms of the GUI, is with the introduction of the topics, repetition and layout managers. Repetition (for loops) offers the ability to add the 100 squares (JButtons) to the problem area, initially, in around six lines of code. This, by default, uses the Flow-Layout manager and does not give the desired layout to the GUI. This leads smoothly onto the need for a way to lay out the various components i.e. the layout managers.

The use of a layout manager (BorderLayout) initially enables the students to arrange the GUI (with center, east and south JPanels) to position

Figure 6. Initial GUI application showing basic visual components

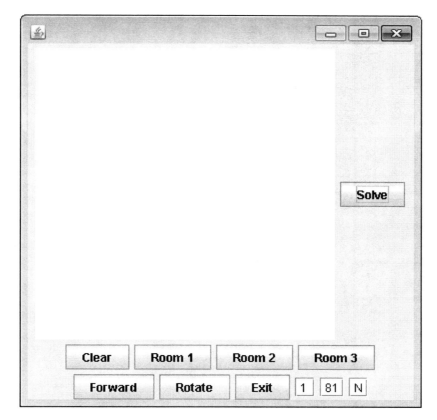

the JButtons to an east JPanel, the JTextFields to a south JPanel and the main rubbish area to the center JPanel. The students then return to the 100 JButtons with the introduction of another layout manager (GridLayout) to the center JPanel. This enables the positioning of the squares to give the required GUI. At this stage, the resulting GUI looks almost complete, as shown in Figure 7.

To complete the GUI, there are two additional sessions that need to be covered, Arrays and 2-D Arrays (Sessions 13 & 14). For simplicity, it is usual to use a one dimensional array where, as in Figure 8 above, 100 JButton objects would be created with the colours applied from a series of selection (if) procedures. The JButtons are created as buttons 0 to 99 (unique objects) but some students do attempt to use a 2-D array. This

is particularly the case with the brighter students, who are encouraged to think ahead and attempt to solve the problem. To complete the GUI, the application frame size would be adjusted to the required size; an icon and title, together with the compass icon (as a JLabel with icon) would also be added.

Only the GUI development has been discussed above, but functionality/complexity would be dealt with as the relevant/appropriate sessions/chapters were covered and revealed - in a similar way to the graphical programming.

It is felt that this visual approach to programming, adopted from the outset, and the transferability of the visual problem-solving to the visual programming task facilitates student engagement, enjoyment, learning and, ultimately, ability to

Figure 7. Developing GUI application using layout managers and repetition

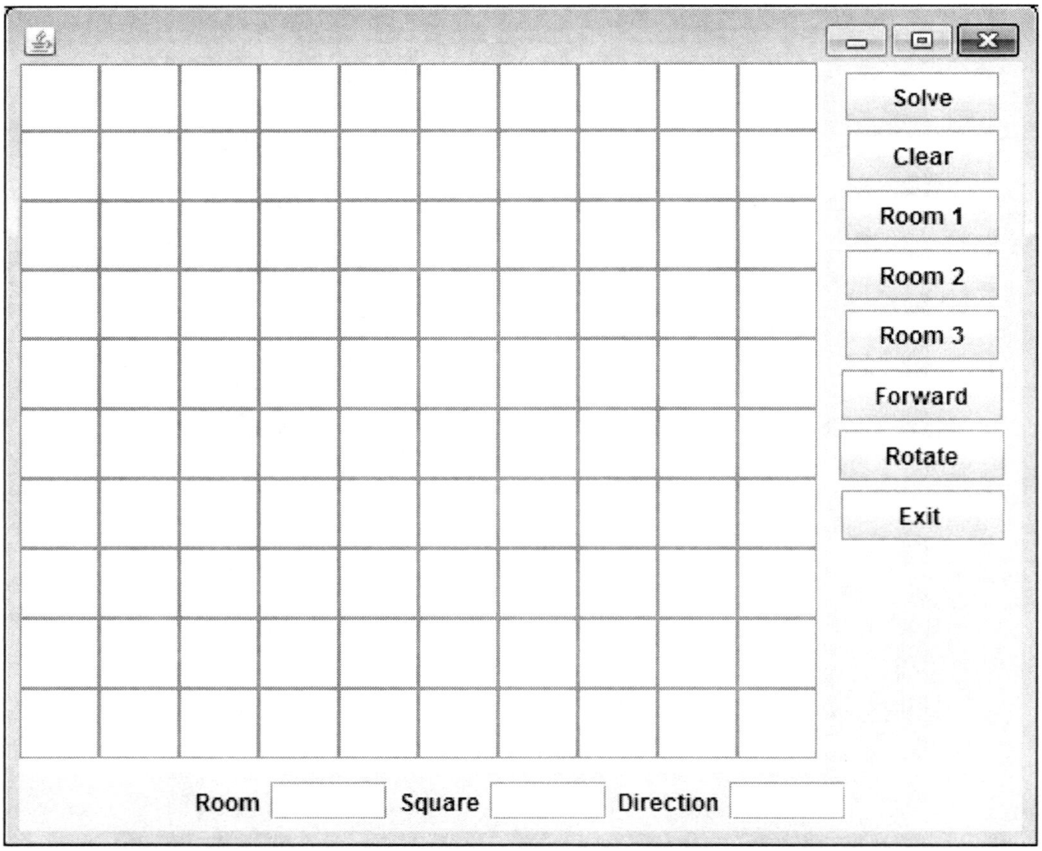

see the relevance to software industry-oriented practices.

SOFTWARE INDUSTRY-ORIENTED RELEVANCE

The Lecturer as the Client

In the previous section, it was mentioned that the task was deliberately prescriptive and aimed at re-using/transferring the skills and techniques developed within the previous section/assignment. This was not the only reason for being prescriptive, or overly explicit. The module tutors adopt a client-developer relationship when discussing the project brief and executing the assignment. Throughout the assignment the relationship between the students and the lecturer is reinforced as a developer-client relationship. Specific time is allocated to the assignment discussions in an attempt to prevent any potential conflict/confusion surrounding the lecturer being the facilitator and the client. The scenario that developed was that the assignment brief was to be exactly what the client required and the client would only pay (in terms of a grade for the assignment) for work requested - not work assumed. It is surprising how some students find it difficult to stick to a given brief. Students would prefer to use their own colours for the JButtons and JPanels and their own names and order of JButtons (on the East side of the JFrame application). They tend to have a desire to add their perceived enhancements or added functionality. It is explained to them that they must produce what the client has requested, but can offer the client any enhancements or added functionality through recommendations in the conclusion of the report. Some examples of enhancements suggested by the developers have been: the accessibility/visibility of some colours (red/green); human computer interaction; timers; instructions to users via a drop-down menu; icons to indicate the orientation of the robot etc.

Figure 8. Lego Mindstorms simulator

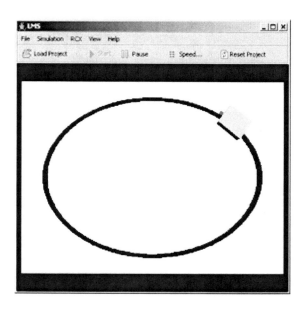

The Student as a Developer

In addition to the client-developer relationship, students are instructed that they are to assume that they are working as part of a software development team. To achieve this the students are given guidance, to ensure that all code meets the following requirements:

- Uses a standard file header: a standard header is explained and a template adopted to clearly indicate: application name; filename/s; author; course; module; tutor; date; version; revisions.
- Clearly referenced: If any material is adopted or used from other sources, such as the course book or the authors, then the students are expected to clearly indicate this within their code. The course team has been optimizing an appropriate method for achieving this, but it reflects various practice from within a development team.
- Clearly commented: The introduction of the different forms of multiple, single,

in-line and special commenting methods are introduced, together with examples of meaningful/helpful commenting.

- Consistent and recognizable coding convention: Here, the existing Java (Oracle, 1999) is introduced and discussed.
- Meaningful variable, object, method (gets and sets) and class names: the expectation is that all variable, object, method (gets and sets) and class names, will use the above coding convention, but must also be meaningful, e.g. button1 should be jB-Clear, to indicate the object type, and its function/use.
- Use of methods and preferably objects: object-oriented programming is encouraged from the outset and additional consideration (for marking) is given to the use of objects and methods. In addition to the *Using Objects* section of the course, students discuss the importance and benefit of using objects.
- Debugging: Students are shown simple methods for debugging their code. In Java, the use of System.out.println at the command prompt or the use of JOptionPane. showMessageDialog are encouraged.
- Implementation with explicit revision history: Students are required to include an implementation section within their project report. They are explicitly informed that this should show a clear morphology of code/prototype application development, via screen shots, and show any revision history in relation to optimization of the code or functionality/complexity.
- Documentation: The generation of automatic Java documentation (via javadoc (Oracle, 2010)) is discussed and demonstrated to illustrate how the application programming interface or implementation documentation could be produced.

By introducing the roles of the lecturer as the client and the student as the developer (as discussed above) it is felt that software industry-oriented practices are further reinforced.

SOLUTIONS AND RECOMMENDATIONS

The main benefit in the problem-solving sessions was that the students consider that robots provide a method to visually and physically see the outcome of a problem. The approach taken in both parts of the module was visually-oriented. The appropriateness of this would appear to be borne out by the student comments. Student satisfaction for both parts of the module was over 92%. One of the comments made was that linking the problem-solving robot task and the programming assignment was popular. This feedback is similar to that reported by other authors when teaching programming using robots (Williams, 2003).

Simulations

A limiting factor, raised in the student's feedback on the problem-solving approach, was the limited availability of the robots. It was not possible for robot kits to be available 24 hours a day, for security reasons, or to be taken home by the students, due to the limited number of kits available. Therefore an alternative approach of using simulators for the Lego robots was considered. One of the requirements/limitations the module tutors imposed on the choice of a simulator was the need to be accessible/free for the students to download and use. This led to two options, Microsoft Robotics Studio (MSRS) and Lego Mindstorms simulator.

Lego Mindstorms Simulator (LMS)

The first option was to use the Lego Mindstorms simulator developed at the University of Paderborn (Straeter & Kuensting, 2007) and this proved useful. This package uses the LeJOS API (Sourceforge, 2006) and Java to simulate these robots. Figure 8 shows an example of a line-following robot in this simulator. The major advantage of this approach is that the code written to control the robots in the simulator can in theory be implemented unchanged on the actual robots.

Though this is very useful software, it did however, have a few drawbacks as often the code required minor modifications to work. In a small evaluation the students found the package a little harder to use than programming the robots directly. Despite this, the potential of this package means work is still on-going on developing its use for this application. This package has since been incorporated into a module on artificial intelligence techniques, where the students have the additional experience needed to be able to use this package.

Microsoft Robotics Studio (MRS)

A series of on-line learning materials has been developed, centred on Microsoft Robotics Studio (Microsoft, 2006), for teaching problem-solving. It had been decided early in the project that the visual programming language, integral to the

MRS, would be used due to its visual nature, shown in Figures 9 and 10.

It was expected that these materials could be integrated into the teaching in sections 1 and 2, that are general problem-solving exercises, and that the materials, although with a programming bias, could be integrated into exercises to enhance these problem-solving skills.

However, evaluation of this package by a group of five students, before they started the problem-solving material, concluded that the visual programming language was not easy to work with, though one of the students who had previous experience of programming did like the package. The major hurdle to its use in the University of Northampton module was that it moves away from the original concept of teaching problem-solving using a language (in this case, Java) which the students would later go on to use to develop their own solutions in a more general way. Nevertheless, the simulation is visually appropriate and interest has been shown in using it with engineering students, where the language choice is less significant.

In summary, though the MRS is a very impressive package for developing pre-programming

Figure 9. Visual programming language example

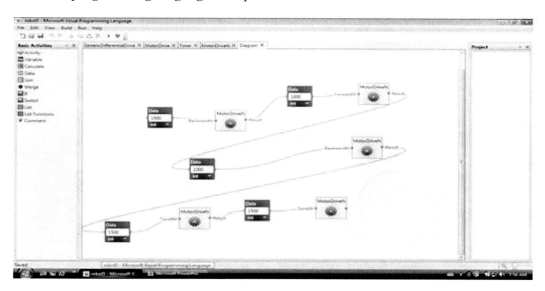

problem-solving skills, the LMS approach is more appropriate where Java is the follow-on programming language. If C# were to be the follow-on language, MRS would show significant potential in this application because of the ability to program the robots in C# through this package.

DISCUSSION

One of the features suggested by the student feedback summary shown in Figure 2 is that the students still see this module as an exercise in programming. Yet over 92% of students expressed satisfaction with the module and the general feedback is similar to other studies on teaching programming using robots (Williams, 2003). There is enough scope in this approach to have different levels of complexity/functionality within an assignment task offering a basic *pass* level for a particular task, but also the scope for those students who desire a greater challenge.

The results suggest that this approach is worth investigating based on the indicative increase in grades and the positive response of students. The improvements suggested by the students can be summarized as more access to the robots, robots with possibly more features, and increased difficulty of the exercises.

The visually-oriented aspect of the approach in both parts of the module was seen by the students as a particular strength.

The limitation in the availability of the robots is in process of being resolved with the use of the Microsoft Robotics Studio package which is free and readily available.

The ongoing developmental activity in this work is focussed on three key areas in the short-term:

- Development of the simulations approaches. Though there are currently problems with the simulator used thus far, these are not insurmountable and their resolution could address some of the issues raised in the evaluation stages.
- Improvement in the physical properties of the robot. The latest version of the Lego Mindstorms robotic kits, Mindstorms NXT (Lego, Denmark), includes features that have the potential to lead to more interest-

Figure 10. Simulator example

ing tasks. The robot construction is also more resistant to falling apart.

- The further development of generic problem-solving skills is seen as an area of development. These techniques have also crossed over into an engineering course. This cross-discipline work is also leading to further feedback on the approach from a different perspective, but also to new ideas that could be incorporated in this work.

A possible further direction of development that is being considered for the problem-solving part is a problem based learning approach (Beaumont & Fox, 2003), which would also help to address the possible concern over the ownership of the problem by moving the problem from one that the tutor sets to being each student's own problem or that of each working group of students.

There are two other areas where this material and this approach can be developed further. The first concerns creativity, which is widely accepted to be a significant element in computing, as indicated, for example, in the work of McGettrick et al. (2005). The use of the embedded simulator can help with developing this capability, by adding the ability to create objects, different robots, etc.. Confidence building is another area for development, as developing more complex simulations with greater functionality can increase the student's confidence to try out different and novel ideas.

CONCLUSION

The experiences described here indicate that the visual and physical nature of using robots is liked by the students. However, students do not appear to invest enough time to the problem-solving element outside the designated session. It would appear that the ownership of the problem continues to present difficulties. Perhaps a freer, student-generated project would be more effective.

This approach has potential in a variety of subjects other than computing, not only in related subjects such as engineering (Adams et al., 2008), but also in other problem-solving subjects. This approach and the concepts surrounding it share an affinity with the idea of computational thinking as an important skill set, fundamental for many disciplines and not only for computing (Wing, 2006).

ACKNOWLEDGMENT

The development of this approach was supported by the HE-ICS Development Fund and the HE-ICS/Microsoft Innovative Teaching Fund.

REFERENCES

Adams, J., Turner, S., Kaczmarczyk, S., Picton, P., & Demian, P. (2008). *Problem solving and creativity for undergraduate engineers: Findings of an action research project involving robots.* Paper presented at the International Conference on Engineering Education (ICEE 2008), Budapest, Hungary.

Beaumont, C., & Fox, C. (2003). Learning programming: Enhancing quality through problem-based learning. In *Proceeding of 4th Annual Conference of the subject centre for Information and Computer Sciences of the Higher Education Academy* (pp. 90-95). Newtownabbey, Northern Ireland: Higher Education Academy.

Bell, D., & Parr, M. (2006). *Java for students* (5th ed.). Upper Saddle River, NJ: Prentice Hall.

Bloom, B. S. (Ed.). (1956). *Taxonomy of educational objectives, handbook I: Cognitive domain.* White Plains, NY: Longman.

Culwin, F., Adeboye, K., & Campbell, P. (2006). POOPLEs: Pre-object-orientated programming learning environments. In *Proceedings of the 7th Annual Conference of the subject centre for Information and Computer Sciences of the Higher Education Academy* (pp. 59-63). Newtownabbey, Northern Ireland: Higher Education Academy.

Fagin, B. (2003). Ada/Mindstorms 3.0. *Institute of Electrical and Electronic Engineering Robotics & Automation Magazine, 10*(2), 19–24.

Lawhead, P. B., Bland, C. G., Barnes, D. J., Duncan, M. E., Goldweber, M., Hollingsworth, R. G., & Schep, M. (2003). A road map for teaching introductory programming using LEGO Mindstorms robots. *Association for Computing Machinery Special Interest Group on Computer Science Education Bulletin, 35*(2), 191–201.

McGettrick, A., Boyle, R., Ibbett, R., Lloyd, J., Lovegrove, G., & Mander, K. (2005). Grand challenges in computing education - a summary. *The Computer Journal, 48*(1), 42–48. doi:10.1093/comjnl/bxh064

Microsoft. (2006). *Microsoft robotics studio.* Retrieved February 14, 2008, from http://msdn2.microsoft.com/en-us/robotics/aa731520.aspx

Oracle. (1999). *Code convention for the Java programming language.* Retrieved October 12, 2010, from http://www.oracle.com/technetwork/java/codeconvtoc-136057.html

Oracle. (2010). *Javadoc – the Java API documentation generator.* Retrieved on October 12, 2010, from http://download.oracle.com/javase/1.4.2/docs/tooldocs/windows/javadoc.html

Price, B. A., Richards, M., Petre, M., Hirst, A., & Johnson, J. (2003). Developing robotics e-teaching for teamwork. *International Journal of Continuing Engineering Education and Lifelong Learning, 13*(1/2), 190–205.

Sourceforge. (2006). *LeJOS: Java for Mindstorms.* Retrieved February 14, 2008, from http://lejos.sourceforge.net/p_technologies/rcx/downloads.php

Straeter, W., & Kuensting, B. (2007). *LMS-Lego Mindstorms simulator.* Retrieved October 31, 2007, from http://ddi.uni-paderborn.de/en/software/lego-mindstorms-simulator.html

Turner, S., & Hill, G. (2008). Robots within the teaching of problem-solving. *Subject Centre for Information and Computer Sciences of the Higher Education Academy, 7*(1), 108–119.

University of Minnesota. (2003). *Five steps in problem-solving.* Retrieved October 10, 2003, from http://cda.mrs.umn.edu/~fauxr/computing/problemsolve.html

Williams, A. B. (2003). The qualitative impact of using Lego Mindstorms robot to teach computer engineering. *Institute of Electrical and Electronic Engineering (IEEE) Transactions on Education, 46*, 206. doi:10.1109/TE.2002.808260

Wing, J. (2006). Computational thinking. *Communications of the ACM, 49*(3), 33. doi:10.1145/1118178.1118215

KEY TERMS AND DEFINITIONS

Computational Thinking: An approach to solving problems and understanding systems, both within and outside of computing, based on concepts that are central to computing.

Graphical Programming: Building systems around graphical tasks to aid student engagement with the tasks with their visual nature (confused with graphical user interfaces).

Lego Based Robots: Robots based around the Lego Mindstorms RCX robotics invention set.

Mindstorm Based Robots: An alternative term used for Lego based robots.

Chapter 8
A New Industry-Centred Module on Structured Parallel Programming

Horacio González-Vélez
Robert Gordon University, UK

ABSTRACT

This work presents the case for the introduction of a new module on parallel programming for the core degree programmes in the School of Computing at the Robert Gordon University, and elsewhere. Having been conceived and designed with the industry-leading tools for structured parallel programming in mind, this module introduces students to parallel architectures, structured parallelism, and parallel programming. The main innovation of our approach is its emphasis on the structured parallelism environments recently released by Google, Microsoft, and Intel.

INTRODUCTION

Knowledge transfer between universities and industries has long been nurtured by different institutional and governmental bodies across the world. While there is an important transfer through journal articles, conferences, projects and dedicated events, the bulk of the conveyance in computer and information science is achieved through university graduates who get degrees and, subsequently, are employed in industry and some of whom return to academia.

Computer science graduates must therefore possess not only solid theoretical foundations, but also transferable job skills and experience to be employable and attractive to the information and communications technology (ICT) industry. Human resource requirements in industry must be swiftly incorporated into the curricula, be-

DOI: 10.4018/978-1-60960-797-5.ch008

cause otherwise graduates risk relegation from the mainstream.

The advent of multi-core processors has strongly impacted industry, as most personal computers now feature multi-core chips and many mobile devices feature low-power multiprocessing units. Furthermore, chip multiprocessors, multi-node clusters, grids, and clouds have sharply increased the number of concurrent processors available for a single application. Accordingly, industry increasingly requires software professionals with parallel programming skills.

Parallel programming aims to capitalise on concurrency, the execution of different sections of a given program at the same time, in order to improve the overall performance of the program, and, eventually, that of the whole system. Despite major breakthroughs, parallel programming is still a highly demanding activity widely acknowledged to be more difficult than its sequential counterpart, and one for which the use of efficient programming models and structures has long been sought. These programming models must necessarily be performance-oriented, and are expected to be defined in a scalable structured fashion to provide guidance on the execution of their jobs and assist in the deployment of heterogeneous resources and policies.

This work presents a proposal for the development of an introductory module on parallel programming, where the main emphasis is on using structured parallelism with an industry-centred approach. Such a module is intended to be incorporated in the undergraduate and post-graduate programmes in the School of Computing at the Robert Gordon University, and in similar programmes internationally.

BACKGROUND

As part of a panel of experts at a recent computer science conference, Ivanov et al. (2008) high-lighted the key factors in the case for teaching parallel computing in universities:

- **Essential**: Parallel computing provides a virtual laboratory for many disciplines such as systems biology, physics, astronomy, meteorology, sociology and anthropology, enabling them to focus on complex problems that would be otherwise unsolvable.
- **Available and Affordable**: Parallel computing is here to stay and expand: every single device is expected to feature parallelism, and some supercomputing facilities have machines with hundreds of thousands of cores. This trend is not expected to change but to permeate still more parts of our lives.
- **Difficult**: Computing has been traditionally taught primarily within a sequential frame of mind, but parallel solutions require a different way of approaching and dissecting a problem. They require a holistic analysis and understanding of the system architecture, the programming paradigm, and the problem constraints. Parallel computing requires calculations to be synchronised, staged, and/or communicated over a number of different phases. Message-passing, threads, load-balancing and semaphores are matters restricted to the expert software developers.

Thus, while we know that parallel computing is a *sine qua non* for many disciplines and is here to stay, the *status quo* tends to render it an experts-only field. But teaching parallel computing ought to be no longer a question of *if*, but of *how soon*. Goth (2009) mentions that computer scientists on university faculties say academia is debating how and when to introduce parallel programming throughout the curriculum, instead of just offering an upper-level course as is now common. It is of interest that the main sources quoted in that article are Intel, Microsoft, and Cilk Arts, an MIT spin-off.

Different institutions have long offered advanced courses on parallel programming covering different aspects of the discipline. The well-known Andrews' textbook (Andrews, 1999) site lists over fifty different higher educational institutions that have adopted the textbook for their parallel programming courses. Wilkinson & Allen (1999b) document an undergraduate course on parallel programming based on their widely used textbook (Wilkinson & Allen, 1999a) and, more recently, their approach has been extended to embrace grid computing education (Wilkinson & Ferner, 2008).

Fekete (2009) has recently reviewed different textbooks and aids for teaching concurrent programming with emphasis on threading. Over the past two decades, different educators and practitioners have described, typically at the annual Technical Symposium on Computer Science Education organised by the Association for Computing Machinery, their particular experiences in teaching parallel programming at different institutions and at different levels (Ben-Ari & Kolikant, 1999; Cunha & Lourenço, 1998; Hartman & Sanders, 1991; Hacker & Springer, 2008; Schaller & Kitchen, 1995; Toll, 1995; Torbert et al., 2010).

While interesting, these mostly describe organically-grown, bottom-up approaches where students are expected to produce and learn parallel programming by coding different computation and communication primitives or by using educational libraries.

However, the ICT industry expects graduates to be able to easily adapt to its best practices. Arguably, this entails the use of pattern-based programming, as it has been the case in sequential programming where the use of design patterns is widely considered the norm, as demonstrated by a myriad of citations to the seminal work of Gamma et al. (1995). The approach presented in this chapter arguably brings a different perspective to teaching concurrency. On the one hand, the

agglomeration of dozens of cores per processor has just increased the complexity of the challenge at hand. The Berkeley report has highlighted the importance not only of producing realistic benchmarks for parallel programming models based on patterns of computation and communication, but also of developing programming paradigms which efficiently deploy scalable, independent task parallelism (Asanovic et al., 2009). Consequently, major software industry powerhouses have acknowledged the need to introduce innovative development tools. On the other hand, the Computing Curricula report (Shackelford et al., 2006) fully embraces the idea of computer scientists and software engineers working on challenging programming jobs. Given that every computer and device is expected to embed parallelism, there is a clear need to teach parallel computing as a core subject using a pattern-oriented approach.

The main contention of this chapter is the need for the adoption of an ICT industry-centred, pattern-based approach to impart parallel programming skills to students in higher education institutions.

INDUSTRIAL INITIATIVES

Developed by Intel, the Intel threading building blocks (TBB) (Reinders, 2007) library helps one to take advantage of multi-core processor performance explicitly. It furnishes different parallel constructs such as reduce, scan, sort, and pipeline.

A major component of the parallel software offering from Microsoft, the task parallel library (TPL), provides concurrency support for the Microsoft.NET framework and does not require any language extensions (Leijen et al., 2009). It furnishes concurrent constructs such as Parallel. For, Parallel.Do, and Parallel.Aggregate which employ work-stealing features in order to keep different thread queues balanced.

Developed by Google for the efficient deployment of computationally-intensive parallel algorithms, MapReduce is a distributed programming model and framework used to compute problems that can be parallelised by mapping a function over a given dataset and then combining the results (Dean & Ghemawat, 2004, 2008). As a framework, it is used to implement MapReduce jobs which encapsulate the features of the model while hiding from users the complexities inherent in parallelism.

In principle, it is expected that developers of efficient parallel applications must be aware of the system conditions, and adapt their execution according to variations in the available computation and communication resources. The challenge is, therefore, to teach students how to produce and support applications which can respond automatically to this variability.

PARALLEL PATTERNS

Parallel patterns can be efficiently designed (Mattson et al., 2004; Ortega-Arjona, 2010), but it is not common practice to teach introductory courses on parallel programming using this paradigm. The industry may well soon require well-trained ICT professionals who can effectively design and deploy structured parallel programs. However, scant research has been devoted to the production of introductory courses on parallel programming with an industrial focus, where parallel patterns are designed, programmed, and re-used as a common practice in software development.

STRUCTURED PARALLELISM

Structured parallelism provides a high-level parallel programming methodology which allows the abstract description of programs and fosters portability by focusing on the description of the algorithmic structure rather than on its detailed implementation. Structured parallelism provides a clear and consistent behaviour across platforms,

with the underlying structure depending on the particular implementation.

Algorithmic skeletons abstract commonly-used patterns of parallel computation, communication, and interaction (Cole, 1989; González-Vélez & Leyton, 2010). While computation constructs manage logic, arithmetic, and control flow operations, communication and interaction primitives coordinate inter- and intra-process data exchange, process creation, and synchronisation. Skeletons provide top-down design, composition, and control inheritance throughout the program structure. As illustrated in Figure 1, by decoupling the behaviour from the structure of a parallel program, skeletons benefit from any performance improvements in the system infrastructure, while preserving the program results.

Structured parallel programs are expressed by interweaving parameterised skeletons in an analogous way to that in which sequential structured programs are constructed. Figure 2 shows the traditional approach to structured parallelism, where a programmer maps a parallel algorithm into a program by selecting a skeleton, or a nesting of skeletons, from a library, and then links the library and the multiprocessing support to produce a skeletal parallel program.

The behaviour-structure decoupling has allowed the structured parallelism paradigm to be seamlessly deployed on different dedicated and non-dedicated architectures including symmetric multiprocessing, massively parallel processing, and clusters (González-Vélez & Cole, 2010; Pelagatti, 1998; Rabhi & Gorlatch, 2003).

A NEW MODULE FOR THE CURRICULUM

The Robert Gordon University (RGU) is a national leader in graduate employability with strong links to the main companies in the oil and gas, healthcare, and ICT sectors. Its study programmes are carefully designed to meet the evolving needs of

Figure 1. The algorithmic skeleton constituents: the behavior. The outcome sought by the application programmer, and the structure. The resource to functionality correspondence.

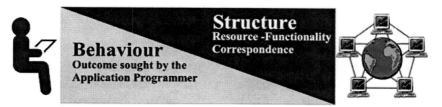

the public and private sectors while maintaining a strong emphasis on teaching quality.

Recognised as the best computer science department of any new United Kingdom University in the Times Good University Guide 2009 and 2010 (Times Online, 2010), the School of Computing at RGU (SoC) has four research themes: knowledge-based systems, computational intelligence, information retrieval, and cognitive engineering. The SoC is an active partner in two major British pooled research initiatives for computer science: the Scottish Informatics and Computer Science Alliance of the leading departments of computer science across Scotland and the Northern Research Partnership.

RGU's Computing Technologies Centre is a purpose-built research infrastructure with facilities providing a creative, supportive environment for all computing researchers, including an IBM JS21 Blade Centre and NVIDIA Tesla C2050 GPU computational facilities. Additionally, the SoC has 12 teaching laboratories with over 250 state-of-the-art Windows, Linux, and Mac workstations.

As part of this vibrant atmosphere, the SoC curricula are continually evolving to meet the requirements of potential employers of graduates. The SoC programmes are designed to respond to the needs of industry through empowering graduates with the adequate skills. There are currently seven accredited undergraduate programmes

Figure 2. The traditional approach to structured parallelism. It does not normally include any provisions for handling resource awareness.

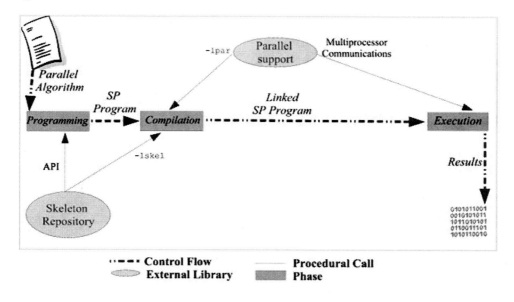

ranging from computer science and networking to multimedia and business information systems. At the postgraduate level, there are five programmes designed to meet the needs of individuals with a strong computing background, or without one, or in search of IT management skills. These programmes have a modular structure to enable students to take courses on different areas that are mapped to the SoC research themes.

Under these conditions the SoC is introducing a new module on parallel programming. Being an introductory course, it is organised in three major blocks: parallel architectures, structured parallelism and parallel programming as illustrated in Figure 3. This 3-block module is designed to be taught in one semester and its learning outcomes are:

- Analyse and discuss techniques and technologies in parallel computing
- Critically review different parallel architectures and organisations, and select the most suitable one for a particular problem
- Design and implement a parallel programming solution for a given problem specification
- Describe and critically evaluate current application areas of parallel computing systems.

As the main innovation of this module is the use of structured parallelism, students are expected to apply the principles of concurrency by utilising different patterns (skeletons) instead of programming applications from scratch. Thence, students are required to use task farms and pipelines to develop coarse-grain parallel applications and scan, reduce, and map constructs to deploy fine-grain parallelism.

The main contributions of this module to the overall programme of study are:

- the establishment of a formal module on parallelism
- the adoption of innovative pattern-based techniques for parallel programming and, ultimately,
- the introduction of ICT industrial practices into the curriculum of a higher-education institution.

Our initial experiences on the use of structured parallelism in student master's degree projects at RGU have been very positive as reflected in interesting, student-led performance evaluation reports (Kontagora & González-Vélez, 2010; Garba et al., 2010). Both of these studies demonstrated the possibility of linking actual calculation needs with student capabilities to develop practical innovative short projects.

CONCLUSION

This module is planned to be first taught at RGU during the academic year 2010/11. As part of the

Figure 3. The organisation of the introductory module on structured parallel programming

Parallel Architectures	Structured Parallelism	Parallel Programming
• Clusters, Clouds, Grids • Multi-core Processors	• Coarse- and Fine-Grain Algorithms • Skeletons and Patterns	• SPMD/MPMD • Message Passing Programming

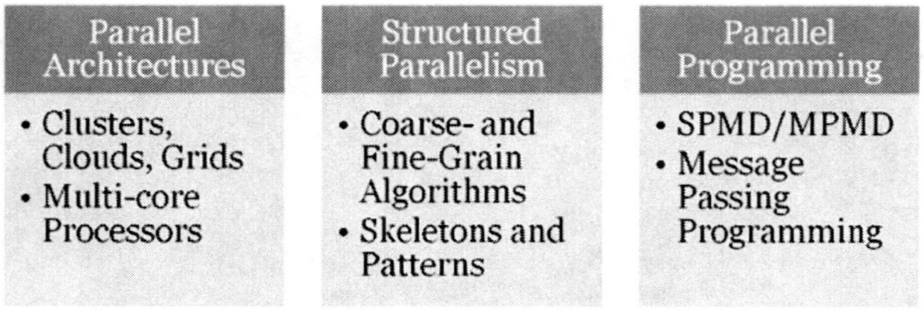

standard RGU feedback process, we expect to receive a report of the students' perception about the utility of the teaching techniques and the didactic approach used in the module. Concurrently, we plan to poll a representative sample of ICT groups at local and national companies in relation to the module in order to gauge their opinion against our expectations.

While we have always expected that this approach will contribute to forming better computer professionals, it will be up to actual employers to assess if our approach is fit for purpose. Following this overall feedback process, the module will be enhanced not only to comply with the leading-edge structured parallelism techniques, but also to satisfy the labour market.

The search for the perfect university module has long occupied educational practitioners. Since there is vastly more material in computer science than a student can possibly assimilate over the four year computing degree programme, there is need to design curricula in which students can acquire core computer science and ICT concepts and skills while also selecting from elective courses to complement and extend their studies. Choosing which topics to include, which to leave out, which to combine with one another, which to make core and which to make elective definitely constitute the great challenge in designing a successful overall computing curriculum.

This work makes the case for a new introductory module on parallel programming, where the emphasis is on the applicability of its materials particularly to the ICT industry. Purely research universities frequently offer a high-end computer science curriculum with a focus on abstraction and research-only subjects. While suitable for some very capable students, the median group of our students is typically more interested in obtaining a successful job following graduation.

Programming in parallel with industry-centred tools can provide these graduates with an attractive profile when seeking employment by start-ups, leading vendors and software developing departments. This is confirmed by recent national initiatives on parallel, multi-core, and cloud computing such as the UK Government Cloud Infrastructure. Therefore, we argue that a module such as this is thoroughly appropriate for undergraduate and postgraduate degree programmes in computing in a professional university.

ACKNOWLEDGMENT

This research was conducted in partial fulfilment of the requirements for the degree of Postgraduate Certificate in Higher Education Learning and Teaching at the Robert Gordon University. Special thanks are owed to Patrik O'Brian Holt and Charles Juwah for their comments to early versions of the manuscript.

REFERENCES

Andrews, G. R. (1999). *Foundations of parallel and distributed programming*. Boston, MA: Addison-Wesley Longman.

Asanovic, K., Bodik, R., Demmel, J., Keaveny, T., Keutzer, K., & Kubiatowicz, J. (2009). A view of the parallel computing landscape. *Communications of the ACM, 52*(10), 56–67. doi:10.1145/1562764.1562783

Ben-Ari, M., & Kolikant, Y. B. D. (1999). Thinking parallel: The process of learning concurrency. *Association for Computing Machinery Special Interest Group on Computer Science Education Bulletin, 31*(3), 13–16.

Cole, M. (1989). *Algorithmic skeletons: Structured management of parallel computation*. London, United Kingdom: Pitman/MIT Press.

Cunha, J. C., & Lourenço, J. (1998). *An integrated course on parallel and distributed processing.* In Association for Computing Machinery (ACM) Special Interest Group on Computer Science Education (SIGCSE 1998): 29th ACM Technical Symposium on Computer Science Education (pp. 217–221). New York, NY: Association for Computing Machinery.

Davey, B. (2010). Special issue on information systems curriculum. *Education and Information Technologies, 15*(4), 237–238. doi:10.1007/s10639-010-9143-7

Dean, J., & Ghemawat, S. (2004). *MapReduce: Simplified data processing on large clusters.* In Operating Systems Design and Implementation (OSDI)'04: Sixth Symposium on Operating Systems Design and Implementation (pp. 137–150). Berkeley, CA: USENIX Association (Advanced Computing Systems Association).

Dean, J., & Ghemawat, S. (2008). MapReduce: Simplified data processing on large clusters. *Communications of the ACM, 51*(1), 107–113. doi:10.1145/1327452.1327492

Fekete, A. D. (2009). Teaching about threading: Where and what? *Association for Computing Machinery Special Interest Group on Algorithms and Computation Theory (SIGACT). News, 40*(1), 51–57.

Finkelstein, A. (1993). European computing curricula: A guide and comparative analysis. *The Computer Journal, 36*(4), 299–319. doi:10.1093/comjnl/36.4.299

Gamma, E., Helm, R., Johnson, R., & Vlissides, J. (1995). *Design patterns: Elements of reusable object-oriented software.* Boston, MA: Addison-Wesley.

Garba, M., González-Vélez, H., & Roach, D. (2010). *Parallel computational modelling of inelastic neutron scattering in multi-node and multi-core architectures.* In Institute of Electrical and Electronic Engineering High Performance Computing and Communications (IEEE HPCC)-10: International Conference on High Performance Computing and Communications (pp. 509–514). Melbourne, Australia.

González-Vélez, H., & Cole, M. (2010). Adaptive structured parallelism for distributed heterogeneous architectures: A methodological approach with pipelines and farms. *Concurrency and Computation, 22*(15), 2073–2094.

González-Vélez, H., & Leyton, M. (2010). A survey of algorithmic skeleton frameworks: High-level structured parallel programming enablers. *Software, Practice & Experience, 40*(12), 1135–1160. doi:10.1002/spe.1026

Goth, G. (2009). Entering a parallel universe. *Communications of the ACM, 52*(9), 15–17. doi:10.1145/1562164.1562171

Hacker, T. J., & Springer, J. A. (2008). *Meeting the data challenge: Curriculum development for parallel data systems.* In Special Interest Group on Information Technology Education (SIGITE)'08: 9th Association for Computing Machinery SIGITE Conference on Information Technology Education (pp. 153–156). New York, NY: Association for Computing Machinery.

Hartman, J., & Sanders, D. (1991). *Teaching a course in parallel processing with limited resources.* In Association for Computing Machinery Special Interest Group on Computer Science Education (SIGCSE)'91: 22nd SIGCSE Technical Symposium on Computer Science education (pp. 97–101). New York, NY: Association for Computing Machinery.

Ivanov, L., Hadimioglu, H., & Hoffman, M. (2008). A new look at parallel computing in the computer science curriculum. *Journal of Computing Sciences in Colleges, 23*(5), 176–179.

Kontagora, M., & González-Vélez, H. (2010, Feb). *Benchmarking a MapReduce environment on a full virtualisation platform.* In Complex, Intelligent and Software Intensive Systemsw (CISIS) 2010: 4th International Conference on Complex, Intelligent and Software Intensive Systems (pp. 433-438). Washington, DC: Institute of Electrical and Electronic Engineering.

Leijen, D., Schulte, W., & Burckhardt, S. (2009). The design of a task parallel library. *Association for Computing Machinery Special Interest Group on Programming Languages Notices, 44*(10), 227–242.

Mattson, T. G., Sanders, B. A., & Massingill, B. L. (2004). *Patterns for parallel programming.* Boston, MA: Addison-Wesley Longman.

Ortega-Arjona, J. L. (2010). *Patterns for parallel software design* (1st ed.). Chichester, UK: John Wiley & Sons.

Pelagatti, S. (1998). *Structured development of parallel programs.* Bristol, UK: Taylor & Francis.

Rabhi, F. A., & Gorlatch, S. (Eds.). (2003). *Patterns and skeletons for parallel and distributed computing.* London, UK: Springer-Verlag. doi:10.1007/978-1-4471-0097-3

Reinders, J. (2007). *Intel threading building blocks: Outfitting C++ for multi-core processor parallelism.* Sebastopol, CA: O'Reilly Media.

Schaller, N. C., & Kitchen, A. T. (1995). Experiences in teaching parallel computing - five years later. *Association for Computing Machinery Special Interest Group on Computer Science Education Bulletin, 27*(3), 15–20.

Shackelford, R., McGettrick, A., Sloan, R., Topi, H., Davies, G., & Kamali, R. (2006). *Computing curricula 2005: The overview report.* In Association for Computing Machinery Special Interest Group on Computer Science Education (SIGCSE)'06: 37th SIGCSE Technical Symposium on Computer Science Education (pp. 456–457). New York, NY: Association for Computing Machinery.

Times Online. (2010). *Good university guide* (report). News International Limited, London, UK: Times Newspapers Ltd. Retrieved from http://www.timesonline.co.uk/tol/life_and_style/education/good_university_guide/

Toll, W. E. (1995). *Decision points in the introduction of parallel processing into the undergraduate curriculum.* In Association for Computing Machinery Special Interest Group on Computer Science Education (SIGCSE)'95: 26th SIGCSE Technical Symposium on Computer Science Education (pp. 136–140). New York, NY: Association for Computing Machinery.

Torbert, S., Vishkin, U., Tzur, R., & Ellison, D. J. (2010). *Is teaching parallel algorithmic thinking to high school students possible? One teacher's experience.* In Association for Computing Machinery Special Interest Group on Computer Science Education (SIGCSE)'10: 41st SIGCSE Technical Symposium on Computer Science Education (pp. 290–294). New York, NY: Association for Computing Machinery.

Wilkinson, B., & Allen, M. (1999a). *Parallel programming: Techniques and applications using networked workstations and parallel computers.* Upper Saddle River, NJ: Prentice-Hall, Inc.

Wilkinson, B., & Allen, M. (1999b). A state-wide senior parallel programming course. *Institute of Electrical and Electronic Engineering (IEEE) Transactions on Education, 42*(3), 167–173. doi:10.1109/13.779894

Wilkinson, B., & Ferner, C. (2008). *Towards a top-down approach to teaching an undergraduate grid computing course.* In Association for Computing Machinery Special Interest Group on Computer Science Education (SIGCSE 2008): 39th SIGCSE Technical Symposium on Computer Science Education (pp. 126–130). New York, NY: Association for Computing Machinery.

KEY TERMS AND DEFINITIONS

Algorithmic Skeletons: Abstractions of commonly-used patterns of parallel computation, communication, and interaction. They provide top-down design, composition, and control inheritance throughout the program structure.

Computing Curricula 2005: A co-operative project of the Association for Computing Machinery, the Association for Information Systems, and the Computer Society of the Institute of Electrical and Electronic Engineering to authoritatively describe undergraduate degree programmes in Computer Engineering, Computer Science, Information Systems, Information Technology, and Software Engineering.

Concurrency: The execution of different sections of a given computer program at the same time.

Parallel Patterns: General reusable solutions to a commonly occurring parallel problem which can be efficiently deployed through concurrency.

Parallel Programming: Creation of a set of instructions (program) to enable a computer to capitalise on concurrency in order to improve the overall performance of such program, and, eventually, that of the whole system.

Pattern-Based Programming: A programming technique where the norm is the use of general reusable solutions to a commonly occurring problem (design patterns).

Structured Parallelism: High-level parallel programming methodology which allows the abstract description of programs and fosters portability by focusing on the description of the algorithmic structure rather than on its detailed implementation.

APPENDIX

Additional Reading

It is widely acknowledged that the best source for curricula development is the Computing Curricula 2005 which covers the undergraduate degree programs in Computer Engineering, Computer Science, Information Systems, Information Technology, and Software Engineering. It is edited by the Joint Task Force for Computing Curricula as a cooperative project of the Association for Computing Machinery, the Association for Information Systems, and the Computer Society of the Institute of Electrical and Electronic Engineering (Shackelford et al., 2006).

The Association for Computing Machinery (ACM) maintains a web page comprising a number of important sources on curriculum development at: http://www.acm.org/education/curricula-recommendations.

Finkelstein (1993) provides a classic comparative analysis of different computing programmes in Europe. While dated, it still provides a good starting point on the subject.

A recent special issue of Education and Information Technologies (Davey, 2010) centres on the development of information systems curricula and provides a wide perspective on recent development in the field.

Chapter 9
Open and Closed Practicals for Enterprise Resource Planning (ERP) Learning

Andrés Boza
Universitat Politècnica de València, Spain

Llanos Cuenca
Universitat Politècnica de València, Spain

ABSTRACT

Enterprise Resource Planning (ERP) systems are implemented in companies to improve their business processes. An ERP system entails extensive functional and technological aspects during its implementation. Teaching ERP systems for computer science students implies addressing these two aspects: ERP functionality and technological features. It is a challenge for teachers to design practical experimentation that students can perform in the teaching environment, due to the prerequisite of a deep understanding of the business processes, business user requirements, and the technological complexity of ERP systems. In order to improve student skills in ERP systems, we encourage active learning among students. In this chapter, we present a methodology using open and closed practicals to learn about both technical and functional aspects of ERP systems. Using these practicals allows us to prepare and organize this teaching/ learning process.

INTRODUCTION

New teaching/learning frameworks encourage students to play a more active role. The Bologna Process for establishing the European Higher Edu-

cation Area considers that appropriate emphasis should be placed on autonomous work (Sorbonne, 1998). Thus, active pedagogical methods receive more emphasis than passive methods. The European Convergence Action Plan at the Universidad Politécnica de Valencia declares that students are the major figures in their educational process and

DOI: 10.4018/978-1-60960-797-5.ch009

that they must acquire new ways of learning and new forms in which to apply it. Although autonomous work by students is guided by teachers, it is a new competency required of teachers. For this reason, it is necessary to design and perform special activities so that students develop meaningful co-operative autonomous learning. Within the University, the School of Computer Sciences is participating in several of these activities and staff from many subject areas are making and testing new proposals along these lines. The Computer Tools for Business course subject is taught in the last year of the computer science engineering degree (year 5) to intensify course subjects on Information Systems. This subject introduces students to ERP systems together with other topics such as business process management, interoperability, enterprise application integration and supply chain management.

Teaching ERP systems for computer science students implies addressing two main aspects:

- ERP functionality, where technical students must deal with the business processes covered by the ERP and business user requirements, and
- technological features, where students deal with the architecture of ERP systems and other complex technical features used in ERP implementation.

The challenge for teachers is significant. On the one hand, the limited previous knowledge that students have of the main business processes makes it difficult to deal with these aspects at an adequately high level of detail. On the other hand, the technological complexity of ERP systems makes it difficult to perform meaningful practical experimentation in the teaching environment.

In order to overcome these difficulties, we encourage active learning among students. Students learn about ERP definitions, features, its implementation processes in a company (selection, customization, configuration, etc.), and the dif-

ficulties in this process, from theoretical classes. However, they need to work with this tool to really improve their skills in ERP systems. In this chapter, we present a methodology using open and closed practicals to learn about ERP systems. In closed practicals, teachers present students with the resolution of a problem that is quite limited in the exposition and in the tools or methods used for its resolution. In the open practicals there is greater freedom in choosing the problem to be solved and the tools or resolution methods to be used to solve it.

ERP EDUCATION

The terms enterprise system and ERP (enterprise resource planning) system are equivalent terms (Davenport, 2000). ERP is an evolution of MRP-II (manufacturing resource planning) and PPC (production planning and control) (Delgado & Marín, 2000; Markus et al., 2000). Nowadays ERP is a generic term for standard software. The ERP system is an enterprise information system designed to integrate the business processes and transactions in a corporation and to optimize them. The ERP is an industry-driven concept and system, and is universally accepted by the industry as a practical solution to achieve integrated enterprise information systems (Moon, 2007).

The following are the main desirable characteristics of an ERP system (Davenport, 2000; Lee et al., 2003; Moller, 2005; Scheer, 1994):

- it integrates all the functions, processes and data of a company by using one single database and by defining individual roles and views
- it is applicable to most economic sectors
- it is modular in design
- it is based on *best practical* process reference models.

ERP II, or extended-ERP represents an expansion of the original ERP. The components that have been included in these newer systems are: the traditional ERP, e-business, enterprise application integration (EAI) features, and collaboration in the supply chain (Kulmar & van Hillegersberg, 2000; Lee et al., 2003; Moller, 2005; Theling & Loos, 2005).

Enterprise resource planning software systems support the comprehensive management of financial, manufacturing, sales, distribution, human resources and other aspects of business processes across the enterprise (Shtub, 2001). This is one of the reasons why ERP systems are being imposed as information systems for business management, due to their ability to automate and integrate the different business processes in the company, and to provide an integrated vision and new advantages in the management of the business (Aguayo et al., 2007).

In the past, companies used to decide how they wanted to do business and then made a decision about a software package that best supported their business processes. This was changed with the emergence of ERP systems that required the business processes to be modified to fit the ERP system chosen (Davenport, 1998). Although sometimes seen as large information systems projects, ERP projects are in fact change management projects where basic business practices are reviewed and changed to align with the *best practice* as defined in the ERP business processes (Carton & Adam, 2003). Unlike other information systems, the major problems of ERP implementation are not technologically related issues such as technological complexity, compatibility, standardization, etc., but mostly about organization and related human issues such as resistance to change, organizational culture, incompatible business processes, etc. (Chakraborty & Sharma, 2007).

The improvement of business processes is the ultimate goal of establishing an ERP initiative. One of the controversial issues in the world of ERP is how much attention should be given to the *as-is*

and the *to-be* business processes. A recent survey shows that while some companies let their ERP systems dictate what the new processes will be, others customize their ERP systems to align with their current business processes. According to this survey, 42% of companies changed their business processes to accommodate ERP functionality. About 27% changed or customized their ERP functionality to accommodate current business processes. Only 9% of companies changed business processes independently of ERP, and then selected or configured the software to align with the new processes. Nearly 22% of companies had very little or no focus on their business processes (Panorama, 2010).

Despite the significant benefits that ERP systems can provide, to deal with an ERP implementation project is a challenge. The statistics show that under 30% of ERP implementations are successful, with the projects completed on time and on budget, and with all features and functions as originally specified (Iskanius, 2009). Furthermore, this challenge continues in the post-implementation phase where the implemented ERP system needs to be continuously reviewed and enhanced in order to meet new user requirements (Peng & Nunes, 2009).

Managers have to learn how to manage operations in a dynamic and uncertain environment, using the model base and database of their ERP systems. In recognition of this need, some schools are considering the installation of a commercial ERP system and training their students in the use of a real system. The amount of time required to learn the details of all the screens and functions of a real ERP system is enormous as these systems are not designed to support teaching (Shtub, 2001). A study among 2800 graduated business students shows that 76% of the respondents are working in a position where IT knowledge is perceived as important or very important. Furthermore, research concludes that IT knowledge is an important selection criterion for employers recruiting business students (Vluggen & Bollen,

2005). Thus, more university faculties are committing to this vision, and coming to believe that a primary mechanism for enlightening business students to information technology and business theory is through enterprise application systems (Hunt et al., 2010; Jæger et al., 2010). Regarding computer science students, Pittarese (2009) indicates that although computer science and information technology programs provide a strong foundation for students in computing skills, students often lack an understanding of the business context in which many of those skills will be used after graduation. In fact, IT firms are looking for employees who can engage the organization at a high level, define comprehensive requirements for large projects, design solutions, and be able to easily develop expertise in multiple areas of the company (Marshall & Roadknight, 2001; Sanders, 2004).

The distinction between ERP training and ERP education defines a division between *know-how* and *know-why*. This distinction allows universities to define their own educational product (Davis & Comeau, 2004).

Although a significant level of such activities are going on in the universities, the number of journal articles on ERP education seems to be relatively few. Perhaps this is an area to which the university community needs to pay attention in order to develop and archive more relevant knowledge (Moon, 2007).

Several studies have covered the introduction of ERP into the curriculum included in business schools (Davis & Comeau, 2004; Hunt et al., 2010; Jæger et al., 2010), the information system and computer science curriculum (Cameron, 2008; Hawking et al., 2001; Pittarese, 2009), the subsequent impact (Boykin & Martz, 2004; Davis & Comeau, 2004; Noguera & Watson, 2004), the costs for universities (Becerra-Fernandez et al., 2000), the implications of implementation in universities (Rabaa'i et al., 2010), inter-university collaboration (Jæger et al., 2010), or the use of an ERP simulation software to avoid failed

implementations of complete ERPs for academic purposes (Lindoo & Wilson, 2010).

There are a number of barriers that hinder teaching ERP systems in universities (Hawking et al., 2001) including the limited knowledge and experience of academic staff charged with the responsibility of integrating ERP into IS courses, and the costs involved in accessing an ERP system to enable students to gain hands-on experience to master the concepts inherent in these types of systems. According to Vluggen & Bollen (2005), the following problems have to be dealt with, overcoming resistance to the use of such software and to the fundamental changes in the existing curriculum (staff), acquiring the necessary (financial) resources for the use of ERP software, composing a multidisciplinary team of faculty members, and implementing and maintaining a technical infrastructure for ERP usage.

In this context, Huynh & Chu (2010) explored the potential of open-source ERP as an alternative to the traditional SAP University Alliances Model. The cost of the latter program remains an inhibiting factor for many universities that are struggling with their already limited resources and budget. By way of conclusion, the authors consider that it is feasible to adopt an open-source ERP system, and to install and deploy it for teaching purposes; however, the faculties that intend to incorporate this open-source ERP may need to spend significant time on developing appropriate content. Although one of the major incentives for adopting open-source software is the absence of license fees, there are other costs to be considered in the adoption of such ERP software and its implementation process (Huynh & Pinto, 2010).

However, it is increasingly accepted that today's globally competitive environment requires technical professionals to move beyond technical expertise and contribute to the strategy and development of dynamic IT systems that are able to support changing business objectives. To prepare students to meet such expectations, IT students must have broad experience in the design, implementation, and integration of such systems (Cameron, 2008). In this sense, theoretical classes and laboratory practical work could improve the knowledge of ERP systems by computer science students as well as their mastery of both underlying business and technical topics.

OPEN PRACTICALS VS. CLOSED PRACTICALS

What students learn is closely associated with *how* they go about learning it (Watson, 2002). Traditional instruction, such as the typical lecture-based session that developed before textbooks were mass-produced, often involves delivering as much information as possible as quickly as possible. The lecture method was one of the most effective and efficient ways to disseminate information and has often been used for this purpose. But, because many faculty members are poor lecturers, and because students are often poor participants in the lecture, this type of instruction has often allowed students to be passive in the classroom. Students, not knowing how to be active participants in the lecture, have relied for learning on transcription, memorization, and repetition (Major & Palmer, 2001).

The literature suggests that students must do more than simply listening, but must read, write, argue, ask questions, or get involved in problem-solving (Oliveira et al., 2006). Active learning is a term used to refer to a range of techniques where students do more than simply listening to a lecture. The key to active learning is that students are doing something that relates to discovering, processing, and applying information (Ishiyama, 2010). Bonwell & Eison (1991) consider five characteristics to be required for learning to be active:

- students are involved in more than listening
- less emphasis is placed on transmitting information and more on developing students skills

- students are involved in higher-order thinking (analysis, synthesis, evaluation)
- students are engaged in activities (reading, discussing, writing)
- emphasis is placed on students' exploration of their own attitudes and values.

As one step forward we found that research suggests that students learn better in the context of a compelling problem (Ewell, 1997) or through experiences (Cross, 1999). One technique used for achieving such a context is problem-based learning (PBL). The main characteristics of PBL are that the tutor's role is as a facilitator of learning, the learners' responsibilities are to be self-directed and self-regulated in their learning, and the essential element of well-designed ill-structured instructional problems to serve as the driving force for inquiry. The challenge for many instructors when they adopt a PBL approach is to make the transition from teacher as a knowledge provider to tutor as a manager and facilitator of learning (Ertmer & Simons, 2006). In a PBL approach, the tutor supports the process and expects learners to make their thinking clear, but the tutor does not provide information related to the problem because that task is the learners' responsibility. Problem-based learning can offer students opportunities to learn how to learn, and to develop key skills, independence of enquiry, and the ability to contest and debate (Savin-Baden, 2000).

Open and closed practicals are related to problem based learning (PBL). In engineering studies, laboratory practicals usually introduce the use of computer science tools for the resolution of problems, which are generally complex and offer great realism (United Nations Educational, Scientific and Cultural Organization, 1996). In a laboratory context, Alemany et al. (2003) distinguish two categories within laboratory practicals: open and closed practicals. In closed practicals, teachers present students with the resolution of a problem limited in terms of the exposition and in terms of the tools or methods to be used for its resolution. In open practicals there is greater freedom for students when choosing the problem to solve and in deciding on the tools or resolution methods to be used.

Open practicals encourage students to find and solve real-life problems that can be solved by means of theoretical knowledge (acquired in class) and commercial computer tools (used in laboratory practicals). Not only do they involve students participating in active and constructive engagement with contents and tools, but they promote skills in identifying and assessing quality resources to address practical problems (Takwale et al., 2007). This is in accordance with the new methodologies that intend to orient teaching toward employment and society. Furthermore, students observe and appreciate the utility of the theoretical contents of the course subjects.

Nevertheless, this type of practical requires considerable effort by students when it comes to solving the real problem. Open practicals are enriching for students and teachers alike. As a result, teachers are challenged to extend their experience and knowledge of real problems and possible solutions to use them for closed practicals or classroom sessions.

USING OPEN AND CLOSED PRACTICALS TO LEARN ABOUT ERP SYSTEMS

General Characteristics

The main goal under consideration here is to introduce students to ERP systems. To go about this, we encourage active learning among students to manage a real ERP system. The challenge for computer science students is twofold: they must acquire new technical skills and must understand the operation of the main business processes (functional skills).

The methodology presented here distinguishes two categories within the practicals (open and closed), and two types of skills (functional and technical). In accordance with this, four kinds of practicals are defined:

- Closed functional practicals
- Open functional practicals
- Closed technical practicals
- Open technical practicals

Closed functional practicals introduce students to the main business processes supported by ERP (procurement, warehouse, sales, production or financial management) and their parameterization in a guided way. Open functional practicals encourage students to define a new closed functional practical. In this practical, they must go deep into new features and define a new functional practical to show new business process behaviours. They must decide which functional areas and which business processes will work.

Closed technical practicals introduce students to the key architecture components used in the ERP development process and the tools to customize the ERP. Finally, open technical practicals encourage students to manage new technical tools in a non-guided way (database administration, export/import processes, configuring and customizing the ERP, etc.). In this case, students decide which technical skill they want and need to study in depth.

Methodology

In this section, we present a methodology for using open and closed practicals to learn about ERP systems. This proposal is a generic methodology that may be used in a wide range of educational situations. The development of the methodology in our academic environment is presented in the following section.

ERP Software Selection

An initial analysis is required to select the ERP software that best fits the purpose of the practicals.

The selected ERP must be appropriate for its use in both open and closed practicals. Besides, this ERP must be used in computer laboratories for students to learn about its functional and technical features; for this reason, selection can be conditioned by computer laboratory equipment. Furthermore, students will explore this ERP in open practicals in a non-guided way. Thus, the selected ERP must be accessible to students and must allow a range of possibilities (beyond those covered in the closed practicals) where students can study both functional and technical aspects in depth.

Workplace Preparation for Closed Practicals

The workplace for closed practicals must include all the necessary facilities so that students can use the ERP as well as the other tools or files they need to perform the closed practicals. This work is done prior to the practicals and may include:

- preparing computer laboratories to make the selected ERP operative
- making the other software tools used in the closed practicals available to students
- providing data files when they are required in the practicals
- preparing the ERP, and other tools and files at the start of the practicals (configuration, parameters, pre-loaded data, etc.).

The detailed preparations depend, among other things, on the ERP selected, its architecture, software licenses, and other services that may be provided by the ERP supplier (like Application Service Providers - ASP). Therefore, this may require installing the ERP (in a server workstation or in a set of PCs), adapting the software or hardware to fulfill the ERP technical requirements or setting up what is required to access it remotely.

Adjust Timing and Student Group Size

It is necessary to plan the number of sessions required to carry out these practicals within the time period available for the practicals within the course subject syllabus. Moreover, given the different types of practicals, it is necessary to set the number of sessions for each type and the time available for each session. As regards the time required to perform them all, it is necessary to identify the time period the students will work in the computer laboratories, plus the time period they will work outside the scheduled sessions (before and after). Finally, it may be possible to choose between individual and group practicals depending on the number of students, the number of sessions, the facilities in the computer laboratories and other factors.

Prepare Guided Worksheet for Closed Practicals

Producing a guided worksheet to be used in closed practicals is necessary. With functional practicals, ERPs support many business processes, and it is possible to choose among a wide range of functional practicals. It is also possible to focus on a module (sales, manufacturing, financials, etc.) or on a complete business process which crosses various functional areas (modules). As regards closed technical practicals, an ERP present a complete technical challenge, ranging from its installation to its customization for an organization, including new functionalities or loading historical data from a legacy system. Obviously, it is necessary to take into account the previous decisions on the features of the selected ERP, the facilities in the computer laboratory, the number of practical sessions and the selection between individual and group practicals, in order to produce the guided worksheets.

Create a Framework for Open Practicals

As stated above, a wide range of functional and technological skills are required in an ERP project. Therefore in order to go deep into ERP training, we propose performing open practicals using aspects that are not covered in the closed practicals. Despite being open practicals, they need to be tutored so that students clearly know the objective of this type of practical. Allowing freedom in many aspects of the practical is possible, but it is necessary to establish a general framework to help students achieve the desired objectives. This framework must establish the set of deliverables to be developed by students to transfer the work done, whether it takes the form of documents (establishing the type of document: summary, software code, screenshots, and so on) or the presentation of the work carried out (establishing rules or suggestions for presentations: power point, screen capture videos, screenshots, limit the time to be used, and so on), or any other kind of deliverable.

Define Evaluation Rules

The evaluation method must be carried out in line with both the objectives set in the practicals and the effort required to meet these objectives. In this sense, the weight and form of evaluation for both open and closed practicals must be established so that students are aware of it in advance.

A scheme of the proposed methodology is shown in the Figure 1.

Experience with Computer Science Students and Results

In this section, we discuss the details and decisions made in implementing open and closed practicals in our course subject. Our students are attending the final year of the computer science engineering degree (year 5) that specializes in information

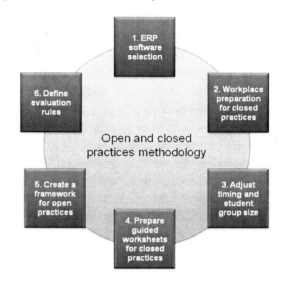

Figure 1. Methodology to use open and closed practicals to learn ERP systems

systems. They have good technological skills, but only a basic level of knowledge of the functional aspects of enterprises. For this reason it was considered necessary to dedicate more sessions to the functional features than to the technical aspects.

ERP Software Selection

As regards selecting the ERP, our course subject includes an introduction to ERP systems; thus, an ERP covering a wide range of functionalities was not necessary, but rather a relatively simple one with the typical business processes supported by ERP systems. Furthermore, we are not conditioned by a decision committee that chooses the best ERP for the enterprise (as in a real enterprise context). So, our judgement was primarily educational: to decide on the best ERP for this teaching/learning process.

The ERP selected for use in the practicals was Openbravo. This ERP allows plenty of versatility for the design of the practicals. Regarding functionalities, it covers the main functional areas that are typically included in ERPs (procurement, warehouse, sales, production and financials). From the global ERP point of view, it includes multi-currency, multi-organization, multi-accounting and multi-language aspects. From the viewpoint of the facilities to be managed by the students, different configurations are possible: a) complete installation on a laboratory server computer and its online use via the web by students, b) complete installation and individualization in all the laboratory PCs (laboratory computers or students' computers), c) use of the Demo Center that Openbravo provides on its website and which includes a fully functional online demonstration. As regards the technological features, this ERP includes advanced technological components like a web applications development framework and modern technologies (Java and Javascript, SQL and PL/SQL, XML and XHTML). In terms of obtaining software and license costs, this is an open-source ERP and it is possible to download it from the network to be employed by the required number of users. We analyzed other ERP products, but our selection was based on the features provided by Openbravo ERP set out above, because it fits the purpose of the practicals and may be used in our computer laboratory.

Workplace Preparation for Closed Practicals

In terms of the workplace for closed practicals preparation, two different environments were prepared: one for functional practicals and the other for technical practicals.

For the functional practicals, the ERP was installed on a server computer where the practical groups were connected via the web. We defined a user/password to the ERP for each student group. We created a company in the system for each group so that each group worked within its own company and had no access to the other groups' information. In this way, all the students were working with the same ERP system but did not share information.

As for the technical practicals, a virtual machine with the ERP installed was used. This virtual machine (downloaded from the Openbravo web site) allowed ERP management in a technical manner without interferences among the student groups.

Adjust Timing and Student Group Size

Practicals were designed to be performed in groups of 2 or 3 students in accordance with both the number of students we had and the characteristics of our computer laboratory. Each practical session lasted two hours, and we planned an introductory session, four sessions for the closed functional practicals, one session for the closed technical practical and two sessions for the open practicals. In the first session, practicals were introduced, groups were formed, and the set of practicals, the schedule and the selected ERP were presented to the students.

Prepare Guided Worksheet for Closed Practicals

The first guided worksheet for the introduction session included access to the ERP, providing a user name and password to each group, a guided tour of the user interface (surfing by the application, making queries, inserting new data, etc.), the components in the menu, the hierarchical information structure following the business structures (entity - representing the entire company, organization - a subdivision of the entity, and warehouse - used in the organizations), user roles, and master data management (business partners and products).

The closed functional practical sessions were distributed in the following way: a procurement management session (purchase orders, receipts, purchase invoices and procurement management reports), a second warehouse management session (warehouses and storage bins, arrivals/departures, physical inventory, movement among warehouses and warehouse management reports), a third sales management session (sales orders, delivery notes, invoicing process and sales management reports), and finally, a production management session (product bill of materials, production plans and production orders). All the sessions included transactional operations and retrieving the introduced information by means of reports.

The closed technical practicals included the installation of the virtual machine with the ERP, creating a new table in the ERP database, creating a user form for data entry and including this new form in the menu.

Create a Framework for Open Practicals

Regarding open practicals, our proposal was for students to prepare a new guided worksheet of some uncovered aspect in the previous practicals. In this case, students did not have a guided worksheet but were provided with general instructions about carrying out this open practical. The topics on which to work and the necessary tools were selected by each group. Students could choose between functional and technical topics. Furthermore, students were provided with a template with the structure to be followed to prepare their guided worksheet. The template structure was similar to that of the guided worksheet in the closed practicals: 1) Objectives of the practical, 2) Summary, 3) Introduction, 4) Development (guided exercises), 5) Review questions.

Students researched the ERP and prepared the guided worksheet outside the laboratory schedule. At the beginning of the open practicals, each group reported the topic they wanted to work on and their objectives. The topics tackled by students in the open practicals were: new functionalities of some of the modules covered in the closed functional practicals (procurement management, warehouse management, sales management, and production management), dealing with new modules (project management and finance) or technological tools

to extract, transform and load data from a legacy system to the ERP.

When the students had started their work, we tutored this work to check the line of work they were following. The students had to prepare a short report on the work carried out until that time, which was discussed in a tutored session.

The deliverables requested at the end of the open practicals were: the new guided worksheet proposed by them, a report about the work done, and a critical analysis of the ERP including the pros and cons found. Furthermore, the students had to synthesize and transfer the knowledge they acquired in their open practical to a public presentation of the work they had carried out. In the last laboratory session they presented their open practical experiences to the other student groups. In this presentation session, the group that was showing their work had an active role, while the audience groups had to participate with their questions in analyzing the work, proposing improvements and evaluating the works presented.

Define Evaluation Rules

Regarding the evaluation of practicals, different weights were established for the closed and open practicals; open practicals had a greater weight, given their difficulty.

In order to evaluate closed practicals, we considered aspects such as successful completion of the proposed activity, completion in time and the synthesis of the activity using review questions. Regarding open practicals, we considered, among others, the difficulty of the selected topic, the depth achieved, the quality of the report about the work done, and the students' abilities to transfer their acquired knowledge.

Our Impressions

The global evaluation of our impressions of the set of open and closed practicals was positive, the selected tool has proved useful for our needs, the planned work for each session matched the scheduled time, and most importantly, the students improved their skills on ERPs from the first guided practical to their own presentation of an ERP topic.

We were also interested in knowing the students' opinions on the set of practicals. Therefore, we conducted an anonymous survey among the students (using a Likert scale) in which they evaluated, among other things, their interest, the level of difficulty involved, the guided worksheets, the presentation session and an overall evaluation. Students' opinions incorporate satisfactory overall evaluation, and were more positive in the case of students who also worked and were in contact with business information systems.

We also included open questions about strengths and weaknesses. The strengths students emphasized were starting with good guided practicals and progressing to the last practicals where they had already acquired good management skills and knowledge of the tool. They also evaluated the use of the open-source software positively. The weaknesses they highlighted were their need for more time for some of the closed practicals and the incidence of some computer bugs in the selected ERP.

FUTURE RESEARCH DIRECTIONS

It is possible to consider this course module as possibly useful in the teaching/learning processes of other business software like SCM (supply chain management) or CRM (customer relations management). Each business software solution has its own features, but this module might be revised in order to create a suitable and equally fruitful methodology for teaching/learning different business softwares.

Another way of learning about ERPs that arises from this experience, would include a research approach in which students would build

a basic ERP. In such a scenario, the activities of an ERP software developer could be simulated in the computer laboratory. Some student groups could develop small modules of an ERP system with basic functionalities. Because of the nature of ERP systems, the different groups (modules) would have to interact, therefore rendering coordination work necessary which could be done by other student groups.

CONCLUSION

Many computer science course subjects focus on technical aspects and do not cover the environments where these technologies will be located. ERP systems clearly locate technology in an enterprise environment. The technological complexity of ERP systems is very great and includes topics such as databases, communications, hardware architectures, etc.. However, the complexity of the business processes supported by ERPs is also vast (procurement management, warehouse management, sales management, production management and finance). Thus, students can observe that technology is used to support business processes, and technological advances are included to improve these processes.

By bearing in mind our objective of students learning about ERP systems, our proposal is to include this topic in theoretical classes and to stress improving students' skills in such systems by means of practical sessions. The combination of open and closed practicals allows students to improve these skills gradually. This teaching/learning process is reinforced where the preliminary closed practicals with guided worksheets lead smoothly into the challenges of ERP management in a non-guided way in the open practicals. Finally, the public presentation of their work enables students to mentally organize the new knowledge learned and to further reinforce this learning.

REFERENCES

Aguayo, M., Luna, P., Ríos, M. A., & Ruiz, J. C. (2007). Aplicación del ECTS a la enseñanza integrada de sistemas de información empresariales mediante páginas HTML. *Revista de Enseñanza Universitaria, 29,* 4–23.

Alemany, M., Cuenca, L., Boza, A., & Ortiz, A. (2003, July). *Education for learning.* Paper presented to the International Conference on Engineering Education (ICEE), Valencia, Spain.

Becerra-Fernandez, I., Murphy, K. E., & Simon, S. J. (2000). Integrating ERP in the business school curriculum. *Communications of the ACM, 43*(4), 39–41. doi:10.1145/332051.332066

Bonwell, C. C., & Eison, J. A. (1991). *Active learning: Creating excitement in the classroom.* Washington, DC: The George Washington University School of Education and Human Development.

Boykin, R. F., & Martz, W. B. Jr. (2004). The integration of ERP into a logistics curriculum: Applying a systems approach. *Journal of Enterprise Information Management, 17*(1), 45–55. doi:10.1108/09576050410510944

Boza, A., & Cuenca, L. (2010). *An educative experience of autonomous workgroups in the subject Enterprise Computer Tools.* In B. Wu & J.-P. Bourrières (Eds.). (2010). *Educate adaptive talents for IT applications in enterprises and interoperability. Proceedings of 5th China-Europe International Symposium on Software Industry Oriented Education* (pp. 23-26). Talence, France: University of Bordeaux.

Cameron, B. H. (2008). *Enterprise systems education: New directions and challenges for the future.* Paper presented at the Association for Computer Machinery Special Interest Group on Management Information Systems Computer Personnel Research Conference on Computer Personnel Doctoral Consortium and Research, Charlottesville, VA.

Carton, F., & Adam, F. (2003). Analysing the impact of enterprise resource planning systems roll-outs in multinational companies. *Electronic Journal of Information Systems Evaluation, 6*(2), 21–32.

Chakraborty, S., & Sharma, S. K. (2007). Enterprise resource planning: An integrated strategic framework. *International Journal of Management and Enterprise Development, 4*(5), 533–551. doi:10.1504/IJMED.2007.013457

Chickering, A. W., & Gamson, A. F. (1987). Seven principles for good practicals in undergraduate education. *The American Association for Higher Education Bulletin, 39*(7), 8–12.

Cross, K. P. (1999). *Learning is about making connections: The Cross Papers Number 3.* Mission Viejo, CA: League for Innovation in the Community College.

Davenport, T. H. (1998). Putting the Enterprise into the Enterprise System. *Harvard Business Review,* (July-August): 1–11.

Davenport, T. H. (2000). *Mission critical: Realizing the promise of enterprise systems.* Boston, MA: Harvard Business School Press.

Davis, C. H., & Comeau, J. (2004). Enterprise integration in business education: Design and outcomes of a capstone ERP-based undergraduate e-business management course. *Journal of Information Systems Education, 15*(3), 287–299.

Delgado, J., & Marín, F. (2000). Evolución en los sistemas de gestión empresarial. Del MRP al ERP. *Economía Industrial, 331*(1), 51–58.

Ertmer, P. A., & Simons, K. D. (2006). Jumping the PBL implementation hurdle: Supporting the efforts of K–12 teachers. *Interdisciplinary Journal of Problem-Based Learning, 1*(1), 40–54.

Ewell, P. T. (1997). Organizing for learning: A new imperative. *American Association for Higher Education Bulletin, 50*(4), 3–6.

Gorgone, J. T., Gray, P., Stohr, E., Valacich, J. S., & Wigand, R. (2006). Master of Science in Information Systems (MSIS) 2006: Curriculum preview. *Communications of the Association for Information Systems, 15*, 544–554.

Guthrie, R. W., & Guthrie, R. A. (2000). Integration of enterprise system software in the undergraduate curriculum. *Proceedings of the Information Systems Education Conference (ISECON 2000), 17*(301).

Hawking, P., McCarthy, B., & Stein, A. (2004). Second wave ERP education. *Journal of Information Systems Education, 15*(3), 327–332.

Hawking, P., Ramp, A., & Shackleton, P. (2001). Information systems IS'97 model curriculum and enterprise resource planning systems. *Business Process Management Journal, 7*(3), 225–233. doi:10.1108/14637150110392700

Hunt, C. S., Regan, E. A., Everett, D. R., Green, D. T., Hunt, D., & Becka, P. (2010). Integrating enterprise systems concepts in the B-school: A regional university perspective. *Information Systems Education Journal, 8*(9), 3–13.

Huynh, M. Q., & Chu, H. W. (2010). Exploring the open-source ERP alternative for teaching business process integration in supply chain management. *Proceedings of the Academy of Information and Management Sciences, 14*(1), 32–36.

Huynh, M. Q., & Pinto, I. (2010). Open source ERP applications: A reality check for their possible adoption and use in teaching business process integration. *Information Systems Education Journal, 8*(69), 3–11.

Ishiyama, J. (2010) What is the Impact of In-Class Active Learning Techniques? A Meta Analysis of the Existing Literature. *APSA 2010 Annual Meeting Paper.* 1-15

Iskanius, P. (2009, July). *The ERP project risk assessment: A case study.* Paper presented to the World Congress on Engineering, London, United Kingdom.

Jæger, B., Rudra, A., Aitken, A., Chang, V., & Helgheim, B. (2010, January). *Teaching business process concepts using enterprise systems in a globalized context.* Paper presented to the 43rd Hawaii International Conference on System Sciences in Koloa, Kauai, Hawaii.

Joseph, G., & George, A. (2002). ERP, learning communities, and curriculum integration. *Journal of Information Systems Education, 13*(1), 51–58.

Kulmar, K., & van Hillegersberg, J. (2000). ERP - experiences and evolution. *Communications of the ACM, 43*(4), 23–26.

Kumar, V., Maheshwari, B., & Kumar, U. (2002). Enterprise resource planning systems adoption process: A survey of Canadian organizations. *International Journal of Production Research, 40*(3), 509–523. doi:10.1080/00207540110092414

Lee, J., Siau, K., & Hong, S. (2003). Enterprise integration with ERP and EAI. *Communications of the ACM, 46*(2), 54–60. doi:10.1145/606272.606273

Lindoo, E., & Wilson, J. L. (2010). Offering process-centric education by way of an SAP simulator. *Journal of Computing Sciences in Colleges, 26*(2), 132–138.

Major, C., & Palmer, B. (2001). Assessing the effectiveness of problem-based earning in higher education: Lessons from the literature. *Academic Exchange Quarterly, 5*(1), 4–9.

Markus, M. L., Tanis, C., & van Fenema, P. C. (2000). Multisite ERP implementations. *Communications of the ACM, 43*(4), 42–46. doi:10.1145/332051.332068

Marshall, I. W., & Roadknight, C. M. (2001, October). *Management of future data networks: an approach based on bacterial colony behavior*. Paper presented at the Institute of Electrical and Electronic Engineering (IEEE) Conference on Systems, Man & Cybernetics, Tucson, AZ.

Meltzer, D. E., & Manivannan, K. (2002). Transforming the lecture-hall environment: The fully interactive physics lecture. *American Journal of Physics, 70,* 639–654. doi:10.1119/1.1463739

Moller, C. (2005). ERP II: A conceptual framework for next-generation enterprise systems? *Journal of Enterprise Information Management, 18*(4), 483–497. doi:10.1108/17410390510609626

Moon, Y. B. (2007). Enterprise resource planning (ERP): A review of the literature. *International Journal of Management & Enterprise Development, 4*(3), 235–264. doi:10.1504/IJMED.2007.012679

Noguera, J. H., & Watson, E. F. (2004). Effectiveness of using an enterprise system to teach process-centered concepts in business education. *Journal of Enterprise Information Management, 17*(1), 56–74. doi:10.1108/09576050410510953

Oliveira, P. C., Oliveira, C. G., Neri de Souza, F., & Costa, N. (2006). Teaching strategies to promote active learning in higher education. In A. Méndez-Vilas, A. Solano Martín, J. A. Mesa González & J. Mesa González (Eds.), *Current developments in technology-assisted education volume 1: General issues, pedagogical issues* (pp. 636-640). Badajoz, Spain: Formatex.

Panorama. (2010). *2010 ERP report: Organizational change management*. Denver, CO: Panorama Consulting Group.

Peng, G. C., & Nunes, M. B. (2009). Surfacing ERP exploitation risks through a risk ontology. *Industrial Management & Data Systems, 109*(7), 926–942. doi:10.1108/02635570910982283

Pittarese, T. (2009). Teaching fundamental business concepts to computer science and information technology students through enterprise resource planning and a simulation game. *Journal of Computing Sciences in Colleges, 25*(2), 131–137.

Rabaa'i, A. A., Bandara, W., & Gable, G. G. (2010). Enterprise systems in universities: A teaching case. *Americas Conference on Information Systems (AMCIS 2010) Proceedings,* paper 171.

Sanders, L. (2004). Strategies for teaching something new. *Science Scope, 28*(1), 26–27.

Savin-Baden, M. (2000). *Problem-based learning in higher education: Untold stories*. Buckingham, United Kingdom: The Society for Research into Higher Education & Open University Press.

Scheer, A.-W. (1994). *Business process engineering: Reference models for industrial enterprises* (2nd ed.). Berlin, Germany: Springer.

Shtub, A. (2001). A framework for teaching and training in the enterprise resource planning (ERP) era. *International Journal of Production Research, 39*(3), 567–576. doi:10.1080/00207540010009714

Sorbonne Joint Declaration. (1998). *Joint declaration on harmonisation of the architecture of the European higher education system*. Paris, France: Sorbonne University.

Takwale, R., Prasad, V. S., Koul, V., Sinclair, P. K., Misra, S., & Kumar, V. … Banerjee, S. (2007). *Open and distance education. Recommendations from the Working Group on Open and Distance Education*. New Delhi, India: National Knowledge Commission.

Theling, T., & Loos, P. (2005). Teaching ERP systems by a multiperspective approach. *Americas Conference on Information Systems (AMCIS) 2005 Proceedings,* paper 151.

United Nations Educational, Scientific and Cultural Organization. (1996). *La educación encierra un tesoro. Informe a la UNESCO de la Comisión Internacional sobre la Educación para el siglo XXI.* Paris, France: United Nations Educational, Scientific and Cultural Organization.

UPV. (2005). *Proyecto general de la UPV para la promoción y dinamización de la convergencia europea.* Retrieved October 30, 2010, from http://www.upv.es/miw/infoweb/pace/ProyectoGeneral.pdf

Vluggen, M., & Bollen, L. (2005). Teaching enterprise resource planning in a business curriculum. *International Journal of Information and Operation Management Education, 1*(1), 44–57. doi:10.1504/IJIOME.2005.007447

Watson, P. (2002). The role and integration of learning outcomes into the educational process. *Active Learning in Higher Education, 3*(3), 205–219. doi:10.1177/1469787402003003002

KEY TERMS AND DEFINITIONS

Autonomous Learning: Learning a course subject in a non-guided way using a self-learning process in order to achieve the theoretical and practical learning objectives of the subject.

Business Process: Series of organized activities that are done in companies for the purpose of adding value and converting inputs (tangibles or intangibles) into value outputs, and may be decomposed hierarchically into sub-processes.

Closed Practicals: Practical in which the teacher presents students with the resolution of a limited problem, and the tools or methods used to resolve it.

Enterprise Resource Planning System: A standard software designed to cover the information requirements of the main business processes in an enterprise in order to collect, integrate and optimize enterprise information.

Functional Practicals: Practicals whose objective is to improve skills in the functional features of the tools used.

Information System: Set of components that participate in the informational needs of one or more organizations that are useful for its/their decision making, coordination, control and operation.

Open Practicals: Practical in which the teacher encourages students to find and solve real-world problems relating to the course subject contents.

Technical Practicals: Practicals whose objective is to improve skills in the technical features of the tools in use.

Chapter 10
Curriculum Issues in Industry Oriented Software Engineering Education

Alok Mishra
Atilim University, Turkey

Deepti Mishra
Atilim University, Turkey

ABSTRACT

Software engineering education has been emerging as an independent and mature discipline. Accordingly, various studies are being done to provide guidelines for the software engineering education curriculum design. This chapter summarizes the case for the need for software industry related courses and discusses the significance of industry oriented software engineering education to meet the educational objectives of all stakeholders. Software industry oriented curricula for the undergraduate and postgraduate levels are discussed. An industry oriented postgraduate level (Master's degree level) software engineering course is also proposed which includes foundational and applied courses to provide effective training to future software engineers. This will lead to the enhancement of their employment prospects in industrial and allied sectors.

INTRODUCTION

Software engineering is becoming popular and moving towards maturity. Innovations and improvements in curricula, instruction and assessment are being directed towards bridging

DOI: 10.4018/978-1-60960-797-5.ch010

the academia-industry gap by projecting the true nature of software development and facilitating the student in acquiring essential knowledge, skills and attitude, that are actually needed by the industry (Shaw et al., 2005). Software engineering deals with the creation and application of engineering fundamentals for the systematic and team-based analysis, development, use, evaluation, etc. of large, software-intensive systems as technical products (Horn & Kupries, 2003). These researchers argued that there is need for highly qualified specialists, capable of mastering, designing, developing and maintaining complex software-intensive systems.

It is common to hear complaints from software engineering companies about the practical knowledge of the new graduates who start working after completion of their academic programmes. While such graduates can have a high level of theoretical knowledge, they often lack practice in solving real-life industrial problems. Complaints about software quality and software failures and even disasters are becoming common and, although these arise from many factors, they are partly due to the shortcomings of the higher education institutions which do not teach essential knowledge and skills (Jaakkola et al., 2006). Many of the challenges associated with software engineering education are due to our inability to provide students with real-life, large-scale software development experience in the academic environment (Su et al., 2007). Therefore, the quality of the software engineering workforce is a strong function of the quality of the software engineering education. Software engineering is the fastest-evolving engineering discipline and most of the tasks of the software development organizations are diverse in nature, provide tools and methods throughout society (Kral & Zemlica, 2008). In this context, it is the task of software engineering education to prepare software engineering professionals adequate to this challenge, by providing them with knowledge and skills to meet the challenging needs of the software industry.

As a result of the gap between software industry needs and the education obtained by prospective software engineers, new graduates tend not to be capable of ready absorption into the industry (Beckman et al., 1997). Frequently it is necessary to provide them with substantial in-house training and orientation before placing them in responsible positions. It is also important that graduates should have experienced significant exposure to a range of different new areas of application. If they are well-versed in emerging technologies the duration of the in-house training in industry will be reduced, thus saving time and money for companies (Mishra et al., 2007). Jaakkola and colleagues (2006) also advocated that the software engineering curriculum should correspond to industry needs, and that only when it did so, would the universities produce appropriately skilled professionals. They further argued that the development of software curricula should take into account standards, frameworks, and recommendations developed by different interest groups.

Software engineering is a multidimensional field that involves activities in many areas and disciplines such as computer science, project management, system architecture, human factors, and technological evolution (Brazilay et al., 2009). Several efforts have been made to map the different dimensions of software engineering and to design a curriculum that addresses them all (SEEK, 2004; Swebok, 2008).

INDUSTRIAL EXPOSURE IN SOFTWARE ENGINEERING EDUCATION

The practical project(s) within a software engineering programme should be assigned to students with the aim of providing hands-on experience of developing a medium-sized software engineering project in a small team of four and five students. The teams should take real-life problems including innovative projects provided by local business organizations to help to give the students industry experience. This would also provide students with an in-depth knowledge of their project domain and give them the confidence and ability to apply that knowledge in practice. Regarding the evaluation of students projects, Hayes et al. (2003) concluded that a good grading scheme must take into account a range of information, and not just rely on the final product. The challenge is to come up with a system of grading the students so that the same assessment criteria can be applied to all, even though they have worked on different projects (Clark, 2005). Gates et al. (2000) identified the importance of structuring individual accountability into the implementation of the project to ensure that all members of the team contribute to the project and receive their appropriate individual gradings. Thus the scheme must include an approach for measuring the individual effort of each team member peer-review. McGourty and colleagues (2000) suggested multisource assessment that would incorporate critical information from several sources, such as peers, industrial colleagues, self and faculty members, on student competencies and specific behaviours and skills, and would provide the student with a better understanding of his/her personal strengths and areas in need of development. The software engineering project should also focus on giving the students opportunities to communicate effectively.

Industrial practices can be included in software engineering curriculum in the following ways:

- process and product development dimensions can be assigned in teams to tackle issues like software process and quality, software architecture and requirements issues
- small projects/assignments should be given as part of a software project management course in which students can use different software project management tools to make different charts and diagrams for decision-making
- class discussions can be related to fundamentals, theory and practice
- industrial trends should be communicated in various ways such as invited talks, mailing lists, technology based forums, industrial internships and others.

According to Brazilay et al. (2009) the four axes of the course framework - the fundamentals of software engineering, practicals and tools, production, and technology evolution - provide educators with a ready means of adapting the elements of the framework as required by adding, removing or changing individual modules, as long as the axis rationale is maintained.

Hilburn et al. (2006) claim that case studies are of special value in problem-based learning, where the concentration is on the development of problem-solving skills and team skills. Group projects are important educational components used for teaching students various teamwork skills (Su et al., 2007). These latter researchers observed however, that the importance of supplying students with a real-life teamwork environment tends to be largely ignored in academic group software development projects. Group projects have been widely adopted in many undergraduate and postgraduate courses in software engineering, computer science and information technology. A major motivation for group projects within higher education is to simulate real-life conditions (Prey, 1995). Industrial case studies can also be helpful in developing understanding of different real-life problems. In summary, industry-relevant case studies and projects, along with industry internship, should be an integral component of the software engineering education curriculum (Saiedian, 1999; Wohlin & Regnell, 1999).

PARTNERSHIP BETWEEN SOFTWARE INDUSTRY AND ACADEMIA

The areas in which managers in the software industry frequently complain of weaknesses in the knowledge and skills of new graduates include key software areas such as software development models, requirements engineering, software architecture and high-level design, software processes, software quality assurance and management, software project management, managing people organizations and working in teams, software testing, and others (Ford & Gibbs, 1996).

Lethbridge added the following topics to this list of deficiency areas that need to be included in the curriculum and that students generally could observe and learn about during an industry internship (Lethbridge, 2000a; 2000b): object-oriented concepts and technologies, requirements gathering and analysis, analysis and design methods, testing verification and quality assurance, human-computer interaction/user interfaces, databases, configuration and release management, ethics and professionalism, technical writing, delivering presentations/seminars to an audience, and leadership skills.

Kitchenham et al. (2005) also supported several of Lethbridge's observations regarding a perceived over-emphasis on mathematical topics in software engineering syllabuses and an under-emphasis on business topics. However, their findings differed from those of Lethbridge as to the topics where new graduates had the greatest knowledge gap. There was no disagreement, however, on the key priority that software engineering students should have the skills to work individually as well as in teams to develop and deliver quality software products (SEEK, 2004).

It is increasingly accepted that the success of software engineering programmes is critically dependent on the involvement and active participation of industry (SEEK, 2004). In this context, Wohlin & Regnell (1999) presented strategies for industrially relevant education for software engineers. There are many ways that industry and academia can co-operate. Many academic institutions have established departmental or institutional industrial advisory boards. These groups, consisting of managers and engineers from industries closely associated with the higher education institution, are one of the vehicles that provide feedback about the direction of an academic programme (Kornecki et al., 2003). Other forms of co-operation are occasional short-term projects to meet the current needs of industry. Such projects allow faculty and students to become familiar with the domain and often contribute to the industrial partner's goals. Other modes of co-operation are student summer internships and faculty internship programmes. These facilitate understanding of industry needs and allow the university to make appropriate programme revisions. All these approaches can be relatively effective but do not provide a permanent solution. Academic institutions should be able to redesign and implement software education curricula that not only emphasize theoretical and technical aspects of computing, but also focus on the practice of software engineering (Dey & Sobhan, 2007).

The most recent Association for Computing Machinery model curricula (ACM, 2005) recognized the different perspectives of academia and industry and recommended teaching in the computing curricula those technical and non-technical skills required for large software development. It has been also suggested that students be exposed to an appropriate range of applications and case studies that relate the theory and skills learned in academia to real-world occurrences to explain their relevance and utility.

The selection of suitable industry partner(s) to provide challenging and motivating projects, including internship within the company for some period, requires that academic coordinating staff be highly motivated to support these projects and prepare for the project prior to the start of each semester. Also it is important that the industry client be prepared to accept that such a project may fail due to time or other limitations (Hogan et al., 2005). Usually students work in teams on projects and different teams may come up with different solutions. These solutions are discussed by the entire class. Students analyze various solutions and present their different approaches. During this process open discussions facilitate learning and the development of communications skills. In most cases industry is interested in application-oriented activities that bring more immediate solutions, help in the implementation of new products, or improve profitability of everyday operations (Kornecki et al., 2003). However industry is also competing for capable graduates with the skills to meet the challenges of developing safety-critical software-intensive systems and the collaboration with students on these projects allows the companies to assess the students as future employees and this can be a strong motivation for the industries to participate in this work.

DEVELOPMENT OF SOFTWARE ENGINEERING CURRICULA

Instructional material design and content creation should take into account Bloom's levels of learning (Bloom, 1956). Since knowledge is assimilated at different levels, learning modules should be constructed so as to take the learner from an elementary knowledge base of information and concepts through application and analysis of the knowledge, and finally towards synthesis and evaluation (Pinto, 2010).

According to Pinto, designing the curriculum should taken following issues into consideration:

- job opportunities and duties involved
- personality traits (soft-skills) required for the job
- the competencies required to perform the job
- the knowledge, know-how and current skills required to achieve these competencies
- the corresponding subject concepts (theory) to acquire the required knowledge base
- assignments (practice) that enhance the *know-how* of the subject
- the skill set (the means) required to perform the assignments

- the reference materials whose subject objectives match the knowledge required in the points above
- assessments that can check a candidate's knowledge at various levels for a given competency.

Although the core conceptual knowledge in IT remains the same, the advances made in the technological area are varied and swiftly changing. Therefore, the skill set that the learner attains must be what the industry is currently using. The curriculum design must be extensible enough to take this into account. Pinto (2010) suggested that a professionally designed curriculum would require inculcating two main types of competencies:

- professional competencies that relate to the knowledge base required and the ability to use this knowledge in the related work area
- personal competencies that represent a set of skills, attitudes and values that enable the professional to work efficiently and adapt to his/her present environment.

Modern software engineering education is driven by an expectation that industry best practice and state of the art software technologies should be an integral part of the curriculum as industrial strength project work is well regarded by potential employers (Hogan et al., 2005). Industry-based projects have students working with real clients who have a significant interest in the results of the projects. Developing software that is of benefit to a real client is in itself a strong motivator for students (Tomayko, 1987), as is the use of leading-edge commercial tools in the projects.

Within the computer science model curricula designed by joint Institute of Electrical and Electronic Engineering Computer Society/Association for Computing Machinery task force, software engineering is divided into eight core areas and four elective areas, thus

Core Areas:

- software design
- using application programming interfaces
- software tools and environments
- software processes
- software requirements and specifications
- software validation
- software evolution
- software project management

Elective Areas:

- component-based computing
- formal methods
- software reliability
- specialized systems development

Koska & Romano (1988) recommended that college curricula substantially change to emphasize skills that require a systems approach on a wide theoretical base so that the graduates would have the knowledge and skills that are required by the industry. According to one approach, it is suggested that the skills and knowledge to be possessed by the graduates be identified and that the curriculum be examined to determine how well it matches the needs of the industry (Waks, 1995). Also, the rapid pace of technological development must be taken into account through continuous updating of educational programmes and the engineering curricula (Waks & Frank, 2000).

CURRICULUM DESIGN

Software engineering deals with the creation and application of engineering fundamentals for the systematic and team-based analysis, development, implementation, evaluation, etc. of large, software-intensive systems as technical products (Horn & Kupries, 2003). The need for highly qualified specialists capable of mastering software systems and adopting different tools throughout the entire process, is the reason for the emergence of soft-

ware engineering as a discipline separate from computer science. Thus, in designing a software engineering curriculum following issues should be considered:

- the curriculum should be designed keeping in mind the needs of the industry which will provide employment to graduates
- the structure of the individual modules (core/compulsory and optional) should follow models suggested by various authorities and should take into account the different prerequisites
- the curriculum should cover the important areas of software engineering
- industrial projects should be an integral part of the curriculum
- students should be able to understand the modules, their significance and relationships.

The curriculum design is somewhat influenced by commercial companies, who offer universities hardware and software at low prices, often together with ready-made courses where this hardware and/or software is used. IBM offers free course material, training and curriculum development to universities in its academic initiative programme (IBM, 2010). Similarly Microsoft has provided financial support for creating software engineering curricula in specific areas (mainly for United States universities) for several years. Currently the company is offering $1.0 million to assist in developing courses in computer science, business and law that focus on secure computing (a popular topic in recent times), while earlier, Microsoft provided about $0.5 million to develop computer gaming curricula (Microsoft, 2006).

While developing the curriculum, it is important to determine its objectives and expected outcomes. Thus, during initiation of a course the stakeholders (particularly academia and industry) need to collaborate in setting the curriculum. At later stages of the development, other interest

Table 1. Core software engineering courses/ modules

Course Title	Credits
Foundations of Software Engineering	3
Software Requirements Engineering	3
Software Project Management	3
Software Engineering Process	3
Software Quality assurance	3
Software Testing and Validation	3
Software Architecture and Implementation	3

Table 2. Advanced software engineering courses/ modules

Course Title	Credits:
Analysis and Design of Information System	Any three courses
Advanced Computer Networks	
Software Technology Management	
Embedded and Real-time Software Engineering	
Computer Animation and Virtual Reality	
Human Computer Interaction	
Distributed Systems	
Software Evolution (Maintenance)	
Engineering Economics for Software	
Cyber Ethics and Laws	
Data Mining and Warehousing	
Emerging Trends in Software Engineering	
Software Industrial Project (5-6 Months duration)	9

groups and accreditation bodies become involved. The Institute of Electrical and Electronic Engineering (SEEK, 2004) provides the latest comprehensive guidelines for undergraduate programmes in software engineering. These include guidelines for curriculum design, delivery, modules and their sequencing. Other programme implementation issues such as faculty, students, infrastructure and industry co-ordination, assessment, and accreditation have also been discussed briefly (Mishra et al., 2007).

An authoritative framework guide to the software engineering body of knowledge-(SWEBOK) (Swebok, 2008) defines the software engineering knowledge that professionals should have after completing a four year undergraduate course. Several software engineering researchers have raised concerns on some aspects of Swebok. For instance it is claimed the Association for Computing Machinery classification and the Institute of Electrical and Electronic Engineering SE 2004 models provide tools to position the contents of the curriculum in the map of computing science in a region specifically important for the research perspective (Jakkola et al., 2006). The Computing Curricula 2005 overview report is a further attempt by the IEEE/ACM joint task force to provide specific guidelines for undergraduate courses in computer engineering, computer sci-

ence, information technology, information systems and software engineering.

Efforts have been also initiated to develop guidelines for postgraduate course(s) in software engineering. Based on the literature and experience in our university, the following tables present recommended mixes of core (Table 1) and optional (Table 2) modules together with industry oriented projects for postgraduate level software engineering education.

FRAMEWORK FOR INDUSTRY-ORIENTED SOFTWARE ENGINEERING (UNDERGRADUATE) CURRICULUM

O'Leary et al. (2006) surveyed software industry employers in Ireland, the UK and China and found that the ability to learn, the ability to adapt to changing circumstances, and the ability to place developments and emerging technologies in context are qualities which employers in industry consider crucial. It is also interesting to note one respondent's comment that over a career, most people will learn any number of new technologies, and it will be much easier to do this if the person has a solid knowledge of the fundamentals.

These researchers also reported on the development and content of the EMERSION project industry-oriented software engineering curriculum, based on collaboration between Dublin Institute of Technology (DIT), Harbin Institute of Technology (HIT) and University of Wolverhampton (UW). This programme was designed to bring a novice through a four-year programme to graduate as an industrially-oriented practitioner. The following was the framework developed for this industry-oriented software engineering curriculum.

The first year objective was to provide the students with foundational programming and problem-solving skills, good communication and presentation skills as well as recognition of the main topics in computing and the role of the software engineer in industry.

During the second year it would be important to develop the students' abilities in developing whole systems, thus introducing the problems related to modular and object-oriented software development. The significance of design approaches and methodologies would be stressed as key at this stage.

In the third year the aim would be to enhance the students' software development skills to the point where they could develop solutions for reasonably large, industrial type problems, thus further developing their problem-solving and software engineering skills.

The task in the final year would be to focus entirely on preparing students for the transition into industry. Successful integration into commercial organizations where the graduate would be in a position to swiftly become productive would be the principal objective of this year. In this year the students would also complete the work placement programme (industry internship) in parallel with preparing an academic dissertation. By requiring students to complete their dissertation while on project placement, with the topic selected and the project supervised (in part) by industrial supervisors, students would be presented with the opportunity to begin their transition from the academic to the industrial environment (O'Leary et al., 2006)

A PROPOSED PLAN FOR THE SOFTWARE INDUSTRY/ ACADEMIC LINKAGE

In the light of the discussion thus far, it is appropriate to outline the desirable features of the linkage between the higher education institution and the software industry.

- There should be a continuous summer student internship programme or a one semester industrial project at the software industry's research and development facilities.
- There should be an exchange programme between academic staff and engineers/ developers from the software industry. The academics might spend their summer or sabbatical leave at the software industry while the industry personnel might be invited to deliver series of lectures on their real-life software projects, challenges, recent advances in software, hardware, tools and other issues affecting the industry.
- The establishment of a professorship with support from the software industry would be helpful to encourage industry-oriented research and exchange of knowledge among academics and engineers from industry.
- The establishment of fellowships, project support, awards and similar financial and other encouragement for students and academic staff, would also assist.
- Continuous transfer of research outcomes, solutions and technologies to industrial

partners from the academic institution could be facilitated.

- The installation of a dedicated laboratory with the support of the industrial partners would encourage the software engineering areas of interest at the university and might be devoted to software engineering related research in areas of mutual interest.

- The inclusion of programme modules consistent with the objectives of the industrial partners could be facilitated.

SOFTWARE ENGINEERING ETHICS AND PROFESSIONAL PRACTICE

Professional practice and continuing education along with computing-software ethics should also be included in the software engineering curriculum for both undergraduate and postgraduate students. These would provide vital elements of the information and procedural skills required of prospective software engineers and managers who have to administer and manage different types of operations, contracts, outsourcing agreements and other such arrangements in the national and international contexts during their careers (Dey & Sobhan, 2007).

Facing ethical dilemmas is an integral part of the software engineer's career and the accreditation standards for software engineering educational programmes also emphasize ethical issues. Institutions seeking accreditation in engineering-related programmes by ABET are asked to specify how the programmes assure the development of an understanding of the ethical, social, and economic considerations in professional practice (ABET, 2002). The teaching of ethics should focus on issues relating to the production of software products and not be confined to the myriad abuses that can occur through the use of computers (Towell, 2003). Students should also be provided with information regarding the handling of confidential information and conflict

of interest situations. The higher education institutions should provide such education and training to prospective software engineers.

ACCREDITATION AND SOFTWARE ENGINEERING PROGRAMMES

Accreditation is one of the major procedures for objectively judging the merits of a programme and benchmarking it against competitor programmes. It allows and encourages universities to review their programmes periodically to keep pace with rapidly changing requirements and changes in business, industry and technology (Dey & Sobhan, 2007; ABET, 2002). The accreditation procedures for undergraduate and postgraduate software engineering programmes is still at the initial stages in many countries. It is expected that national and international accreditation organizations will assist in the development of the vision for industry-oriented programmes and projects, not only for the higher education institutions and the software industry but for wider industry and society, including governments and students.

CONCLUSION

Software engineering is rapidly becoming a mature discipline, increasingly vital and critical to all parts of society, in all part of the world. The demand for software engineering is increasing and so there is an increasing demand for efficient and knowledgeable software engineers. The collaboration between the software industry and higher education departments can lead to synergies for both in accomplishing their objectives. The university has a role in research and financial support for that research should come from industry. Such collaborations can provide real-life project handling experience as well as financial incentives to students. The academic staff can engage in applied research and contribute to the solution of software industry problems. Theoretical research can then find applications in practical software problems and projects. The results of the research laboratory activities can be used in the classrooms for discussions and further enrichment of the curriculum.

There are many reasons for incorporating real-life industry projects in software engineering education, including increased student motivation and confidence, exploration by students of ICT areas not covered directly in the curriculum or only covered in summary fashion, and development of increased problem-solving and critical thinking skills, communication skills and business vision among the students (Clark, 2005). The development of the social, technical and ethical skills of teamwork and accountability can also build on and add considerable value to the key technical skills of software engineering to produce a graduate with strong career credentials.

REFERENCES

ABET (Accreditation Board for Engineering and Technology). (2010). *ABET self-study questionnaire: Template of the computing self-study report.* Baltimore, MD: ABET.

Association of Computing Machinery/Institute of Electrical and Eelectronic Engineeering. (2005). *Joint task force on computing curricula: 2005 - overview report.* Retrieved March 23, 2007, from http://www.acm.org/education/curricula.html

Beckman, K., Coulter, N., Khajenouri, S., & Mead, N. (1997). Collaborations: Closing the industry–academy gap. *Institute of Electrical and Electronic Engineering Software, 14*(6), 49–57.

Bloom, B. S. (Ed.). (1956). *Taxonomy of educational objectives, handbook 1: Cognitive domain.* White Plains, NY: Longman.

Brazilay, O., Hazzan, O., & Yehudai, A. (2009). A multidimensional software engineering course. *Institute of Electrical and Electronic Engineering (IEEE) Transactions on Education, 52*(3), 413–424. doi:10.1109/TE.2008.930094

Clark, N. (2005). Evaluating student teams developing unique industry projects. In A. Young, & D. Tolhurst (Eds.), *Proceedings of the 7th Australasian Conference on Computing Education* (pp. 21-30). Darlinghurst, Australia: Australian Computer Society.

Dey, S. K., & Sobhan, M. A. (2007, December). *Guidelines for preparing standard software engineering curriculum: Bangladesh and global perspective.* Paper presented to 10th International Conference on Computer and Information Technology, Dhaka, Bangladesh.

Ford, G., & Gibbs, N. E. (1996). *A mature profession of software engineering* (Technical Report CMU/SEI-96-TR-004, ESC-TR-96-004). Pittsburgh, PA: Carnegie Mellon University, Software Engineering Institute.

Gates, A. Q., Delgado, N., & Mondragon, O. (2000). A structured approach for managing a practical software engineering course. In *Proceedings of the 30th Annual Frontiers in Education Conference* (1, pp. T1C/21-T1C/26). Washington, DC: Institute of Electrical and Electronic Engineering Computer Society.

Hayes, J. H., Lethbridge, T. C., & Port, D. (2003). Evaluating individual contribution toward group software engineering projects. In *Proceedings of the 25th International Conference on Software Engineering* (pp. 622-627). Washington, DC: Institute of Electrical and Electronic Engineering Computer Society.

Hilburn, T. B., Towhidnejad, M., Nangia, S., Li, S., & Hilburn, T. (2006, October). *A case study project for software engineering education.* Presented at the 36th Annual American Society for Engineering Education/Institute of Electrical and Electronic Engineering (ASEE/IEEE) Frontiers in Education Conference, San Diego, CA.

Hogan, J. M., Smith, G., & Thomas, R. (2005). Tight spirals and industry clients: The modern software engineering education experience. In A. Young & D. Tolhurst (Eds.), *Proceedings of the 7th Australasian Conference on Computing Education* (pp. 217-222). Darlinghurst, Australia: Australian Computer Society.

Horn, E., & Kupries, M. (2003). A study program for professional software engineering. In *Proceedings of the 16th Conference on Software Engineering Education and Training (CSEE&T 2003)* (pp. 298-308). Washington, DC: Institute of Electrical and Electronic Engineering Computer Society.

International Business Machines (IBM). (2010). *IBM academic initiative.* Retrieved October 15, 2010, from http://www.ibm.com/developerworks/university/academicinitiative

Jaakkola, H., Henno, J., & Rudas, I. J. (2006). *IT curriculum as a complex emerging process.* Paper presented at the Institute of Electrical and Electronic Engineering International Conference on Computational Cybernetics (ICCC 2006), Tallinn, Estonia.

Kitchenham, B., Budgen, D., Bereton, P., & Woodall, P. (2005). An investigation of software engineering curricula. *Journal of Systems and Software, 74*(3), 325–335. doi:10.1016/j.jss.2004.03.016

Kornecki, A. J., Khajenoori, S., Gluch, D. P., & Kameli, N. (2003). On a partnership between software industry and academia. In *Proceedings of the 16th Conference on Software Engineering Education and Training (CSEE&T 2003)* (pp. 60-69). Washington, DC: Institute of Electrical and Electronic Engineering Computer Society.

Koska, D. K., & Romano, J. D. (1988). *Countdown to the future: The manufacturing engineer in the 21st century.* Dearborn, MI: Society of Manufacturing Engineers.

Kral, J., & Zemlicka, M. (2008, May). *Engineering education: A great challenge to software engineering.* Paper presented at the 7th Institute of Electrical and Electronic Engineering/Aassociation for Computer Information Systems (IEEE/ACIS) International Conference on Computer and Information Science (ICIS 2008), Portland, OR.

Lethbridge, T. C. (2000a). What knowledge is important to a software professional? *Institute of Electrical and Electronic Engineering Computer, 33*(5), 44–50.

Lethbridge, T. C. (2000b). Priorities for the education and training of software engineers. *Journal of Systems and Software, 53*(1), 53–71. doi:10.1016/S0164-1212(00)00009-1

McGourty, J., Dominick, P., & Reilly, R. R. (1998). Incorporating student peer review and feedback into the assessment process. In *Proceedings of the 28th Annual Frontiers in Education Conference* (1, pp. 14-18). Washington, DC: Institute of Electrical and Electronic Engineering Computer Society.

Microsoft. (2006). *Computer game production curriculum 2004 RFP awards.* Retrieved October 15, 2010, at http//research.microsoft.com/ur/us/fundingopps/Gaming_curriculumRFP_awards.aspx

Mishra, A., Cagiltay, N. E., & Kilic, O. (2007). Software engineering education: Some important dimensions. *European Journal of Engineering Education*, *32*(3), 349–361. doi:10.1080/03043790701278607

O'Leary, C., Lawless, D., Gordon, D., Haifeng, L., & Bechkoum, K. (2006). Developing a software engineering curriculum for the emerging software industry in China. In *Proceedings of the 19th Conference on Software Engineering Education and Training* (pp. 115-122). Washington, DC: Institute of Electrical and Electronic Engineering.

Pinto, Y. (2010). A strategy, implementation and results of a flexible competency based curriculum. *ACM Inroads*, *1*(2), 54–61.

Prey, J. C. (1995, November). *Co-operative learning in an undergraduate computer science curriculum.* Paper presented at the 25th Annual American Society for Engineering Education/Institute of Electrical and Electronic Engineering (ASEE/IEEE) Annual Frontiers in Education Conference, Atlanta, GA.

Saiedian, H. (1999). Software engineering education and training for the next millennium. *Journal of Systems and Software*, *49*, 113–115. doi:10.1016/S0164-1212(99)00082-5

SEEK. (2004). *Curriculum guidelines for undergraduate degree programs in software engineering.* Retrieved October 20, 2010, from http//sites.computer.org/ccse/

Shaw, M., Herbsleb, J. D., & Ozkaya, I. (2005, May). *Deciding what to design: Closing a gap in software engineering education.* Paper presented to the 27th International Conference on Software Engineering (ICSE 2005), St. Louis, MO.

Su, H., Jodis, S., & Zhang, H. (2007). Providing an integrated software development environment for undergraduate software engineering courses. *Journal of Computing Sciences in Colleges*, *23*(2), 143–149.

Swebok. (2008). *Software engineering body of knowledge.* Retrieved October 20, 2010, from http://www.swebok.org/index.html

Tomayko, J. E. (1987). *Teaching a project-intensive introduction to software engineering.* (Technical Report SEI-SR-87-1). Pittsburgh, PA: Software Engineering Institute, Carnegie Mellon University.

Towell, E. (2003). Teaching ethics in the software engineering curriculum. In *Proceedings of the 16th Conference on Software Engineering Education and Training (CSEE&T 2003)* (pp. 150-157). Washington, DC: Institute of Electrical and Electronic Engineering Computer Society.

Waks, S. (1995). *Curriculum design: From an art towards a science.* Hamburg, Germany: Tempus.

Waks, S., & Frank, M. (2000). Engineering curriculum versus industry needs - a case study. *Institute of Electrical and Electronic Engineering Transactions on Education*, *43*(4), 349–352.

Wohlin, C., & Regnell, B. (1999). Strategies for industrial relevance in software engineering education. *Journal of Systems and Software*, *49*(2-3), 125–134. doi:10.1016/S0164-1212(99)00085-0

KEY TERMS AND DEFINITIONS

Accreditation: The granting of approval (recognition) to a higher education institution by an official review board after the institution/school has met specific requirements, for the award of a degree or other award(s).

Professional Practice: Where a student is required to develop and acquire knowledge and skills within a practical/industrial software environment, for instance through a period of internship.

Software Engineering Curriculum: Programme curriculum that includes technical (core and optional) and other courses required to train graduates to engineer large complex software systems.

Software Engineering Education: Programmes that deal with the creation and application of engineering fundamentals for the systematic and team-based analysis, development, use, evaluation (testing and quality assurance), etc., of software-intensive systems.

Software Ethics: The morals relating to computer/software usage, including the set of proper (ethical) practices relating to software development and implementation to be followed by software engineers.

Software Industrial Project: The creation of new software for an application or system domain and the maintenance and implementaion of this software.

Software Industry: Includes functions involved in the development, maintenance, implementation and promulgation of computer software using different business models, including software services, training, documentation, and consulting.

Section 4
International Academic Quality Assurance

Chapter 11
Seven Factors for the Quality Assurance of International Higher Education

Ciarán O'Leary
Dublin Institute of Technology, Ireland

ABSTRACT

As education becomes accepted as a service like any other, the market for trade of education services has developed significantly, with a diversity of providers competing to provide education outside their national boundaries. As well as providing an international experience to students, this can facilitate the sharing of expertise among students, educators, and policy makers who can learn from successes in other countries. This appears to be particularly important in the education market for software engineers and computing professionals, where the knowledge base is rapidly evolving. This requires, however, careful management of the service provision, which results in increased focus on quality assurance. Assuring quality is made difficult by many factors, some shared with quality assurance of education in general, and others unique to the international context. We present seven factors that represent the core challenges for the quality assurance of international higher education, and as such, represent a valuable tool for computing educators and others either currently involved in, or intending to become involved in, the international education market.

INTRODUCTION

The Single European Act (European Community, 1986) recognised the European Union as an area for free movement of goods, persons, services and capital. Twenty years later, the EU Services Directive (European Commission, 2006) defined a path into the future where education services are provided outside of the national context within which the qualifications to which they lead are awarded. This mirrors the effect of the World Trade Organisation's General Agreement on Trade in Services (World Trade Organisation, 1995) which first recognised education as a service in the international context, and attracted a diversity

DOI: 10.4018/978-1-60960-797-5.ch011

of education providers to the international market to compete for students and status.

Countries with large, established education systems such as the United States (US) and the United Kingdom (UK) have been the most significant participants in the international education market, with other countries, which benefit from their geographic location, such as Australia, matching both the US and the UK for innovation outside their national boundaries. More recently, countries such as Ireland have increased their efforts to engage with the international provision market. The motivation for participation in this market is driven by both financial and academic considerations. Clearly, the ability to charge fees to students and attract students to the home campus to pay international fees is a key motivator for this provision. However, it is also the case that engagement with this type of provision has the potential to develop and share expertise in various aspects of education, including curriculum design, learning and teaching methods and specific research areas. It also offers the potential for countries to share education experiences and learn about each other's successes and routes to success.

The past two decades have seen a significant increase in focus on quality assurance for education, whereby methods such as external review, audits, self-study and performance indicators have been employed to ensure that the service provided by an institution is of an appropriate standard. This has led to a series of debates about what quality means in the context of education, with some authors arguing that quality, like beauty and excellence, is something without tangibility that can only be assessed subjectively (Doherty, 2008). The more widely accepted definition of quality is as *fitness for purpose* whereby a programme, team, department or institution is assessed on its ability to meet a specific need in a type of graduate, with the need often encoded in a framework of qualifications or set of learning outcomes.

Outside of the national context, we must examine how the definition of quality as *fitness for purpose* impacts on quality assurance of education provision in the international context. Does the programme designed by the European provider which is being delivered in Africa, for example, address the needs of the local market, the European market, or both? Is the education being provided as a European education, and if so, is this even possible when it is removed at such distance from Europe? Is it important that the education is delivered by staff from the source country, or is it more important that the source institution is involved in the design of the programme and its outcomes? These questions address the purpose for international education, and until we understand the purpose for the provision, we do not have a means to assess or assure its quality.

Countries such as Ireland which emerged in the 1990s as important and influential participants in specific markets, such as the software market, attributed much of their success to the quality of their education system. Now as Ireland looks to share its lessons internationally by providing education outside its boundaries, informed by its own experience, it needs to develop its understanding of the context within which that education will be delivered. This approach represents a valuable approach to internationalization of education, and a great opportunity for countries to learn from each other. However, for education to be a success it must be appropriately supported by quality assurance methods, and it is perhaps these methods which currently represent the weakest link in the international education chain.

We propose seven factors which must be considered by teams, departments or institutions which engage with the international education market. These seven factors frame quality assurance, providing a framework within which international provision can be evaluated. The factors, listed below, form the core contribution of this chapter, with a discussion of each expanding and highlighting how the debate about quality might usefully be conducted in the international context.

1. *Motivation*: What is the main reason for the partnership or programme?
2. *Purpose*: What purpose is the programme designed to meet?
3. *Team*: How is the team designing and delivering the programme comprised?
4. *Environment*: How is the learning environment developed and supported?
5. *Methods*: What are the learning, teaching and assessment methods?
6. *Fitness*: Is the programme fulfilling its purpose, and to what degree?
7. *Safety*: How is risk being managed?

This chapter is organised as follows. First we introduce some important terminology to be used in the chapter. International education and quality assurance are both heavily freighted with terms which take on a specific meaning in a specific context. It is therefore important to explain precisely what our understanding of each relevant term is. The next section provides some background on quality assurance of education and associated methods, independently of the international context. This sets the scene for the introduction of the Seven Factor Model, which is again explained without reference to the international context, to illustrate its relationship to the general case of quality assurance of education. The following sections then distinguish clearly between international education and the non-international case, and also provide background on the quality assurance methods employed for the international case. This leads to the core contribution of this chapter, which is the Seven Factor Model implemented for the international context. Each of the seven factors is explained in detail, with a grading system provided for most of them, which can be used to both guide the design of an international education programme, and facilitate its assessment.

Of the programmes that are being currently brought to the international market, those in software engineering, information and communications technology and computing in general are among the most popular. It is a widely held belief that computing education serves are a foundation for development, either out of poverty (the well known *global digital divide*) or towards greater prosperity. As education providers seek to meet the global need for high quality education in computing and software engineering, there is a pronounced need to maintain a focus on the requirement to assure quality. The seven factor model introduced in this chapter seeks to provide a route towards the desired high quality.

TERMINOLOGY

We distinguish, first of all, between the *source country* and the *implementation country*. The source country is the country from which the award for the education programme is being made. In the case of joint programmes, awards are made from both (or all) countries involved in the programme, in which case the source country is determined by perspective, it being the country of the focal awarding body. The implementation country is the country where the students taking the programme are located. It may be the case that there are several implementation countries, and it may also be the case that a source country is also an implementation country.

We prefer these terms to the more typical *provider* and *receiver* which imply, in our opinion, activity on behalf of the provider and passivity on behalf of the receiver. Rather, in a partnership, we see the source as the starting point for the programme, since the award is typically the driving force for a programme, and the implementation involves the delivery and assessment components of the programme.

There are various practical components in the programme which introduce terminology which will be used throughout this chapter. These are depicted graphically in Figure 1, and explained in detail below. Those terms underlined identify

Figure 1. Programme components in source and implementation countries

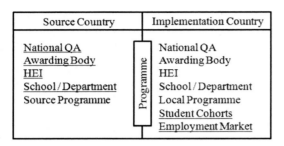

components which are always present in the *source* or *implementation* country as depicted, and which define the core of our understanding of the international education model. Those components which are not underlined are sometimes present, and sometimes not, in the *source* or *implementation* country as depicted. These represent variations outside of the core of our understanding of the international education model.

National QA is the quality assurance agency which takes overall responsibility for the assurance of quality in education in the respective country. Implementation countries may or may not have such an agency, or agencies, and the programme may or may not be subject to national QA rules and authority in the implementation country, but in all cases, such programmes will be subject to national QA authority in the source country.

The *awarding body* is the entity which has the legal authority to make the award. This may be a higher education institution (HEI) involved in delivery or it may be a body specifically created for the award of qualifications. Technically, where an awarding body is involved, there is not a specific requirement for a HEI to also be involved, though this is rarely the case. Similarly a *department* or sub-section of the HEI is always involved as the holders of domain knowledge specific to the programme in question. To avoid

cumbersome terminology, we will use the terms *source HEI*, *implementation HEI*, *source department* and *implementation department* with their obvious meanings.

In certain cases, an awarding body from the implementation country is also involved, for example in the case of dual degrees (where successful students are eligible for two awards) and joint degrees (where two awarding bodies collaborate to make an award). Similarly, a HEI and department or sub-section may not be required in the implementation country, where for example, the HEI from the source country establishes a branch campus or works with a private company in the implementation country, but in most cases, international education of this sort involves a partnership between HEIs in two or more countries.

The *programme* is depicted as shared between the source and implementation countries, suggesting a shared ownership between the HEIs involved in both countries. Individually, they each will typically have their own programmes in their respective departments, which may be replicas of the focal programme. In the case of franchise arrangements, the shared programme is usually a copy (to some extent) of a successful programme in the source HEI. In the case of accreditation, the shared programme is either a copy of, or is the only instance of, a programme which was designed and often previously running, in the implementation HEI, and which was approved by the source HEI for the relevant award.

The *student cohort* will be recruited from the implementation country, and as graduates they will be recruited into the *employment market* in that country, notwithstanding the overall internationalisation agenda in higher education which motivates an international outlook for curriculum design, facilitating international mobility pre- and post-graduation.

QUALITY ASSURANCE
OF EDUCATION

Quality can have a variety of meanings and interpretations. One important distinction is between *quality* as a noun and *quality* as an adjective. A product or service can be high quality or low quality, implying that when quality is used as a noun its meaning is closest to *goodness* and its level is variable, ranging from *low* to *high*. A product, then, can be low quality. A quality product, however, is one that has high quality, suggesting that when *quality* is used as an adjective its meaning is closest to *excellent*. These are two clearly contrasting interpretations for quality, and it is important that in any discussion on quality the interpretation being used is clearly understood (Poole, 2010).

In the field of educational quality assurance, there are several interpretations for and understandings of quality (Campbell & Rozsnyai, 2002; Harvey & Knight, 1996). The first interpretation, as discussed, is of *quality as exceptional*, where it meets or needs high standards - the standards required for excellence, exclusive or elite, as explained in terms of the use of quality as an adjective above.

The second definition is of *quality as perfection*, or absense of defects. This is derived from the manufacturing process where a set of requirements are set and the goal is to consistently meet those requirements by producing instances of the product with zero deviations from the exemplar. A quality culture in this context is one which leads to correction of processes which led to defects, so that the perfect product is produced every time in the future. This interpretation is consistent with the *Six Sigma* and *Total Quality Management* interpretations of quality (Dahlgaard & Dahlgaard-Park, 2006).

The third definition of quality is *quality as fitness for purpose*. This is a distant definition from the first one where quality is associated with excellence or exceedingly high standards. Rather, in this case, quality is about something doing the job for which is it intended. The challenges identified with this approach arise from the understanding of the two core parts of the definition, specifically, what is the purpose of the product or service, and how is its fitness measured? This approach is consistent with the outcomes-based approach to education, judging quality as the meeting of a need (Biggs, 2003).

The fourth definition of quality is *quality as value for money*, which looks at quality from the perspective of those who hold the purse strings. Where the government funds public education, they require assurance that the investment provides a return to the public. The complication arises through the agreement on appropriate performance indicators - for example, number of graduates, average grades, etc.. Where the government focuses on the accountability of the provider, there is the recurring danger that what gets measured, gets done (Westerheijden 2010), suggesting that superficial performance indicators are insufficient to determine quality.

The fifth and final definition for quality is *quality as transformation*. This focuses specifically on the student and their personal educational journey. Education is about the contribution, or value added, to the individual. This is seen as the trigger for lifelong learning, where students are empowered to take ownership and control of their own learning. The performance indicators in this case measure the effectiveness of the methods used for transformation of the individual, their empowerment and the impact they have long-term, post-graduation (Harvey & Knight, 1996).

Quality, then, can be interpreted in many ways, but is largely associated with the final result, or output. Quality assurance plays the role of assuring that when the process leading to the output concludes, the output is of the required quality. Quality assurance, then, is largely about the process, and is implemented through the monitoring and improvement of the process. Quality assessment is a measurement of the quality of the product or service. Quality assessment plays a role in quality assurance, as it provides a means of identifying poor quality, which can then feed back into the redesign of the process which led to that outcome. Quality enhancement and quality improvement are terms which are acquiring increased popularity because of the focus they put on the improvement of quality suggesting that where quality of the output is a variable, the processes must be continuously improved to achieve higher and higher standards. This is popularised with the Japanese *kaizen* approach to continuous improvement in manufacturing processes (Imai, 1986).

Quality assurance for education, thus, can require a selection of the appropriate definition for quality, a means of measurement or appreciation for an output that achieves that quality (quality assessment), a means of assuring that inputs to the system which pass through the entire process to become outputs will have achieved that quality (quality assurance), and a means of constantly improving the process to achieve higher levels of quality (quality enhancement). In reality, the term quality assurance has come to be interpreted as a synonym for, or at the very least, an umbrella term for, all aspects of quality achievement as discussed.

QUALITY ASSURANCE METHODS

The Quality in Higher Education (Harvey et al., 1993) project conducted in the United Kingdom in the early 1990s identified ten assessment criteria for quality education:

1. There are adequate physical resources (library, workshops, IT, etc.) to support teaching and learning
2. There are adequate human resources to support teaching and learning (and staff are properly qualified)
3. The programme has clear aims and objectives which are understood by staff and students
4. The subject content relates to the programme's aims and objectives
5. Students are encouraged to be actively involved in, and given responsibility for, learning
6. The standard of the programme is appropriate to the award
7. Assessment is valid, objective and fair
8. Assessment covers the full range of course aims and objectives
9. Students receive useful feedback from assessment (and are kept informed of progress)
10. Students leave with transferable knowledge and skills.

These criteria recognise the primacy of assessment above other aspects of the programme, as the final threshold prior to a graduate becoming output from the system. It identifies outcomes as the core definition for the programme, and incorporates key transferable skills as important for the breadth and depth of the graduate skill set. The environment and staff quality are seen as important in achieving the outcomes. With some variations, these criteria are more or less the foundation for most of the instruments of external quality assessment by quality assurance agencies in the United Kingdom and Ireland.

Much of the same territory is covered by the more recent European Standards and Guidelines for Quality Assurance in Higher Education (ENQA, 2005), broadening the scope to incorporate the interests of various stakeholders, from the programme level to the agency level.

The Input-Process-Output framework for quality classification (Chua, 2004) neatly organises the various elements concerning academic quality into sets according to whether they concern the input to the system, the process at the centre of the system or the output, suggesting means through which the output can be measured. The classification is important, the authors argue, because different stakeholders prioritise different aspects of the system. Parents, the state and the market view

Figure 2. The input–process–output framework of quality classification (Chua, 2004)

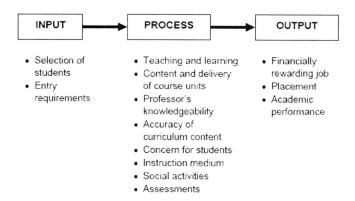

the system as a black box, monitoring input and output but taking little interest in the process in their assessment of quality. Students, as participants in the system, prioritise the process. This classification is given in Figure 2.

The European Framework for Quality Management (EFQM) excellence model has been applied to higher education for the purpose of quality assurance and management (Arjomandi et al., 2009; Calvo-Mora et al., 2006; Hides et al., 2004). This TQM framework is a goals- and results-oriented approach, focussing on leadership and management. This represents one of several perspectives from which quality assurance can be viewed.

The methods employed for quality assessment primarily revolve around external review, of which there are three main models (Woodhouse, 1999):

- Audit: A check of the institution's claims about itself
- Assessment: A process resulting in a score, according to criteria
- Accreditation: An evaluation of a suitability to maintain or achieve a status.

While external quality assessment typically takes place on a quinquennial basis, ongoing quality assurance occurs at the institutional, departmental and programmatic level through:

- Annual monitoring: Annual reports completed by programme teams
- External examination: Peer review of the assessment components of a programme
- Programme committees: Involving staff and students in reflection on quality.

There are three main views on the role of quality assurance and quality assessment. First, *quality assurance for trust* relates to the public perception of the service provided by a HEI, and the degree to which employers, society and individuals can be sure that a graduate with a specific award has met a certain standard. This motivation has taken on particular importance as access to higher education and the number of education providers have increased in recent decades. Where institutions have not existed for long enough, or have not occupied a particular position in society for long enough, they have not had the opportunity to acquire the needed reputation to generate trust. This is true both for private institutions and public institutions that have emerged in recent times. In this case, the government or their agencies perform quality assurance to assure the public of the quality of the institution's awards.

Qualifications frameworks, both national and international, have played a key role in this respect, where an independent agency assures that the awards being provided by institutions are appropriate for a given level on a qualifications framework. Young (2005) writes convincingly about the role of qualification frameworks for creating trust in developing countries, but notes also that the institutional context is important and often neglected. This can be interpreted as seeing qualifications frameworks as a means for providing quality assurance for trust, where quality is more accurately fitness for purpose. The institutional context is more closely concerned with an additional layer where quality assurance by the institution generates trust in the institution's excellence, building a reputation independent of, or in addition to, the qualifications framework.

Secondly, a widely held perception, and reality in many cases, is *quality assurance for control*, where quality assurance is employed as a managerial method to keep an eye on what is taking place at different positions in the organisational hierarchy. This relates to the definition of quality as value for money, and is employed to identify how and whether funding, for example, should be allocated.

Finally, as discussed earlier, *quality assurance for improvement*, or *quality enhancement*, is the motivation for continuous improvement in quality.

Kells (1995) identified two main trends in the approaches to quality assurance in the 1990s which mirror the final two points above:

- Schemes move towards more internally driven concerns, putting more emphasis on self-evaluation, self-regulatory activity and the institutional infrastructure for it
- Schemes become less related to government influence, and more related to improvement, management and strategy, with more feedback from clients.

Kells (1999) later tried to relate the external quality assurance schemes of different countries using cultural indices (Hofstede, 1980) to justify diversity and explain commonality, but his approach was criticised as selective and incomplete by Billing (2004), who, in turn, presented a general model for external quality assessment in education.

In the next section we introduce an outline model for quality assurance in education, which frames much of the work which follows.

THE SEVEN FACTOR MODEL

The seven factor model being developed puts a structure on the main aspects of a programme of education (although equally it could be considered at a coarser level of granularity) which ought to be considered within quality assessment and quality assurance processes. It will be used as a starting point for this research, serving as a base for the international model to be presented later.

The seven factors are:

1. Motivation
2. Purpose
3. Team
4. Environment
5. Methods
6. Fitness
7. Safety.

We briefly discuss each of these factors below, identifying how and why they are relevant to the quality assurance and quality assessment of an academic programme.

Motivation

Academic departments create programmes of study primarily to attract students to their department, but they can also develop programmes which are representative of their academic speciality, or to attract specific types of student, or to respond to national priorities. We loosely suggest at this point four main motivations for the provision of academic programmes:

- Core function: The core function of an academic department, as well as - but often ahead of - research, is the provision of undergraduate education at the core of the discipline. Few academic departments exist without at least one undergraduate programme from their discipline, and so this provision is simply motivated.
- Profit: The provision of programmes beyond the core of the discipline is often related to the need to attract more funding from the state, or more fees from international students.
- Status: Or expansion. Providing more programmes can make the department more powerful, and consequently eligible for more staff, or floor space, or senior posts.
- Research speciality: Often academic departments will provide education programmes directly related to their area of research speciality, thus allowing them to disseminate their research and possibly recruit talented students to the area.

There is no ideal motivation for a programme, but it is simply important that the motivation for the programme be known by staff involved in the programme, and, indeed, by students on the programme as well. Without understanding the motivation for the programme, it is difficult to evaluate it.

Purpose

If education is a process, then it produces an outcome. Like the manufacturing process, the design process or the creative process, it leads to something. That *something* is the outcome which serves a purpose. If the motivation is the managerial perspective on academic programmes, the purpose is the educational perspective. This can simply be viewed as the learning outcomes for the programme. In evaluating a programme from an academic perspective, the outcomes may

state the expectation that the graduate will be able, for example, to integrate into a professional environment, to demonstrate high quality ability and effectively document and record their work. The purpose of the programme is then to meet the needs of the employment market from which those outcomes were derived.

Some obvious purposes for a programme include:

- Meeting employment market needs: This, obviously, is the main purpose of an academic programme in the modern educational environment.
- Preparing students for further study: This is directly related to the qualifications framework model.
- Develop society: The goal of universities was always to develop the citizens of the country, as thinkers, as doers and as talents who could develop the country. This purpose for education has probably not been given the same explicit priority in modern education as it has previously, but it usually remains an implicit purpose of academic programmes.

Qualifications frameworks attempt to capture as learning outcomes those outcomes which serve a multitude of purposes. However they often fail to articulate the purpose for a programme or for a level of study.

We contend that *learning outcomes* represent one aspect of what should be considered for a programme's purposes, with other aspects including, for example, the *admissions policy and requirements*.

Again, it is important that the purpose be understood by all participants in the programme, and the relationship that exists between the outcomes and the purpose for the graduate. Rather than simply accepting outcomes as documented, or deriving outcomes from the qualifications framework, the programme should be developed and implemented in a way that clearly addresses the purpose for the graduate.

Team

An effective programme or department will require an effective team. Effective teams are *communicative* teams, teams with *clear goals*, teams with *ownership* over their project and teams with *effective* leadership (West, 2004). For the purposes of curriculum design and implementation it is important that members of the team cooperate along the dimensions of 3D-Alignment or some similar model or philosophy (O'Leary et al., 2006).

Academic programmes and departments cannot operate without a team, so any evaluation of a programme should include not simply an assessment of the team's *qualifications*, or *background* or *development policy*. It needs to examine how the team operates as a whole, how they understand the purpose of the education process they are involved in, how they are aligned and how they solve problems collectively.

Environment

The environment usually includes the library, the computer laboratories, the classrooms and so on. Increasingly, the environment incorporates the virtual environment, which includes access to online information, online support for students through virtual learning environments and so on. The additional functions provided by the HEI are often included here, including social and sports clubs, mentoring and support and so on.

Methods

Methods in this case refers to learning, teaching and assessment methods which are implemented by the team in their environment to meet the outcomes defined by the purposes of the programme, and as such includes the content of the programme, such as the modules and syllabuses.

Constructive alignment (Biggs, 2003) and 3D alignment (O'Leary et al., 2006) and related philosophies obviously have a role to play here, with effective methods being ones which are appropriately aligned with each other and with the outcome of the programme.

Fitness

A programme which is effective is one which, according to the chosen definition for quality, is *fit for purpose*. In evaluating a programme, it is necessary to examine how the programme itself is quality assured during delivery, such that those involved in the programme can assure that the team, the environment and the methods employed are fit for the purposes identified for the programme.

Methods often employed by teams include many of the following (ENQA, 2005):

- committees including student representation
- annual monitoring reports to management
- benchmarking and standards.

Methods for assuring fitness from outside the team typically include quality assessment methods such as programme review and assessments by professional bodies. In turn, the fitness methods employed must themselves be assessed and assured as *fit for purpose*.

Safety

Safety is usually a managerial concern, as with the programme's motivation. It concerns the effect of a programme failing a quality assessment and reflects a need for awareness among those involved in the programme of those effects. For the quality assurance process, it is important that there be a policy in place to deal with such situations, especially when there are students on a programme which is no longer deemed *fit for purpose.* Safety is about an awareness of the risk involved in a programme and how that risk is managed.

INTERNATIONALISATION OF HIGHER EDUCATION

Internationalisation is one of the most overloaded and ambiguous terms in education, often confused with the more sinister-sounding globalisation (Knight, 1999). Distinguishing between internationalisation at home and internationalisation abroad, de Wit (2005) identifies activities such as the internationalisation of curricula, cultural and ethnic education and the attraction and integration of international students as valuable approaches and strategies for developing an international ethos without activity outside of the national borders. Internationalisation abroad, he contends, has become synonymous with the cross-border trade in education whereby HEIs become active in other countries for the purposes, generally, of attracting fees from students who may never need to visit the home country of the HEI in order to gain an award from that same institution. Although he argues that this definition is too narrow, the need to focus our research and unambiguously define our terminology, the default interpretation for *international education* in this work is *the provision of awards for higher education by a HEI outside of their national territory.* The terms *cross-border provision,* and *transnational-provision* are popular synonyms for *international education* in this context.

Altbach & Knight (2007) argue that the full implementation of the World Trade Organisation's General Agreement on Trade in Services (GATS) (World Trade Organisation, 1995), which removes or reduces barriers to international trade, has the effect of encouraging the following approaches to the internationalisation of education:

- Cross-border supply, or overseas provision, such as the franchising of programmes of study, but also the provision of education at distance using electronic means
- Consumption abroad, or quite simply student mobility across borders for the purposes of education
- Commercial presence abroad, or the establishment of campuses abroad by institutions

The main motivations for internationalisation (Altbach & Knight, 2007) are:

- Profits: Clearly the main motivation and reason for institutions to engage with the international market, it could be argued that overseas provision, or transnational education in most markets is motivated entirely by the opportunity it affords institutions to increase numbers and attract fees from students who would not otherwise have been able to travel to the provider's country for education.
- Access Provision and Demand Absorption: Some countries have extremely high demand for education which cannot be met by local providers. This is particularly so in countries where there is a very young education system, which has grown at a pace beyond that which can be supported by people qualified to teach, or providers able to enroll students.
- Traditional Internationalisation: Or historical motivation, based on links that have existed for a long period of time.
- European Internationalisation: The countries of the European Union and its neighbours represent a closely connected set of nations, which while independent, are constantly seeking means to integrate more closely on areas of common interest. One such area is education, where the establishment of the Bologna Process and its ef-

fects, such as shared qualifications frameworks, credit transfer systems and overall harmonisation of the education systems of European countries has resulted in an increasingly integrated pan-European education system. Europe's motivation is due to the Lisbon agenda which seeks to establish Europe as the world's leading knowledge economy.

- Developing-Country Internationalisation: The role of internationalisation in support of development is somewhat controversial, particularly given the first motivation above and its conflict with development. Some authors view with scepticism the motivation for education providers to seek markets in developing countries, whereas others view this engagement as a means to drive development towards the Millennium Development Goals (un.org/millenniumgoals). Some extraordinary successes such as the Dutch-South African SANPAD PhD programme (sanpad.org.za) demonstrate the true potential for the development motivation for internationalisation.

- Individual Internationalisation: This refers to self-funded students who cross national boundaries for a host of reasons.

Knight (2006) provides a useful taxonomy trying to capture the entirety of international education, including *people*, *programmes*, *providers* and *projects*. Our interest lies solely in the *types* of programmes, which Knight identifies as *twinning*, *franchises*, *validated and articulated*, *joint and double awards* and *online and distance*. These programmes are positioned across a spectrum of motivations ranging from *development co-operation* on the left, through *educational linkages* to *commercial trade*. Our intent is to dig deeper into the classification of the programmes, incorporating their *partnership type* and *motivation* as above, developing it as necessary to describe the totality of programme arrangements in Irish HEIs.

QUALITY ASSURANCE OF INTERNATIONAL EDUCATION

The provision of education outside of an institution's national context necessarily complicates the quality assurance process. Van der Wende (1999) questions whether some providers have an *export quality* distinct from the quality of their local product. This is clearly a concern for quality assurance agencies, with some, such as the United Kingdom's Quality Assurance Agency documenting a clear code of practice (Quality Assurance Agency, 2004), and increasing the attention it pays to international provision. The United Nations Educational, Scientific and Cultural Organization (UNESCO/OECD, 2005) similarly provides guidelines to governments, student bodies and providers, identifying for example the needs to:

- Ensure that the programmes they deliver across borders and in their home country are of comparable quality and that they also take into account the cultural and linguistic sensitivities of the receiving country. It is desirable that a commitment to this effect be made public.

- Recognise that quality teaching and research is made possible by the quality of faculty and the quality of their working conditions that foster independent and critical enquiry.

- Consult competent quality assurance and accreditation bodies and respect the quality assurance and accreditation systems of the receiving country when delivering higher education across borders, including distance education.

There are many different types of programme, including but not limited to those listed below. Each type introduces different challenges for quality assurance.

- Direct franchise: The programme is an exact copy of the programme delivered in the source HEI's base campus, but is delivered mostly or exclusively by staff at the implementation HEI. The award is made always by the source. In some cases, the assessment is taken in parallel by students on the source's base campus and students on the franchise programme.
- Mutual design: The programme is designed by a team comprised of members at both the source HEI and the implementation HEI, taking into consideration the requirements of both.
- Accredited programme: The programme is designed and delivered by the implementation HEI, but is judged by the provider as being of appropriate content and quality to lead to their award.
- Extended classes: The programme at the source HEI's home campus is made available to students elsewhere through remote communications technology and electronic learning. All students attend the same classes, albeit virtually, and take the same assessment.

The core philosophy for quality assurance of international education is simply that *quality assurance must travel*. This, however, is complicated by the unique challenges of internationalisation. While some have argued for closer international cooperation and international quality assurance schemes (Van Damme, 2002), those international networks which exist such as the International Network for Quality Assurance Agencies in Higher Education (Harvey, 2007) operate mainly on quality assurance at the local level, outside of the international challenge.

In Ireland, although the National Qualifications Authority of Ireland has asked HEIs to provide more transparency with respect to the quality assurance of international provision, they are asked to do so independently of strict guidelines or codes of practice. Ireland's Higher Education Training and Awards Council (HETAC) has recently produced a *Policy for collaborative programmes, transnational programmes and joint awards* informed by the United Kingdom approach, with efforts currently underway for this policy to be implemented in the various HEIs under its authority (HETAC, 2008).

Quality assurance for international education requires a specific awareness of a range of challenges and issues. In the next section we revisit the seven factors from the previous section with a specific view of the requirements for quality assurance in the international context.

THE SEVEN FACTOR MODEL (INTERNATIONAL)

In each of the sub-sections below, we consider one of the seven factors of the quality assurance and quality assessment policy model in depth, in relation to their application to international education, identifying issues that can arise and some approaches that are popular for addressing each of them.

Motivation

From a source HEI's perspective, the two main motivations for becoming involved in transnational education are *trade* and *aid*. Trade, or profit, is the primary motivation in most cases, and results from the facility to charge fees to HEIs for the franchise of their programme and to students for enrolment in their HEI, and also the facility to recruit international students to register on the home campus and pay full international fees. Aid is increasingly considered a motivation for transnational delivery (Altbach & Knight, 2007), where education systems in developing countries are not capable of supporting the higher education requirements of their citizens or the needs of their industry. Not all education provided in developing countries could be considered aid, indeed much of the profit gained from international provision comes from developing countries with underdeveloped education systems.

The recruitment of high quality international students for postgraduate study serves as an additional motivation, particularly in HEIs with a strong research profile and focus. However, it is often the case that such HEIs can effectively recruit without the need to engage in delivery elsewhere. The access that international provision provides to specific global regions and to the development of name recognition in that region, however, may serve as a motivation for such provision.

As education systems globally become more internationalized, cross-border provision gives HEIs an opportunity to develop their understanding of how best to facilitate the learning of students with diverse learning styles. This can help with the development of expertise and consequently an enhancement in the status associated with the HEI's international delivery. Education is increasingly an active area of research in its own right, and is supported by funding agencies. Expertise in this area provides access to such funding.

From an implementation HEI's perspective, it is often the case that the partnership is formed simply because they are unable to make the types of awards that the provider can make. Institutions which do not have degree awarding status often make agreements with institutions that do, such that those degree awards can be made to their own graduates. While this sometimes arises when the source simply accredits an existing programme, in other cases a new programme is designed by both partners or a programme is transplanted from the source HEI's context. In all cases, the qualifications of the source HEI become available to students in the implementation HEI.

In some cases, the implementation HEI simply perceives that the status attached to an award from the providing HEI is greater than the status attached to their own award, and seeks the partnership in order to assist with the recruitment of students and the development of their own status and the perception of their provision in their own market.

The provision of international awards and the consequent effect on status is probably the main motivation from perspective of the implementation HEIs, although the development of expertise and learning from international providers is another important motivation. Partnerships which begin through joint provision can also develop over time into broader partnerships incorporating research stretching across disciplines. This future potential can motivate the development of international provision.

It is important to note that motivation can be very difficult to establish. There is the *motivation as presented*, which is the motivation that is spoken of by management in HEIs and that is often used in marketing literature. It may be believed by those presenting it that that is the real motivation, but it may contrast with the *motivation as perceived* by staff at the operational level, by students on the programme, by the partner HEI and by the government and public. The *motivation as discovered* through investigation and analysis may match with either the motivation as presented or as perceived, or may fall somewhere in between, but regardless, this is the motivation which needs to be understood by all those involved.

Partnerships will be successful when win-win outcomes can be achieved, but a win can only be understood when the motivation of each partner is known. It is important that rather than simply relying on superficial statements of commitment and motivation, the team involved in the programme on each side clearly understands why both they and their partners are involved in the partnership. Often, the real motivation needs to be discovered.

We identify broadly five motivations for involvement in cross-border provision, from the perspective of the source and implementation HEIs:

- Profit: Typically just from the source's perspective, but occasionally from the implementer's as well, which can recruit students locally and attract their fees.

- Awards: Typically just from the implementer's perspective who can make awards (indirectly) previously unavailable to them, but occasionally from the source's who may be assessed or measured partly according to their volume of graduates annually.
- Expertise: Partners can develop their expertise of international education, learning styles and various approaches to education, now an active area of research.
- Access: Partners can gain access to remote geographical regions and possibly funding available for the area. They may also gain access to expertise in the partner's HEI, leading to the possibility of future involvement with research and other activities.
- Status: Either partner may gain status through involvement with higher profile HEIs elsewhere, or simply through the development of international links.

Where the primary motivations are well understood, they can be characterised using the above terminology e.g. *profit-award* partnerships where the source is primarily motivated through the opportunity to recruit international students and gain profit, while the implementer is primarily motivated through the opportunity to make awards from a HEI in a different country. The partnership's strength is based on the success and persistence of both motivations.

Motivations ought to be *motivations as discovered* through analysis, discussion and reflection, rather than simply those motivations presented or perceived.

Purpose

The purpose of the programme can roughly be considered to be the learning outcomes with justification. Considering an outcomes-based philosophy of education, the learning outcomes are statements of what the graduate of the programme can do. They are supported by quality assurance agencies and governments for the clarity of communication they provide, mapping the work of the higher education sector clearly onto the requirements of industry and society. They can, consequently be used to attract investors into a state by clearly articulating what the graduate workforce can do. They form the basis of national qualifications frameworks, which identify in a general domain way the knowledge, skills and abilities of the graduate, often to be later distilled into domain specific statements of outcomes, in turn to form the basis of programme learning outcomes. Using the language of Bloom's Taxonomy, learning outcomes have a sound foundation in cognitive psychology and their tiered approach derives from the constructivist approach to education. Critics of outcomes based education argue that it diminishes the role of education to that of a manufacturing process, where all that is important is the destination, with no consideration given to the transformation of the learner, apart from their ultimate skill set.

However, in Europe the outcomes based approach is by far the most popular approach to monitoring and assessment of education, as well as mapping and equivalency. Equivalency is particularly important in the context of international education, where delivery and assessment in one national context leads to an award from another. Within the Bologna process, and within the European Union, two meta-frameworks have been provided which endeavour to provide an inter-lingua for the discussion of levels of knowledge and skill (Maguire, 2010). Individual states can map their local framework to these meta-frameworks, thus facilitating student and graduate mobility across Europe, but also allowing joint programmes to fit into a higher level framework with a shared understanding of the level of award and the expectation of the graduate.

Outcomes are important, but outcomes need to be designed. Biggs' approach (2003) to *constructive alignment* stresses the cyclical nature of the design of learning outcomes where their design cannot be separated from the context of their delivery. Identifying *learning outcomes* as one third of the design process, partnered with *assessment methods* and *learning and teaching methods*, Biggs discusses how *learning outcomes* cannot be designed without consideration of how they will be assessed, nor can they be designed independently of how learning and teaching takes place. We will return to this in the next section, but the consequence of this is simply that any change in assessment or learning and teaching methods, will likely result in a change to learning outcomes. This is a point often overlooked in relation to international provision.

The primary means for the design of learning outcomes, however, is concerned with an assessment of a need. Programme teams and academic management involved in the design of curricula will usually survey industry, conduct expert panels, monitor recruitment policies, review government policy, incorporating relevant agencies, assess requirements for progression to postgraduate study, identify expertise available in the HEI or department, and study the requirements and recommendations of professional bodies. As already discussed, the appropriate national qualifications framework also has an overarching role. The outcome of this work is usually the set of learning outcomes in first draft, which are then reviewed and revisited as the assessment strategies and learning and teaching methods are decided upon.

Clearly, many of the inputs to this process are localised to the specific context of the programme's delivery. Industry requirements, for example, will be different in different countries. The same applies to government policy and available expertise. Qualifications frameworks and quality assurance requirements may also differ. This does not mean that there is not a great deal to be learned from the development of shared programmes, it simply

means that the transplanting or direct franchising of programmes outside of the context within which it is designed runs a risk of providing a programme whose purposes are misaligned with the local requirements.

Similarly, recognising the role of the awarding body in the source country, it is important to understand that designing without consideration of the requirements from the quality assurance agencies of the source country is also likely to lead to problems, where occasionally the programme can no longer lead to the award that triggered its development.

Both sides need to be involved in the development of the programme. Neither transplanting from the source's context nor ignorance of the same context can lead to an effective design of the programme's purposes. In designing the purpose for the programme, both the implementer's context and the source's context need to be understood, the implementer's because it will presumably serve as the main employer for graduates, and the source's because graduates will carry that brand on their degree qualification, and will as a consequence give rise to certain expectations from both employers and postgraduate recruiters in contexts where the provider, or even simply their qualification when placed on a framework, is known.

We provide a continuum and identify three points on the continuum. When designing the purpose for the programme, designers should ideally strive for the centre point.

- Transplant (source-aligned, implementer-misaligned): At one extreme on the continuum is the transplanted programme, or complete franchise. Students on this programme are being equipped with the knowledge and skills required to function as graduates in a different national context. The entire programme was designed without any input from the local context, which will serve as the main consumer of the graduates.

- Aligned (source-aligned, implementer-aligned): The programme has been designed to meet the requirement of the local context, in terms of market demands and government policy, for example, and also to meet the requirements of the source's context to meet the level of skills and knowledge required for the award for which it is designed.
- Transformed (source-misaligned, implementer-aligned): At the other extreme is the transformed programme. This programme is designed completely for the local context, without any recognition of the source's requirements. The programme is independent of the qualifications framework of the source's country and as such cannot lead to the award for which it was intended.

Team

The team is the core implementing component of the programme, and as such it has the primary role in quality assurance. Teams will be discussed in greater detail in the next section, but some of the important issues to consider with respect to the formation of teams for international programmes are the following:

- Involvement of staff from the source HEI: At one extreme the entire programme may be delivered by staff from the source HEI, either remotely or in person. At the other extreme, no staff members from the source HEI are involved in the programme, and it is effectively running as an accredited programme. In between, various approaches can involve occasional or partial delivery by staff from the source HEI, either of whole modules or partial modules, in partnership with or independent of staff from the receiving HEI.

- Training and development of staff in the implementation HEI: Staff in the implementation HEI are sometimes considered staff of the source HEI while delivering their programmes, and as such are invited to training programmes to develop their skills in line with the education philosophy of the source HEI. Where the sharing of expertise and skill in learning, teaching and assessment is one of the motivations for the programme, such training is highly important.

As a final point, there exists in some cases a question over the ownership of the programme, with staff in the implemention HEI sometimes considering the programme as *someone else's*. It is important that staff feel involved in the programme and that the ownership of the programme is seen to be shared between both sides. A careful understanding of the motivation helps this, as does clarity of the purpose, but most important is the staff's involvement in localising the programme's delivery and assessment method, and their involvement in the team structure which runs the programme.

Environment

The environment is important, as always, including library, laboratories, classrooms and other elements. In the case of international programmes, the facilities in the implementation HEI may often be of a lesser standard than in the source HEI, particularly in the case of developing countries. Additionally, there may be a need to incorporate elements of the source environment into the implementation environment, through online delivery and access to resources such as the online library in the source HEI.

Methods

As with the programme's purposes, the learning and teaching methods and the assessment methods must find the balance between the source's requirements and the implementer's context. In cases of remote delivery or remote assessment, students in the implementation country use technology such as video conferencing to attend classes, and/or are assessed using matter designed by the source, often for students on the source's home campus. One of the benefits of the international approach is the opportunity it affords students to benefit from innovative learning and teaching methods employed elsewhere. Indeed, one of the main motivations for international education is the sharing and development of expertise in learning, teaching and assessment.

In many ways, the methods employed for international delivery represent the most difficult aspect of the design of transnational programmes. The question of localisation is somewhat easily addressed for the purposes or outcomes of the programme, but much more care needs to be taken when looking at localisation of learning and teaching methods and assessment methods.

Some of the important issues to consider are the following:

- Use of language: The language of delivery and assessment is of crucial importance. From the source's perspective, the use of the language of instruction from the source HEI is essential for quality assurance and frequently also represents one of the purposes of the programme. Certainly, if a student was studying in the home campus of the HEI they would be expected to obtain a high level of skill in the language of instruction, so this aspect of the programme is something that would be expected to travel. On the other side, where a cohort of students all speak the same language as the instructor, and where this language is different to the expected language of instruction it is likely that they will revert to the local language, and indeed, this may well represent an important part of the learning and teaching process. Getting the balance right here, and finding the correct approach represents one of the biggest localisation challenges.

- Localisation of learning and teaching methods: The methods employed ought to be chosen according to the philosophy of the source HEI, as this represents one of the most important aspects of the programme design. Also, however, the staff in the implemention HEI have a specific knowledge of the approaches expected by students in their context, given their schooling and culture. Again, an important balance needs to be reached here, which can be found over time through communication between team representatives from both partners.

- Localisation of assessment methods: Some programmes operate as a mirror of a base programme, with the same forms of assessment delivered in parallel with the base programme. This can make it easier to assure the quality in an outcomes based approach, where all cohorts of student take the same assessment, but it does not provide the assessor with an opportunity to localise any of the tasks given to the student. Where a distinction is made between formative and summative assessment, it should at least be expected that local assessors can make their own decision about how to implement and handle the formative part of the assessment, tied as it is to feedback and monitoring of students.

Again, we present a methods continuum, where the optimal position is in the centre.

- Locally impossible (source-aligned, implementer-misaligned): The learning, teaching and assessment methods are inappropriate for the local context and serve as a barrier to learning. It is not possible for the students to meet the outcomes of the programme or to be accurately assessed on the outcomes of the programme using these methods.
- Locally informed (source-aligned, implementer-aligned): The background, language and learning styles of the local cohort inform the learning, teaching and assessment methods employed, such that they are still transparent to the source's quality assurance processes, and are appropriately aligned with the purposes for the programme in the local context.
- Localised with loss (source-misaligned, implementer-aligned): The methods have been adapted to the local context such that there is a significant loss to the programme and its outcomes. For example, through the exclusive use of the local language, it is no longer possible for the provider to stand over the quality of the graduates of the programme.

Fitness

Fitness requires an involvement from team members in both partners. How they interact, how they perceive each other, how they trust each other, will all effect the means through which they can work on the quality of the programme as it is running, and develop outcomes, teams, environments and methods which are fit for purpose.

Continuing the theme of the earlier factors, we present a continuum for fitness methods, with the ideal again being in the centre.

- Form-filling: This approach to quality assurance often misses the point, with par-

ticipants in the process seeing quality assurance as something which simply needs to be completed on occasion, rather than viewing it as an ongoing process. Forms and documents are necessary, but ought to be seen as a reflection of a much larger and much deeper process, rather than as an end in themselves. Any problems which exist for standard programmes can be multiplied several times in the international context.

- Team based: Adaptive, evolving and continuously improving programmes require active teams, communicating effectively and performing as a well organised team. This clearly relates to the team factor discussed above.
- Interfering: In contrast to the passive form-filling approach to quality assurance, approaches which have a constant and ongoing interference from the authority responsible for assessing quality is likely to cause disruption to the team and create opposition to the quality assurance process.

Safety

As outlined earlier, safety is concerned with the risk management. Where a team is formed across organisations and across national boundaries, it is inevitable that there is a risk involved. Safety can be arrived at through the generation of trust within the team and among the management of the programme, even though made difficult by the boundaries which separate the membership of the team. Rather than avoiding risk, the effective team will need to innovate to allow the programme to evolve, and learn from the outcomes of the innovation, without causing breakdown of trust, and consequently the breakdown of the partnership or programme.

For this final factor, we again identify three points on a continuum and highlight the centre point as the ideal.

- Unsafe: In this case there is a risk-taking culture but little or no consideration for the management of risk. Likely, the partnership was started without sufficient knowledge of the motivations of the stakeholders, or the purpose of the programme, leading to requirements to shift goalposts and make quick, ill-considered decisions, which can in turn have an effect on the contract entered into with students, and between the partners. The lack of agreement on how to handle situations such as that can effect the quality of the programme, or lead to the failure of the programme.

- Safe: Where safety is present, risks and innovation can take place, but the required procedures are in place to handle those risks carefully, including exit strategies if required. The safest programmes are those which carry the most trust and the right form of trust, where trust is earned through behaviour, rather than blindly awarded.

- Oversafe: In this case, one or both partners is unwilling to take any risk to innovate or adapt the programme or modify or improve the partnership. This is often as a result of poor trust between partners regarding their motivations or their ability to follow through on commitments. Like the unsafe scenario, this can lead to a programme's failure either through breakdown or outdatedness.

DISCUSSION AND FUTURE WORK

The model presented here represents a proposal which will be subjected to testing in the near future. The model draws from the author's experience of international education and quality assurance through various projects and partnerships, as well as the referenced literature. It is reflective of the need to identify international education as a special case of education, and that it is insufficient to simply require that *quality assurance must travel*. Indeed it must, but on its journey, it must evolve in each of the seven ways outlined above.

For the model to be tested appropriately, it is important to identify the various sources of international education, in Ireland and more broadly, particularly with respect to software education, and the degree to which they are appropriately positioned for each of the factors identified. The success (to whatever degree) of programmes and partnerships provides reinforcement for the systems and processes in place for that programme or partnership, often reducing the stimulus for identification of areas of improvement. As discussed, quality assurance is best situated when it is used towards improvement, and it is in this respect that the model presented is intended to guide the development and ongoing monitoring of academic programmes.

This chapter has taken the approach of first providing a foundation upon which the model ultimately rests. This in turn simply represents a foundation upon which possible successive versions are built, to reflect over time the evolving nature of higher education in the international market.

Education in software engineering and computing represents a tightly market-driven sector, requiring it to respond regularly to a rapidly changing employment market, in ever mobile and fluid economies. The ability to respond and adapt is one of the great strengths of software education providers, but it also introduces many challenges for quality assurance, and consequently for the reputation of the provider. These challenges are magnified still more in the international context. Perhaps now is the time, after much successes in international education provision for the software market, to focus on how to develop appropriate methods to assure students, customers, partners and governments that the product they are buying is not just the right quality, but also the right product.

REFERENCES

Altbach, P. G., & Knight, J. (2007). The internationalization of higher education: Motivations and realities. *Journal of Studies in International Education, 11*(3-4), 290. doi:10.1177/1028315307303542

Arjomandi, M., Kestell, C., & Grimshaw, P. (2009). An EFQM excellence model for higher education quality assessment. In *Proceedings of the 20ᵗʰ Annual Conference of the Australasian Association for Engineering Education Conference,* (pp. 1015-1020). Adelaide, Australia: University of Adelaide.

Biggs, J. (2003). *Teaching for quality learning at university* (2nd ed.). Buckingham, United Kingdom: Open University Press.

Billing, D. (2004). International comparisons and trends in external quality assurance of higher education: Commonality or diversity? *Higher Education, 47*(1), 113–137. doi:10.1023/B:HIGH.0000009804.31230.5e

Calvo-Mora, A., Leal, A., & Roldan, J. L. (2006). Using enablers of the EFQM model to manage institutions of higher education. *Quality Assurance in Education, 14*(2), 99–122. doi:10.1108/09684880610662006

Campbell, C., & Rozsnyai, C. (2002). Quality assurance and the development of course programmes. In L. C. Barrows (Ed.), *Papers on higher education.* Bucharest, Romania: United Nations Educational, Scientific and Cultural Organisation (UNESCO), Centre européen pour l'enseignment supérieur (CEPES).

Chua, C. (2004). Perception of quality in higher education. In R. Carmichael (Ed.). *Proceedings of the Australian Universities Quality Forum 2004: Quality in a Time of Change* (pp. 181–187). Adelaide, Australia: Australian Universities Quality Agency.

Dahlgaard, J. J., & Dahlgaard-Park, S. M. (2006). Lean production, six sigma quality, TQM and company culture. *The Total Quality Management (TQM) Magazine, 18*(3), 263–281.

de Wit, H. (2005). *Higher education in Latin America: The international dimension.* Washington, DC: World Bank Publications. doi:10.1596/978-0-8213-6209-9

Doherty, G. D. (2008). On quality in education. *Quality Assurance in Education, 16*(3), 255–265. doi:10.1108/09684880810886268

European Association for Quality Assurance in Higher Education (ENQA). (2005). *Standards and guidelines for quality assurance in the European higher education area.* Helsinki, Finland: European Association for Quality Assurance in the European Higher Education.

European Commission. (2006). *Services directive.* Retrieved August 6, 2010, from http://ec.europa.eu/internal_market/services/services-dir/index_en.htm

European Community. (1986). *Single European Act.* Retrieved October 4, 2010, from http://eur-lex.europa.eu/en/treaties/index.htm

Harvey, L. (2008). International network of quality assurance agencies in higher education. *Quality Control and Applied Statistics, 52*(6), 619–620.

Harvey, L., Green, D., & Burrows, A. (1993). Assessing quality in higher education: A trans-binary research project. *Assessment & Evaluation in Higher Education, 18*(2), 143–148. doi:10.1080/0260293930180206

Harvey, L., & Knight, P. (1996). *Transforming higher education.* Buckingham, United Kingdom: Open University Press and Society for Research into Higher Education.

Hides, M. T., Davies, J., & Jackson, S. (2004). Implementation of EFQM excellence model self-assessment in the UK higher education sector: Lessons learned from other sectors. *The Total Quality Management (TQM) Magazine, 16*(3), 194–201.

Higher Education & Training Council (HETAC). (2008). Policy for collaborative programmes, transnational programmes and joint awards. Retrieved August 6, 2010, from http://www.hetac. ie/docs/Policy%20for%20collaborative%20programmes,%20transnational%20programmes%20 and%20joint%20awards.pdf

Hofstede, G. (1980). Culture and organizations. *International Studies of Management & Organization, 10*(4), 15–41.

Imai, M. (1986). *Kaizen: The key to Japan's competitive success.* New York, NY: McGraw-Hill.

Kells, H. R. (1995). Building a national evaluation system for higher education: Lessons from diverse settings. *Higher Education in Europe, 20*(1), 18–26. doi:10.1080/0379772950200104

Kells, H. R. (1999). National higher education evaluation systems: Methods for analysis and some propositions for the research and policy void. *Higher Education, 38*(2), 209–232. doi:10.1023/A:1003704015735

Knight, J. (1999). Internationalization of higher education. In *Quality and internationalisation in higher education* (pp. 13–28). Paris, France: Organisation for Economic Co-operation and Development (OECD) Publishing.

Maguire, B. (2010, April). Issues arising from qualifications frameworks in Europe. In the *Proceedings of the Irish Bologna Experts Conference.* Dublin, Ireland.

O'Leary, C., Lawless, D., Gordon, D., Carroll, D., Mtenzi, F., & Collins, M. (2006). *3D alignment in the adaptive software engineering curriculum.* Paper presented at the 36th Annual American Association for Engineering Education/Institute of Electrical and Electronic Engineering (AAEE/IEEE) Frontiers in Education Conference. San Diego, CA.

Poole, B. (2010). Quality, semantics and the two cultures. *Quality Assurance in Education, 18*(1), 6–18. doi:10.1108/09684881011015963

Quality Assurance Agency. (2004). *Code of practice for the assurance of academic quality and standards in higher education: Collaborative provision and flexible and distributed learning* (including e-learning). Retrieved August 6, 2010, from http://www.qaa.ac.uk/academicinfrastructure/codeOfPractice/section2/collab2004.pdf

United Nations Educational, Scientific and Cultural Organization (UNESCO)/Organization for Economic Co-operation and Development (OECD). (2005). *Guidelines on quality provision in cross-border higher education.* Retrieved August 6, 2010, from http://portal.unesco.org/education/en/ev.php-URL_ID=29228&URL_DO=DO_TOPIC&URL_SECTION=201.html

Van Damme, D. (2002). Trends and models in international quality assurance in higher education in relation to trade in education. *Education Management and Policy, 14*(3), 93–136. doi:10.1787/hemp-v14-art21-en

Van der Wende, M. (1999). Quality assurance of internationalisation and internationalisation of quality assurance. In *Quality and internationalisation in higher education* (pp. 225–235). Paris, France: Organisation for Economic Co-operation and Development (OECD) Publications.

West, M. A. (2004). *Effective teamwork: Practical lessons from organizational research* (2nd ed.). Chichester, United Kingdom: Wiley-Blackwell.

Woodhouse, D. (1999). Quality and quality assurance. In *Quality and internationalisation in higher education* (pp. 29–40). Paris, France: Organisation for Economic Co-operation and Development (OECD) Publishing.

World Trade Organisation. (1995). *General agreement on trade in services.* Retrieved August 6, 2010, from http://www.wto.org/english/tratop_e/serv_e/gatsintr_e.htm

Young, M. (2005). *National qualifications frameworks: Their feasibility and effective implementation in developing countries.* Geneva, Switzerland: International Labour Organisation.

KEY TERMS AND DEFINITIONS

Aligned Programme: A programme aligned with the source HEI and with the implementation HEI. The programme has been designed to meet the requirement of the local context, in terms of market demands and government policy, for example, and also to meet the requirements of the source's context to meet the level of skills and knowledge required for the award for which it is designed.

Implementation Country: The country where the students taking the programme are located. (or HEI or department)

International Education: The provision of awards for higher education by a higher education institution (HEI) outside of the national territory where the student working towards the award is located. (within the context of this work, aka transnational education)

Quality Assessment: Measurement of the quality of the product or service.

Quality Assurance: Assuring that when the process leading to the output concludes, the output is of the required quality.

Quality Enhancement/Improvement: Where the quality of the output is a variable, the processes must be continuously improved to achieve higher standards.

Source Country: The country (or HEI or department) from which the award for the education programme is being made.

Transformed Programme: A programme misaligned with the source HEI but aligned with the implementation HEI. This programme is designed completely for the local context, without any recognition of the source's requirements. The programme is independent of the qualifications framework of the source's country and as such cannot lead to the award for which it was intended.

Transplanted Programme: A programme aligned with the source HEI but misaligned with the implementation HEI. Students on this programme are being equipped with the knowledge and skills required to function as graduates in a different national context. The entire programme was designed without any meaningful input from the local context, which is to serve as the main consumer of the graduates.

Section 5
E–Learning and Support Tools

Chapter 12
An Ontology-Based Learning System in IT Project Management

Constanta-Nicoleta Bodea
Academy of Economic Studies, Romania

ABSTRACT

This chapter presents a Web-based learning system in IT project management, capable of building and conducting a complete and personalized training cycle, from the definition of the learning objectives to the assessment of the learning results for each learner. The focus is on the content management solution, using an educational ontology and a competency catalogue, both of them developed by the author in line with the ICB 3.0 competency standard. Ontology-based learning is considered in the context of competency-based learning. The competency catalogue allows the identification of a possible gap between the reference and the actual competency profiles and the identification of the training requirements. An ontology-based project management learning approach allows one to find the most suitable educational programmes and training when there is a similarity but not an exact match between education and training offers and the competency gap.

The development process is based on the state of the art IT technologies (metadata and ontology for knowledge manipulation, Web services, learner model, and intelligent tutoring systems). Besides interoperability and personalization, the proposed approach brings additional advantages, including: unitary interpretation of the content structure by different user categories or content providers; explicit specification of the knowledge domain, allowing the updating of the domain definition without major changes of e-learning tools and programmes; reuse of the learning objects with economical advantages by saving costs of (re)writing the content for the different course forms and strategies; reuse of the created tools in one domain in other domains; promoting the competency-based learning through the domain ontology and the relations between concepts and competencies. The results obtained in practice are very encouraging and suggest several future developments.

DOI: 10.4018/978-1-60960-797-5.ch012

INTRODUCTION

The importance of education is becoming more and more widely accepted. The 21st century is considered the education century (Shi & Tsang, 2008) because education is becoming a vital and continuous process, and a crucial element in order to survive in the knowledge society. Huggins (2004) identified the following three reasons to get involved in learning activities: personal and professional potential benefits, opportunities for learning and external factors. According to the Huggins's study, when individuals are engaging in learning activities, they are looking for personal development, performance at work, confidence and promotion. Other studies stress the financial and non-financial benefits of education (Demirel, 2009; Fabra & Camisón, 2009). As non-financial benefits, the following are often mentioned: more interesting and stimulating work, higher stability and autonomy of the job, safer working conditions. Demirel emphasizes that people should be engaged in learning activities in order to cope with the constantly changing environment. In this context, they should constantly renew their existential perspective, behaviour and values.

The software industry is currently governed by several major forces: global competition (software companies compete globally, national boundaries become less visible), interdependence between many sectors, a high rate of innovation, significant risk exposure and a high degree of professionalization.

In the software industry, the human resources are subject to a continuous process of improvement. Otherwise, they quickly become obsolete and are released. According to Morris (2009), investment in skills development remains a long-term imperative and co-ordinated efforts among governments, universities and IT firms are needed to improve the quality of technology training and expand the pool of potential recruits. Education and training need to address the competencies required by the software industry.

The pillars of a competency-based education are the skills and traits (knowledge, experience, attitude and abilities) that individuals use to perform successfully. The identification, modeling and assessment of competencies represents the foundation of a competency-based education.

Project management is a core competency in the software industry. The correlation between business performance and project success can not be disputed (Ling et al., 2009). Extensive research has been done on this topic, but project management is a highly dynamic field. Several categories of key factors have been revealed, relating to project management actions, project related factors, project procedures, human factors and environmental factors. All of these factors are described in standardized guides and codes of practice. Prominent among these codes is the IPMA Competency Baseline, Version 3.0, developed by the International Project Management Association (2006).

The increasing need for IT education and the demand for more flexible ways of acquiring competencies are forces that motivate the use of e-learning. Due to the technological explosion, e-learning has gained an important position among the range of educational tools. It offers convenience, flexibility, mobility and adaptability. In consequence, e-learning has become a strategic vector in the development of the knowledge-based economy (Charpentier et al., 2006). This change in education and training has resulted in the intensification of research on e-learning. Researchers seek to discover students' preferences for various tools and e-learning platforms, the relationships between online learning and other learning styles, and the factors affecting student performance and satisfaction in the online environment (McFarland & Hamilton, 2006).

E-LEARNING STANDARDS

As a consequence of the spread of e-learning systems, e-learning standards emerged in order to assure the conditions for running applications in different environments, and for exchanging digital content between different applications

The airline industry computer-based training committee (AICC) standard is the oldest e-learning standard and emerged from the need to create a training system specific to this industry. The AICC objectives were to assist operators in developing guidelines to promote computer training sites, interoperability, a forum for discussions on the computer-based training and information technology applied in education.

Advanced distributed learning (ADL) is a United States Government initiative, providing access to education and training of high quality, tailored to the individual needs, and delivered effectively anywhere anytime. ADL strategy is based on the use of distributed environments, creating reusable content that is not dependent on a given platform, promoting extensive co-operation to meet common needs, developing common specifications for multiple platforms, improving performance by using emerging technologies, and providing incentives for organizational and cultural changes.

The sharable content object reference model (SCORM) specification is a collection of good practices from a number of e-learning standards to bring interoperability, accessibility and reusability of content to systems used in web-based learning. SCORM integrates industrial specifications from many organizations (AICC, Instructional Management Systems (IMS), Institute of Electrical and Electronic Engineering (IEEE)), to provide a unified system of learning content and define a standard web environment, the first step toward defining an architecture for e-learning. It is an e-learning standard based on clear specifications for metadata and for how communication between the learning management system and the back-end applications should take place.

The Instructional Management System (IMS) learning design standard, developed by the IMS global learning consortium (IMS, 2003) allows the use of a diversity of pedagogical models and innovations, as well as interoperability of the educational resources. Additionally, this standard offers the possibility of specifying personalization aspects, so that the educational content and the activities can be adapted with regard to the preferences, portfolio, prerequisites, educational requirements and situational circumstances of the user. The unit of the learning model (course, module and lesson) includes roles, resources, activities and methods as shown in Figure 1.

The IMS model is based on the following pedagogical approach: a *person* carries out a *role* in the teaching-learning process, most frequently that of *learner* or of didactic *staff*. In this role the person wants to obtain some *outcome*, executing one or more *activities* using one or more *environments*. An environment is composed of several *learning objects* and *services* provided to the persons, according to their roles. Through *method* or by *notifications* it can be established which roles begin the action and which are the activities they give rise to at a given moment. The method is aimed at achieving the *learning objectives* and assumes the existence of some *prerequisites*. The method consists of one or more concurrent *plays*; a play consists of one or more sequential *acts*; an act represents the execution of some *role-parts*. This results in associating an activity or *activity structure* with each role. Each role can have sub-roles with specific activities. A method can contain conditions (Boolean expressions) by defining *properties*, such as *If-Then-Else* rules that define the visibility of the activities and environment entities on persons and roles. The properties can be grouped in *property-groups* and can be *global* or *local*, *personal* or depending on roles. A notification is started by a result and can trigger a role to execute a new activity. The person who makes

Figure 1. Conceptual model: IMS learning design (source: IMS, 2003)

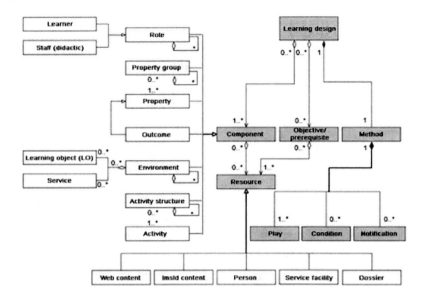

the notification does not have to be the person who obtains the result.

Other e-learning standards are the institutional alliance of remote authoring and distribution network for Europe (ARIADNA), an industry association, the Institute of Electrical and Electronic Engineering learning technology standards committee (IEEE LTSC), the International Organization for Standardization (ISO)/International Electrotechnical Commission (IEC) joint technical committee 1 (JTC 1) subcommittee 36 (SC 36) (information technology for learning, education and training (ITLET)), and the advanced learning infrastructure consortium (Alice).

THE LEARNING SYSTEM ARCHITECTURE

The proposed learning system architecture, presented in Figure 2, is based on the SinPers system (Trandafir & Borozan, 2006). During 2005-2008, the author was involved in the development of this system, being responsible for the design and development of the educational content (Bodea,

2007a; 2007b). The objective of the SinPers project was the development of an e-learning platform, centred on the learner and based on advanced technologies. The main research objective was personalization, as a solution to satisfy individual user needs, by adjusting the learning content and services to a learner's objective and preferences for competency, skills and performance enhancement. During 2009-2010, the author adapted the educational content for the IT sector, studying the applicability and the relevance of the system content with the specific competency requirements of the IT domain (Bodea & Dascalu, 2009, 2010a; 2010b).

The proposed learning architecture brings new conceptual approaches and technical solutions for three basic elements of the system, the teaching/learning process (learning and support activity flows, delivery conditions, triggers, notifications or timed events), the learning content (domain ontology, learning object and metadata) and the actors-roles. The development process uses state of the art IT technologies (metadata and ontology for knowledge manipulation, web services, learner model, and intelligent tutoring systems).

Figure 2. The e-learning system architecture

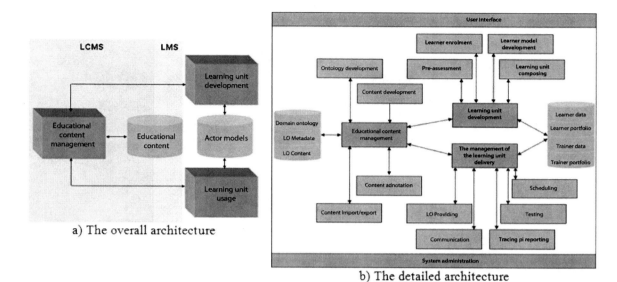

a) The overall architecture

b) The detailed architecture

The educational content management is based on the first comprehensive project management course ontology aligned with the ICB 3.0 standard (International Project Management Association, 2006). An original solution for integrating the educational ontology with a competency ontology also in line with the ICB competency standard is proposed by the learning architecture. The competency ontology allows the identification of a possible gap between the reference and the actual competency profiles and the identification of the project management training requirements.

The learning system architecture is based on the following elements: infrastructure, services and the educational content. E-learning infrastructure includes two major software categories of applications, clearly distinguished and complementary:

- LCMS, the learning content management system
- LMS, the learning management system.

The services assure the successful implementation of an e-learning technology, including efficient resource planning, adapting to the organizational context and/or to the individual preferences of the student, application integration and management, and expert consultancy.

Referring to the content, it has been observed that currently, organizations prefer more and more to purchase a pre-existing content delivered by a third party, or to reuse some parts by import and export. This explains the tendency towards specialization of some content suppliers and the creation and maintenance of the large collections/ warehouses of digital educational content. The interoperability of these warehouses depends on some standards, for which the project team selected the recommendations of the IMS digital repository.

The learning management system (LMS) is a system having the following functions: enrolment and administration of learners, courses and curriculum planning, delivery of lessons, development of learner progress reports, communication support, testing and assessment of knowledge. The learning content management system (LCMS) is a multi-user content management system (CMS),

Figure 3. The LMS: LCMS integration

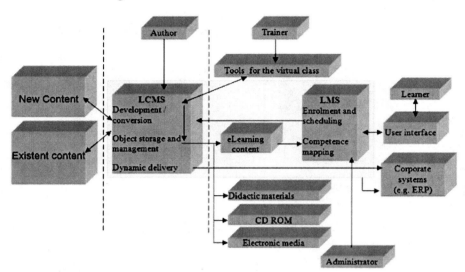

which can assist in the development, re-usage, management and delivery of the digital content based on a central repository of learning objects.

LMS and LCMS are complementary components of the learning system. They exchange information with benefits for the learner and the training administrator. An LMS can manage a community of users, allowing each of them to obtain the most appropriate learning objects according to their needs. Along with the content delivery, an LCMS can assess the progress of each

student, record and report the test score back to the LMS. Figure 3 shows the flow and exchange of information between these components in the learning system.

For this integration to be effective it is necessary that the two systems be interoperable. In these circumstances, the two key benefits of using learning objects, interoperability and reuse, are based on XML standards and known metadata standards (SCORM, IMS, IEEE).

Figure 4. The content semantic annotation

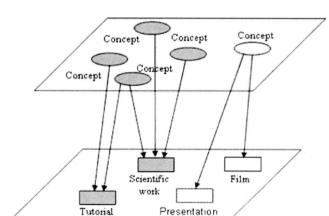

Figure 5. The learning path

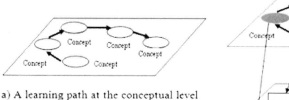
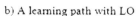

a) A learning path at the conceptual level

b) A learning path with LO

STRUCTURE OF THE EDUCATIONAL CONTENT: AN ONTOLOGY-BASED APPROACH

The structuring of the course content (knowledge) is done on several distinct levels:

- educational ontology (concepts and relations between concepts)
- learning objects (support of the concepts)
- metadata (object attributes).

The ontology-based modeling can be accomplished on two levels of knowledge organization as shown in Figure 4:

- upper level: the concept set selected from the domain concepts

- lower level: learning resources (books, web presentations, movies) associated with the upper level concepts; the ontology may be used as a semantic index for accessing the resources.

In the course development phase, learning paths can be created at the conceptual level based on semantic relations between the concepts, as in Figure 5. In this phase

- a sequence of concepts is obtained by browsing the domain ontology, which then gives the access order to the learning objects
- the corresponding learning objects sequence, which is related to the ontology

Figure 6. The learning path development

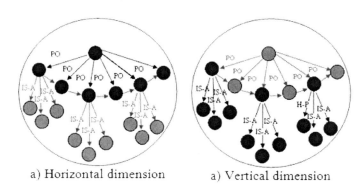

a) Horizontal dimension   a) Vertical dimension

concepts and which constitute the personalized course, is obtained.

At the conceptual level, the learning paths can be developed based on semantic relations between the concepts, on the two dimensions, horizontal and vertical, shown in Figure 6.

On the horizontal dimension, the learning sequence is established by moving from a given concept (the main subject), and the ontology is browsed by following the decomposition relations (PO – part of relation). On the vertical dimension, the ontology is browsed on the specialized connections (the IS-A relationship) with different results based on the direction, from down to up (synthesis and topic completion) and from up to down (topics development).

Several learning systems, listed below, are based on ontologies and standards that have an important role in the representation of learning objects and repositories:

- *CIPHER* (http://www.cipherweb.org) supports the exploration of national and regional heritage resources.
- *Connexions* (http://cnx.rice.edu) is an open source project that provides learning objects, a repository, a mark-up language and a set of tools for authoring, composing modules into courses and navigating through these courses.
- *Conzilla* (http://www.conzilla.org/) is being developed as part of the PADLR project (Knowledge Management Research Group, 2002) as a means of accessing and annotating learning objects. It is a concept browser that allows the user to navigate through a space of context maps to access associated content. While the context maps are not referred to as ontologies, the two may be considered equivalent.
- *Edutella* (http://edutella.jxta.org) is a project that provides an infrastructure for peer-to-peer systems for exchanging educational resources. Edutella uses metadata based on standards such as Institute of Electrical and Electronic Engineering learning objects metadata (IEEE LOM) to describe resources.
- *EML (Educational Modelling Language)* (http://eml.ou.nl/introduction/explanation.htm) is a notational system developed at the Open University of the Netherlands as a means of representing the content of a study unit and the students' and teachers' roles, relations, interactions and activities. It now forms the basis for the IMS Learning Design Specification. As with many extensible mark-up language (XML)-based approaches, ontologies are not mentioned. However, the study units, domain and learning theory models can be contrued as a set of ontologies.

Applying this type of approach to the IT project management domain requires the adoption of a standard for the domain concepts and project manager competencies. The standard used here is ICB 3.0, the international competency baseline of the International Project Management Association (2006). The ontology of the IT project management course contains more than 200 concepts and 3 types of relationship between concepts: *has-part, is-required-by* and *suggested-order*. Figure 7 (a) presents the overall view of the ontology and Figures 7 (b), (c) and (d) present detailed views of the ontology.

The system ontology was developed using Protégé editor (Protégé 2000 User Guide, 2000). Figure 8 presents a fragment of the OWL code.

The link between the concepts and the learning objects, depending on the type of object (expositive object or assessment), is shown in Figure 9.

According to the Instructional Management Systems (IMS) recommendation (IMS Global

Figure 7. The ontology of the IT project management course: detailed views

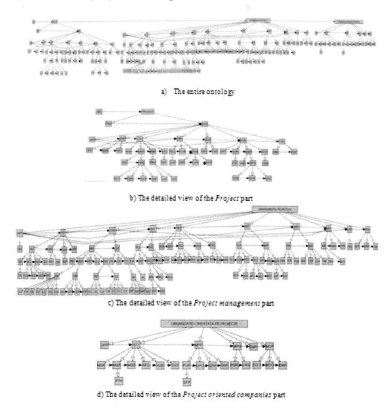

a) The entire ontology

b) The detailed view of the *Project* part

c) The detailed view of the *Project management* part

d) The detailed view of the *Project oriented companies* part

Figure 8. OWL code of the project management course ontology: an extract

```
<?xml version="1.0"?>
<rdf:RDF
  xmlns:rdf="http://www.w3.org/1999/02/22-rdf-syntax-ns#"
  xmlns:xsd="http://www.w3.org/2001/XMLSchema#"
  xmlns:rdfs="http://www.w3.org/2000/01/rdf-schema#"
  xmlns:owl="http://www.w3.org/2002/07/owl#"
  xmlns="http://www.owl-ontologies.com/unnamed.owl#"
  xml:base="http://www.owl-ontologies.com/unnamed.owl">
  <owl:Ontology rdf:about=""/>
  <owl:Class rdf:ID="Obiectivele_proiectului">
    <rdfs:label
rdf:datatype="http://www.w3.org/2001/XMLSchema#string"
      >Obiectivele proiectului</rdfs:label>
    <rdfs:subClassOf>
      <owl:Class rdf:ID="Entitatea_proiect"/>
    </rdfs:subClassOf>
  </owl:Class>
  <owl:Class rdf:ID="Tehnici_de_stimulare_a_creativității">
    <rdfs:label
rdf:datatype="http://www.w3.org/2001/XMLSchema#string"
      >Tehnici de stimulare a creativității</rdfs:label>
    <rdfs:subClassOf>
      <owl:Class rdf:ID="Generarea_ideii_de_proiect"/>
    </rdfs:subClassOf>
  </owl:Class>
  <owl:Class rdf:ID="Exprimarea_obiectivelor">
    <rdfs:label
rdf:datatype="http://www.w3.org/2001/XMLSchema#string"
      >Exprimarea obiectivelor</rdfs:label>
    <rdfs:subClassOf rdf:resource="#Obiectivele_proiectului"/>
  </owl:Class>
  <owl:Class
```

```
rdf:ID="Asociații_profesionale_de_managementul_proiectelor">
    <rdfs:label
rdf:datatype="http://www.w3.org/2001/XMLSchema#string"
      >Asociații    profesionale    de    managementul
proiectelor</rdfs:label>
    <rdfs:subClassOf>
      <owl:Class
rdf:ID="Cariera_in_managementul_proiectelor">
    <rdfs:subClassOf>
  </owl:Class>
  <owl:Class rdf:ID="Manageri_de_produs_și_de_proces">
    <rdfs:label
rdf:datatype="http://www.w3.org/2001/XMLSchema#string"
      >Manageri de produs și de proces</rdfs:label>
    <rdfs:subClassOf>
      <owl:Class
rdf:ID="Influențe_constrângeri_organizaționale">
    <rdfs:subClassOf>
  </owl:Class>
  <owl:Class rdf:ID="Consultare">
    <rdfs:subClassOf>
      <owl:Class rdf:ID="Consolidarea_echipei">
    <rdfs:subClassOf>
  </owl:Class>
  <owl:Class rdf:ID="Proceduri_de_negociere_a_contractelor">
    <rdfs:subClassOf>
      <owl:Class rdf:ID="Achiziții_și_contracte">
    <rdfs:subClassOf>
    <rdfs:label
rdf:datatype="http://www.w3.org/2001/XMLSchema#string"
      >Proceduri de negociere a contractelor</rdfs:label>
  </owl:Class>
```

Figure 9. Conceptual schema of the educational content

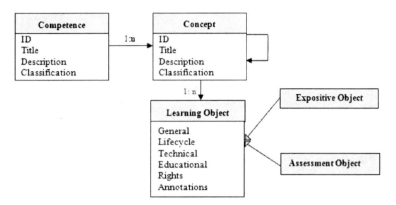

Learning Consortium, 2003), each learning object has different characteristics (metadata):

- *General:* groups information describing the learning object as a whole (e.g. *title, catalogue entry, language, description, keyword, structure*)
- *Lifecycle:* history and current state of the resource (e.g. *version, status, contributions*)
- *Technical:* technical features of the learning object (e.g. *format, size, location, technical requirements, installation remarks*)
- *Educational:* educational or pedagogic features of the learning object (e.g. *type of resource, language, description, interactivity type, interactivity level, semantic density, end-user role intended, age range of users, difficulty, context, learning time*)
- *Rights:* conditions of use of the resource (e.g. *cost, copyright and others restrictions, description*)
- *Annotations:* comments on the educational use of the learning object.

COMPETENCY-BASED STRUCTURE OF THE EDUCATIONAL CONTENT

The competency ontology, known also as competency catalogue defines the employee competency profiles (the actual competencies of the employees) and/or the reference position competency profiles (the list of competencies that are needed to fulfil the working requirements of the individual positions) (Biesalski & Abecker, 2005; Schmidt & Kunzmann, 2006). The competency ontology should be in line with a competency standard. Afterwards, these two types of profile allow a matching process to be done for the identification of a possible gap between the reference and the actual competency profiles and identification of the project management training requirements.

The use of competency ontologies has several benefits such as:

- Competency groups or clusters can easily be defined since the competency ontologies are taxonomies. A hierachy can be easily exploited to aggregate competencies to a more abstract level and build up competency groups.
- An ontology component can be integrated from another information source (e.g. the domain ontology) using ontology mapping techniques.
- Similarity measures can easily be calculated to define the gap between the reference and the actual competency profiles.
- A similarity-based search of the most suitable educational programs or training

Figure 10. The connection between the educational ontology (a) and the project management competency catalogue (b)

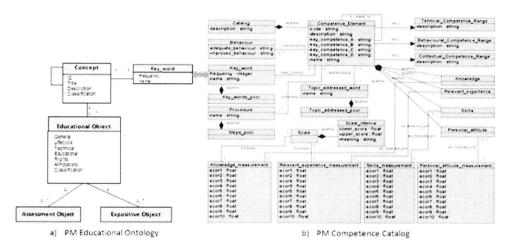

a) PM Educational Ontology

b) PM Competence Catalog

activities can be used to recommend programmes and training schemes.

The proposed educational ontology is connected with the project management competency *PMCatalog*, shown in Figure 10, and developed by the author based on the ICB 3.0 (Bodea et al., 2010). The *PMCatalog* has four abstract classes and 11 concrete classes. The abstract classes are set in a taxonomic hierarchy. The class *Catalogue* is the super-class for the other three classes, *Technical_Competence_Range*, *Behavioural_Competence_Range* and *Contextual_Competence_Range*. The sub-classes correspond to the three groups of competencies: 20 technical competencies, 15 behavioural competencies and 11 contextual competencies. The *Catalogue* class has only one slot, named *description*, which explains the motivation for using the ICB 3.0. Furthermore the IPMA competency baseline is the common framework document that all IPMA Member Associations and Certification Bodies abide by to ensure that consistent and harmonised standards are applied (International Project Management Association, 2006).

The connection between educational ontology and the competency catalogue is achieved using the key words, which are related to the Concept IDs. Table 1 presents this connection.

Assuring this connection, it is possible to consider the educational content as having a competency-based structure. A competency-based structure of the educational content allows one to find the most suitable educational programmes and training activities when there a similarity but not an exact match between training offers and the competency gap.

THE LEARNING SYSTEM APPLICATION

Based on different pedagogical methods, several use cases have been defined. Table 2 presents a comparison between different use cases.

Figure 11 presents the use case (Figure 11 (a)) and the e-learning scenario (Figure 11 (b)) adopted as the system application solution.

The e-learning scenario includes the following steps:

Table 1. Connection between educational ontology and the competency catalogue

Key words in competency catalogue	ID Concept in the Educational ontology	Key words in competency catalogue	ID Concept in the Educational ontology
Project management success	INT, PRJ, SCS, DSC, FSP, SUC	Assertiveness	CO4
Interested parties	MSP, MSE, PIN, RMS, ACO, QAD, AAN, SRP	Relaxation	CO5
Project requirements and objectives	ENT, ASI, STO, RST, OBV, OOB, DOB, OBP, OSA, NOB	Openness	CO6
Risk & opportunities	MRO, IER, ACA, MOC, PMM	Creativity	CO7
Quality	MCP, PCP, PPR, PCR, PCM, ASC, ADP, CON, COA	Results orientation	CO8
Project organizations	SOP, ORG, OPR, RPR, PRP, MGP, CMP, STP, ASO, CER, FDP, CAM, MEP, COL, EPR	Efficiency	CO9
Teamwork	FEP, CEP	Consultation	C10
Problem resolution	MPR, CRD, PSO	Negotiation	C11
Project structures	GRP, CXP, STR, SPR	Conflict & crisis	C12
Scope & deliverables	SFC, REZ, WBS, WBI, SPA, CPA, RPA, IPA	Reliability	C13
Time & project phases	DIT, FPP, CVP, FZP, MTP, PLC, PJA, JAL, DGT, ADC, DRA, DEP, RDD, DRC, ALG	Value appreciation	C14
Resources	RES, NOR, ESR, ALR, MLR, OAR	Ethics	C15
Cost & finance	MCF, COS, TCO, CEN, PCO, ECO, BPR, MFP, SFP, PFN	Project orientation	OPP
Procurements & contract	ACC, NAP, SFR, NCO, DCA	Programme orientation	MPG, PGR, OPG
Changes	MSH, MSC, MSR, MSF	Portfolio orientation	MMP, GRU, LAN, CLP, MPP, POP, SPP, OPO, GPP, TPP
Control & reports	CCT, RPT, ACP, CRE, RCR, DUR, CCO, RPC, AEV, CFN, RAF, TMC, CTR	Project, programme & portfolio implementation (PPP implementation)	TIP, DIM, DSP
Information & documentation	IDP, SMD, SMP, SIP, BDP	Permanent organization	ICO, DMP, MOP, COO, MMO, EMP
Communication	COP, STC, TIC, SWP	Business	IPR, INV, IDE, CRV, SFZ, ACB, AEC, ASZ, ARC, SWO
Start-up	DDI, DIP, PRO, CPR, DDP, EEP, ATP	Systems, products & technology	PTH
Close-out	TPR, DOF, APR, LIN	Personnel management	MGF, MGE, MGR
Leadership	CO1	Health, security, safety & environment	SSS
Engagement	CO2	Finance	AFC
Self-control	CO3	Legal	AJD

- the specification of the personal training options (e.g. entire course, one module, competency acquirement), personal data (e.g. studies/qualifications, age, activity domain) and personal preferences (e.g. learning style, hardware-software support)
- the updating of the learner model
- unit of learning completion, with specific sub-phases for a computer assisted course,

Table 2. Alternative use cases: a comparison

Use Case	Actors	Learner Choices	Trainer Actions	Pre-Assessment	Personalization Information
1. Customization of learning units by learner objectives	Trainer Single learner	Learning outcomes	Outcomes identification (Propose other outcomes)	Test (prerequisites fulfillment for a given outcome)	Test result Learner model
2. Knowledge improvement	Single learner	Course/ module/ subject/ competence	-	Knowledge test (specific for the selected course/ module/ subject/ competence)	Test result Learner model
3. Collaborative learning (by roles)	Groups of learners Trainer	-	Assign roles	-	Roles by group
4. Recommendation of a learning path	Single learner Trainer	Prior knowledge test Tests selection (Complementary courses studied)	(Transmit the pre-assessment test) (Compose the learning path and transmit the homework)	Knowledge is set (on the selected domain)	Test results Domain content (structured by LO)
5. Adaptive learning	Single learner Operational LMS systems/ service providers	Preferences (learning style, content presentation style, etc.)	-	Setting up preferences	Preferences (Learner model) LO metadata LO sequence

Figure 11. The system application solution

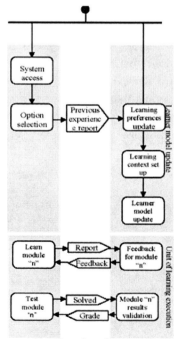

Primary actors: learner, LMS
Pre-requisites:
The learner is already knowledgeable to use the system (from a preliminary „face to face" lesson, or from a manual user instructions published on the website). The educational content is available.
Start: The learner accesses the system
Success scenario:
1. The learner accesses the system using id and password.
2. The systems presents the menu with options referring to course personalization and presentation:
   • desired objective / outcomes,
   • knowledge enhancement in the desired sub-domain,
   • customization of the learning path according to learner profile (initial knowledge level, preferences).
3. The learner selects a menu option.
4. The system updates the learning preferences, based on the *previously services used* by the learner.
5. The system composes the learning context (using a *context-informed adaptive service*).
6. The system composes the learner profile (using *a user modeling exchange service*)
7. The system composes the learning path.
8. The system presents to learner the description of the personalized learning path.
9. The learner goes over the learning path and submits the results to the system (exercises, reports, case studies, projects etc.). In this step all the "n" modules of the personalized learning path are delivered.

a) The use case description

b) The e-learning scenario

Figure 12. The development cycle of the e-learning system

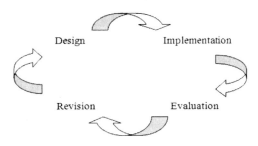

including learning object delivery and intermediate assessment.

This e-learning scenario requires the use of different services in order to compose the learning context and the learner profile.

THE LEARNING SYSTEM EVALUATION

Evaluation is an important phase of the e-learning development cycle that is shown in Figure 12.

The traditional evaluation of the e-learning system focused on measuring the participant reaction to the training sessions (Shepherd, 2010). The customer satisfaction could be seen as a valid measure of the e-learning system quality. The evidence shows that those who are trained and have positive opinions about the experience

of training do not necessarily provide greater productivity when they return to work. It can be said that they have the necessary experience to judge the effectiveness of the complex design decisions in the training but that perceptions gathered at the end of a training programme can be influenced by factors not related to a training system that is effective at improving performance at work. Therefore trainees' perceptions are only a limited part of the entire evaluation. Kirkpatrick proposed a training evaluation model as given in Table 3.

Different experiments were designed in order to evaluate the e-learning system at all four levels in this table. One of these experiments is presented below.

The experiment was based on the following research question: *How does e-learning in project management influence the performance of the organizations?* The following performance indicators were selected:

- wage increases
- customer retention rate
- number of employees who obtained professional certifications.

The subjects of the study were the users of the e-learning system, coming from different Romanian companies and enrolled in the certification program of the Romanian Project Management Association. The users can be classified according

Table 3. Kirkpatrick's training evaluation model (Source: http://www.businessballs.com)

Level	What is measured?	Evaluation description and characteristics	Evaluation tools and methods (example)
1	Reaction	Reaction evaluation is how the delegates felt about the training or learning experience.	- *Happy sheets*, feedback forms. - Verbal reaction, post-training surveys or questionnaires.
2	Learning	Learning evaluation is the measurement of the increase in knowledge - before and after.	- Typically assessments or tests before and after the training. - Interview or observations
3	Behavior	Behavior evaluation is the extent of applied learning back on the job - implementation.	Observations and interview.
4	Results	Results evaluation is the effect on the business or environment by the trainee.	Measures are already in place via normal management systems and reporting - the challenge is to relate to the trainee.

Table 4. The user profiles

IPMA Level	No. Users	No. Respondents
A	0	0
B	11	2
C	35	11
D	106	64

Table 5. Profiles of case study subjects

Business sector	No. Firms	No. Subjects
IT	7	32
Consulting	9	29
Other sectors	3	16

to the level of their abilities in project management activities from level A to D. As instruments of research, we mainly used the questionnaire and, sometimes, interviews and informal e-mails.

The study hypotheses were the following:

- There is a connection between the period spent using the e-learning system and the wage increases for the users.
- There is a relationship between the number of clients who returned to the company and the use of the e-learning system by the company' employees.
- There is a connection between the number of certified people and the use of the e-learning system by those people.
- The impact of the e-learning system on the company's performance depends on the business sector of the company.

In order to establish the relationship between the use of the e-learning system (the dependent variable) and the Romanian companies' performance (the independent variable), 153 users of the e-learning system were questioned through questionnaires sent to them. The response rate was 50.32%, meaning that 77 users responded. Details about the respondents' profiles are provided in Table 4. The affiliation of the trainees to the same company or to the same business sector was also taken into account, as indicated in Table 5.

The experiment revealed that 35% of the subjects got an IPMA certification as a result of their use of e-learning system, with most of these from the IT sector. The main reason for starting to use

the system was their desire to get certifications. This desire included the need to get professional recognition, to have a higher level of well-being and to improve the firms' portfolio. The fact that most of the individuals who completed their work with the e-learning system were from the IT sector indicates the ambition driving Romanian IT firms to achieve improved performance.

Most of the subjects said that the customer retention rate in a six-month period was about 55%, which is a high level. Most subjects who stated this were from the consulting sector. This observation may be explained by the duration of IT projects, which usually last longer than the six-month period. When we asked if they thought that their improved skills, as a result of the e-learning system, had any impact on clients' returning rate, 60% of them gave a definite *yes* and the other 40% claimed a certain level of impact.

Just 9% of our subjects got a wage rise after using the e-learning system. This low result may be due to the recession. 50% of those who received a rise named the competency development through the e-learning system as one important reason for it. Those who made this statement were mainly from different business sectors.

The results of the experiment broadly indicated a positive link between the use of the e-learning system and the growth of performance indicators at the firms.

FUTURE DEVELOPMENT

A very interesting topic to be followed in the future is how to share the learning objects within and across learning object repositories. An ontology-based solution would be expected to be helpful in this regard, because ontology provides a shared understanding of common domains.

With the proliferation of different ontologies for the same domain, a mapping process to perform interoperability needs to be defined. Although many efforts at ontology mapping have already been tried, few of them use resource properties to generate relations between local concepts. Our plan is to seek to define these properties and use inference rules to obtain correspondences and relationships between concepts from source and target ontology.

CONCLUSION

This chapter brings new conceptual approaches and technical solutions forward for three basic elements of the e-learning system: the teaching-learning process (learning and support activity flows, delivery conditions, triggers, notifications or timed events), the learning content (domain ontology, learning objects and metadata) and the connection with the required competencies.

The novelty of the approach is provided by the following innovative elements:

- project management training personalization, providing facilities for building learning paths for each student depending on his/her profile, preferences and organizational objectives. The personalization is possible by structuring course content on multiple levels of abstraction and modeling knowledge about students.
- the application of innovative teaching methods based on constructivist learning theory
- a new approach to knowledge management and a semantic-based approach in e-learning systems

- e-learning community promotion, offering new facilities for communication between different roles involved in the training process with similar goals and profiles
- the adoption of widely circulated e-learning international standards, in order to ensure interoperability with other systems and reuse of components.

The project management educational ontology and the competency catalogue were developed based on ICB 3.0. The integration of the ontology-based learning with the competency management is described. The competency ontology allows the identification of a gap between the reference and the actual competency profiles and the identification of the appropriate project management training requirements. An ontology-based project management learning approach allows one to find the most suitable training when there a similarity but not an exact match between training offers and the competency gap.

REFERENCES

Biesalski, E., & Abecker, A. (2005). Human resource management with ontologies. In *Lecture Notes in Computer Science (LNCS), 3782/2005* (pp. 499–507). Berlin, Germany: Springer Verlag.

Bodea, C. N. (2007a, August). *An innovative system for learning services in project management.* Paper presented at the Institute of Electrical and Electronic Engineering/INFORMS International Conference on Service Operations and Logistics, and Informatics (SOLI), Philadelphia, PA.

Bodea, C. N. (2007b, June). *SinPers - an innovative learning system in project management.* Paper presented at the 21st International Project Management Association (IPMA) World Congress on Project Management, Cracow, Poland.

Bodea, C. N., & Dascalu, M. (2009, October). *Competency-based e-learning in the framework of knowledge management.* Paper presented at the 4th International Conference on Business Excellence, Brasov, Romania.

Bodea, C. N., & Dascalu, M. (2010a, April). *Competency-based e-assessment in project management and firm performance: A case study.* Paper presented to the 4th European Computing Conference (WSEAS), Bucharest, Romania.

Bodea, C. N., & Dascalu, M. (2010b, May). *Modeling project management competencies: An ontology-based solution for competency-based learning.* Paper presented at the 1st International conference on Technology Enhanced Learning: Quality of Teaching and Educational Reform (TECH-EDUCATION 2010), Athens, Greece.

Bodea, C. N., Elmas, C., Tanasescu, A., & Dascalu, M. (2010). An ontological-based model for competencies in sustainable development projects: A case study for a project's commercial activities. *Amfiteatru Economic, 27*, 1–14.

Charpentier, M., Lafrance, C., & Paquette, G. (2006). *International e-learning strategies: Key findings relevant to the Canadian context.* Retrieved November 10, 2010, from http://www.ccl-cca.ca/ pdfs/ Commissioned Reports/ John Biss International ELearning EN.pdf

Demirel, M. (2009). Lifelong learning and schools in the twenty-first century. *Procedia - Social and Behavioral Sciences, 1*, 1709–1716.

Fabra, E., & Camisón, C. (2009). Direct and indirect effects of education on job satisfaction: A structural equation model for the Spanish case. *Economics of Education Review, 28*(5), 600–610. doi:10.1016/j.econedurev.2008.12.002

Huggins, K. (2004). Lifelong learning-the key to competence in the intensive care unit? *Intensive & Critical Care Nursing, 20*(1), 38–44. doi:10.1016/j.iccn.2003.10.001

Instructional Management Systems (IMS) Global Learning Consortium. (2003). *IMS learning design: Information model*, version 1.0 final specification. Retrieved October 15, 2010, from http://www.imsglobal.org/

Instructional Management Systems (IMS) Global Learning Consortium. (1999-2007). *Website.* Retrieved October 15, 2010, from http://www.imsglobal.org/

International Project Management Association. (2006). *IPMA Competency Baseline (ICB) version 3.0.* Nijkerk, The Netherlands: International Project Management Association.

Knowledge Management Research Group. (2002). *Personalized access to distributed learning resources (PADLR).* Retrieved October 15, 2010, from http://kmr.nada.kth.se/

Ling, F. Y., Low, S. P., Wang, S. Q., & Lim, H. H. (2009). Key project management practices affecting Singaporean firms' project performance in China. *International Journal of Project Management, 27*(1), 59–71. doi:10.1016/j.ijproman.2007.10.004

McFarland, D., & Hamilton, D. (2006). Factors affecting student performance and satisfaction: Online versus traditional course delivery. *Journal of Computer Information Systems, 46*(2), 25–32.

Morris, I. (2009). *Resilience amid turmoil: Benchmarking IT industry competitiveness 2009.* The Economist Intelligence Unit. Retrieved October 15, 2010, from http://global.bsa.org/ 2009eiu/ study/ 2009_eiu_global.pdf

Protégé. (2000). *Protégé 2000 user guide.* Retrieved October 15, 2010, from http://protege.standford.edu/ doc/ users_guide/ index.html

Schmidt, A., & Kunzmann, C. (2006). Towards a human resource development ontology for combining competence management and technology-enhanced workplace learning. In *Lecture Notes in Computer Science (LNCS), 4278/2006* (pp. 1078–1087). Berlin, Germany: Springer Verlag.

Shepherd, C. (2010). *Evaluating online learning*. Retrieved October 15, 2010, from http://www2.warwick.ac.uk/ services/ ldc/ resource/ evaluation/ elearning/

Shi, Y., & Tsang, M. (2008). Evaluation of adult literacy education in the United States: A review of methodological issues. *Educational Research Review, 3*(2), 187–217. doi:10.1016/j.edurev.2007.10.004

Trandafir, I., & Borozan, A.-M. (2007, March). *E-learning design based on personalization requirements*. Paper presented to the International Technology, Education and Development (INTED 2007) Conference. Valencia, Spain

ADDITIONAL READING

Brew, L. S. (2008). The role of student feedback in evaluating and revising a blended learning course. *The Internet and Higher Education, 11*(2), 98–105. doi:10.1016/j.iheduc.2008.06.002

Brown, M., Anderson, B., & Murray, F. (2007, December). *E-learning policy issues: global trends, themes and tensions*. Paper presented to the Conference of the Australian Society for Computers in Learning in Tertiary Education (ASCLITE), ICT: Providing choices for learners and learning. Singapore. Retrieved October 30, 2010, from http://www.ascilite.org.au/ conferences/ singapore07/ procs/ brown-m.pdf

Casanova, D., Holmes, B., & Huet, I. (2009). Aiding academics to move from knowledge management to knowledge creation: conceptualisation of a personal academic environment (PAE*)*. In Méndez-Vilas, A., Solano Martín, J. A., Mesa González, J. A., & Mesa González, J. (Eds.) *Research, Reflections and Innovations in Integrating ICT in Education (Proceedings of Cinference on Multimedia, Information and Communication Technologies (MICTE 2009),* 1, pp. 481-486). Badajoz, Spain: Formatex.

Chen, L.-J., Chen, C.-C., & Lee, W.-R. (2008). Strategic capabilities, innovation intensity and performance of service firms. *Journal of Service Science and Management, 1*(2), 111–122. doi:10.4236/jssm.2008.12011

Commission of the European Communities. (2005). *Proposal for a Recommendation of the European Parliament and of the Council on Key Competences for Lifelong Learning*. Brussels, Belgium: European Commission.

Cruz Natali, A. C., & de Almeida Falbo, R. (2002). *Knowledge management in software engineering environments*. Retrieved October 30, 2010 from www.inf.ufes.br/ ~falbo/ download/ pub/ Sbes2002.pdf 9

Dittmann, L. (2004). *Ontology-Based Skills Management*. Work Report no. 22. Institute for Production and Industrial Information Management. Duisburg, Germany: University of Duisburg-Essen.

Garcia, A. C. B., Kunz, J., Ekstrom, M., & Kiviniemi, A. (2003). *Building a Project Ontology with Extreme Collaboration and Virtual Design & Construction Abstract, Center for Integrated Faculty Engineering (CIFE) Technical Report #152*. Stanford, CA: Stanford University.

Garofano, C., & Salas, E. (2005). What influences continuous employee development decisions? *Human Resource Management Review, 15*(4), 281–304. doi:10.1016/j.hrmr.2005.10.002

Hitt, M. A., Ireland, R. D., & Lee, H.-U. (2000). Technological learning, knowledge management,firm growth and performance: an introductory essay. *Journal of Engineering and Technology Management, 17*(3-4), 231–246. doi:10.1016/S0923-4748(00)00024-2

Kanellopoulos, D., Kotsiantis, S., & Pintelas, P. (2006, February). *Ontology-based learning applications: a development methodology.* Paper presented to the International Association of Science and Technology for Development (IASTED) International Conference on Software Engineering, Innsbruck, Austria.

Kröll, M. (2007, September). *Limits and possibilities for competence development in firms.* Paper presented to the European Conference on Educational Research (ECER). Ghent, Belgium.

Lundin, J. (2005). *Talking about Work: Designing Information Technology for Learning in Interaction, Gothenburg Studies in Informatics, Report 34.* Gothenburg, Sweden: University of Gothenburg.

Marimuthu, M., Arokiasamy, L., & Ismail, M. (2009). Human capital development and its impact on firm performance: evidence from developmental economics. *Journal of International Social Research, 2*(8), 265–272.

Markulla, M. (2006). *Creating favorable conditions for knowledge society through knowledge management, egovernance and elearning.* Retrieved October 30, 2010, from http://www.fig.net/ pub/monthly_articles/ june_2006/ june_2006_markkula.pdf

Raymond, L., Croteau, A.-M., & Bergeron, F. (2009, May). *The integrative role of IT in product and process innovation: growth and productivity outcomes for manufacturing.* Paper presented to the 11th International Conference on Enterprise Information Systems, Milan, Italy.

Stergiou, N., Georgoulakis, G., Margari, N., Aninos, D., Stamataki, M., & Stergiou, E. (2009). Using a web-based system for the continuous distance education in cytopathology. *International Journal of Medical Informatics, 78*(12), 827–838. doi:10.1016/j.ijmedinf.2009.08.007

Suikki, R., Tromstedt, R., & Haapasal, H. (2006). Project management competence development framework in turbulent business environment. *Technovation, 26*(5-6), 723–738. doi:10.1016/j.technovation.2004.11.003

Turner, J. R. (1996). International Project Management Association global qualification, certification and accreditation. *International Journal of Project Management, 14*(1), 1–6. doi:10.1016/0263-7863(96)88794-1

Vannakrairojn, S. (2003). *E-learning standard.* Retrieved November 10, 2010, from www.su.ac.th/ html_broadcast/ 2.ppt

KEY TERMS AND DEFINITIONS

Competency: A specific, identifiable and measurable knowledge, skill, ability and/or other deployment-related characteristic (e.g. attitude, behavior, physical ability) which a person may possess and which is necessary for, or material to, the performance of an activity within a specific business context.

Competency Catalogue: Defines the employee competency profiles (the actual competencies of the employees) and/or the reference position competency profiles (the list of competencies that are needed to fulfil the working requirements of the individual positions).

E-Learning: A type of distance education teaching-learning interaction mediated by an environment set up by new information and communication technologies, in particular the Internet. The Internet is both the material environment, as well as the communication channel between the actors involved.

Learning Content Management System (LCMS): A multi-user content management system (CMS), which can assist the development, reuse, management and delivery of the digital content based on a central repository of learning objects.

Learning Management System (LMS): A system having the following functions: enrolment and administration of learners; courses and curriculum planning in order to meet the learner's requirements (teaching material, trainer), lessons delivery, development of learner progress reports; communication support; testing and assessment of knowledge.

Learning Ontology: An explicit formal specification of how to represent the learning objects, learning concepts (classes) and other entities and the relationships between them. It describes the learning terms and the relationships between them and provides a clear definition of each term used.

Ontology: A set of representational primitives with which to model a domain of knowledge or discourse. The representational primitives are typically classes (or sets), attributes (or properties), and relationships (or relations among class members).

Compilation of References

ABET (Accreditation Board for Engineering and Technology). (2010). *ABET self-study questionnaire: Template of the computing self-study report.* Baltimore, MD: ABET.

Adams, J., Turner, S., Kaczmarczyk, S., Picton, P., & Demian, P. (2008). *Problem solving and creativity for undergraduate engineers: Findings of an action research project involving robots.* Paper presented at the International Conference on Engineering Education (ICEE 2008), Budapest, Hungary.

Aguayo, M., Luna, P., Ríos, M. A., & Ruiz, J. C. (2007). Aplicación del ECTS a la enseñanza integrada de sistemas de información empresariales mediante páginas HTML. *Revista de Enseñanza Universitaria, 29,* 4–23.

Alemany, M., Cuenca, L., Boza, A., & Ortiz, A. (2003, July). *Education for learning.* Paper presented to the International Conference on Engineering Education (ICEE), Valencia, Spain.

Alix, T., Jia, Z., & Chen, D. (2009). Return on experience of a joint master programme on enterprise software and production systems. In B. Wu & J.-P. Bourrières (Eds.), *Educate adaptive talents for IT applications in enterprises and interoperability. Proceedings of 5th China-Europe International Symposium on Software Industry Oriented Education* (pp. 27-36). Talence, France: University of Bordeaux.

Altbach, P. G., & Knight, J. (2007). The internationalization of higher education: Motivations and realities. *Journal of Studies in International Education, 11*(3-4), 290. doi:10.1177/1028315307303542

Andrews, G. R. (1999). *Foundations of parallel and distributed programming.* Boston, MA: Addison-Wesley Longman.

Archer, W., Garrison, D. R., Anderson, T., & Rourke, L. (2001, March). *A framework for analyzing critical thinking in computer conferences.* Paper presented at the European Conference on Computer-Supported Collaborative Learning (Euro-CSCL 2001), Maastricht, Netherlands.

Aritzeta, A., Swailes, S., & Senior, B. (2007). Belbin's team role model: Development, validity and applications for team building. *Journal of Management Studies, 44*(1), 96–118. doi:10.1111/j.1467-6486.2007.00666.x

Arjomandi, M., Kestell, C., & Grimshaw, P. (2009). An EFQM excellence model for higher education quality assessment. In *Proceedings of the 20th Annual Conference of the Australasian Association for Engineering Education Conference,* (pp. 1015-1020). Adelaide, Australia: University of Adelaide.

Asanovic, K., Bodik, R., Demmel, J., Keaveny, T., Keutzer, K., & Kubiatowicz, J. (2009). A view of the parallel computing landscape. *Communications of the ACM, 52*(10), 56–67. doi:10.1145/1562764.1562783

Association of Computing Machinery/Institute of Electrical and Eelectronic Engineeering. (2005). *Joint task force on computing curricula: 2005 - overview report.* Retrieved March 23, 2007, from http://www.acm.org/education/curricula.html

Baan, A. Z. (2003, March). *IDEAS roadmap for e-business interoperability: Interoperability development for enterprise application and software – roadmaps (IST-2001-37368).* Paper presented at the e-Government Interoperability Workshop, Brussels, Belgium.

Barrick, M. R., & Mount, M. K. (1991). The big five personality dimensions and job performance: A meta-analysis. *Personnel Psychology, 44,* 1–26. doi:10.1111/j.1744-6570.1991.tb00688.x

Beaumont, C., & Fox, C. (2003). Learning programming: Enhancing quality through problem-based learning. In *Proceeding of 4th Annual Conference of the subject centre for Information and Computer Sciences of the Higher Education Academy* (pp. 90-95). Newtownabbey, Northern Ireland: Higher Education Academy.

Becerra-Fernandez, I., Murphy, K. E., & Simon, S. J. (2000). Integrating ERP in the business school curriculum. *Communications of the ACM, 43*(4), 39–41. doi:10.1145/332051.332066

Beckman, K., Coulter, N., Khajenouri, S., & Mead, N. (1997). Collaborations: Closing the industry–academy gap. *Institute of Electrical and Electronic Engineering Software, 14*(6), 49–57.

Belbin, R. M. (1981). *Management teams: Why they succeed or fail.* London, United Kingdom: Heinemann.

Bell, D., & Parr, M. (2006). *Java for students* (5th ed.). Upper Saddle River, NJ: Prentice Hall.

Ben-Ari, M., & Kolikant, Y. B. D. (1999). Thinking parallel: The process of learning concurrency. *Association for Computing Machinery Special Interest Group on Computer Science Education Bulletin, 31*(3), 13–16.

Biesalski, E., & Abecker, A. (2005). Human resource management with ontologies. In *Lecture Notes in Computer Science (LNCS), 3782/2005* (pp. 499–507). Berlin, Germany: Springer Verlag.

Biggs, J. (2003). *Teaching for quality learning at university* (2nd ed.). Buckingham, United Kingdom: Open University Press.

Billing, D. (2004). International comparisons and trends in external quality assurance of higher education: Commonality or diversity? *Higher Education, 47*(1), 113–137. doi:10.1023/B:HIGH.0000009804.31230.5e

Bloom, B. S. (Ed.). (1956). *Taxonomy of educational objectives, handbook I: Cognitive domain.* White Plains, NY: Longman.

Bodea, C. N., Elmas, C., Tanasescu, A., & Dascalu, M. (2010). An ontological-based model for competencies in sustainable development projects: A case study for a project's commercial activities. *Amfiteatru Economic, 27*, 1–14.

Bodea, C. N. (2007a, August). *An innovative system for learning services in project management.* Paper presented at the Institute of Electrical and Electronic Engineering/INFORMS International Conference on Service Operations and Logistics, and Informatics (SOLI), Philadelphia, PA.

Bodea, C. N. (2007b, June). *SinPers - an innovative learning system in project management.* Paper presented at the 21st International Project Management Association (IPMA) World Congress on Project Management, Cracow, Poland.

Bodea, C. N., & Dascalu, M. (2009, October). *Competency-based e-learning in the framework of knowledge management.* Paper presented at the 4th International Conference on Business Excellence, Brasov, Romania.

Bodea, C. N., & Dascalu, M. (2010a, April). *Competency-based e-assessment in project management and firm performance: A case study.* Paper presented to the 4th European Computing Conference (WSEAS), Bucharest, Romania.

Bodea, C. N., & Dascalu, M. (2010b, May). *Modeling project management competencies: An ontology-based solution for competency-based learning.* Paper presented at the 1st International conference on Technology Enhanced Learning: Quality of Teaching and Educational Reform (TECH-EDUCATION 2010), Athens, Greece.

Bonwell, C. C., & Eison, J. A. (1991). *Active learning: Creating excitement in the classroom.* Washington, DC: The George Washington University School of Education and Human Development.

Boykin, R. F., & Martz, W. B. Jr. (2004). The integration of ERP into a logistics curriculum: Applying a systems approach. *Journal of Enterprise Information Management, 17*(1), 45–55. doi:10.1108/09576050410510944

Boza, A., & Cuenca, L. (2010). *An educative experience of autonomous workgroups in the subject Enterprise Computer Tools.* In B. Wu & J.-P. Bourrières (Eds.). (2010). *Educate adaptive talents for IT applications in enterprises and interoperability. Proceedings of 5th China-Europe International Symposium on Software Industry Oriented Education* (pp. 23-26). Talence, France: University of Bordeaux.

Brazilay, O., Hazzan, O., & Yehudai, A. (2009). A multidimensional software engineering course. *Institute of Electrical and Electronic Engineering (IEEE) Transactions on Education, 52*(3), 413–424. doi:10.1109/TE.2008.930094

Broucek, W., & Randall, G. (1996). An assessment of the construct validity of the Belbin self-perception inventory and observer's assessment from the perspective of the five-factor model. *Journal of Occupational and Organizational Psychology, 69*(4), 389–405.

Calvo-Mora, A., Leal, A., & Roldan, J. L. (2006). Using enablers of the EFQM model to manage institutions of higher education. *Quality Assurance in Education, 14*(2), 99–122. doi:10.1108/09684880610662006

Cameron, B. H. (2008). *Enterprise systems education: New directions and challenges for the future.* Paper presented at the Association for Computer Machinery Special Interest Group on Management Information Systems Computer Personnel Research Conference on Computer Personnel Doctoral Consortium and Research, Charlottesville, VA.

Campbell, C., & Rozsnyai, C. (2002). Quality assurance and the development of course programmes. In L. C. Barrows (Ed.), *Papers on higher education.* Bucharest, Romania: United Nations Educational, Scientific and Cultural Organisation (UNESCO), Centre européen pour l'enseignment supérieur (CEPES).

Carroll, D., Lawless, D., Hussey, M., O'Leary, C., Mtenzi, F., Gordon, D., & Collins, M. (2005). Stakeholders in the quality process of software engineering education. In *Proceedings of the 2nd China-Europe International Symposium on Software Industry-Oriented Education.* [New Series]. *Journal of Harbin Institute of Technology, 12,* 88–93.

Carroll, D., Lawless, D., Hussey, M., Gordon, D., O'Leary, C., Mtenzi, F., & Collins, M. (2006, November). *Assuring quality in Chinese IT education.* Paper presented at the Asia-Pacific Education Research Association Conference, Hong Kong, China.

Carton, F., & Adam, F. (2003). Analysing the impact of enterprise resource planning systems roll-outs in multinational companies. *Electronic Journal of Information Systems Evaluation, 6*(2), 21–32.

Centre International de la Pédagogie d'Enterprise (CIPE). (2008b). *Jeu de la GPAO* (gestation de la production assistée par ordinateur). Retrieved October 30, 2010, from http://www.cipe.fr

Centre International de la Pédagogie d'Entreprise (CIPE). (2008a). *Manufacturing resourses planning software package.* Retrieved October 30, 2010, from http://www.cipe.fr

Chakraborty, S., & Sharma, S. K. (2007). Enterprise resource planning: An integrated strategic framework. *International Journal of Management and Enterprise Development, 4*(5), 533–551. doi:10.1504/IJMED.2007.013457

Charpentier, M., Lafrance, C., & Paquette, G. (2006). *International e-learning strategies: Key findings relevant to the Canadian context.* Retrieved November 10, 2010, from http://www.ccl-cca.ca/pdfs/CommissionedReports/JohnBissInternationalELearningEN.pdf

Chen, D., & Vallespir, B. (2009). MRPII learning project based on a unified common case-study: Simulation, reengineering and computerization. In B. Wu & J.-P. Bourrières (Eds.), *Educate adaptive talents for IT applications in enterprises and interoperability. Proceedings of 5th China-Europe International Symposium on Software Industry Oriented Education* (pp. 233-240). Bordeaux, France: University of Bordeaux.

Chen, D., Vallespir, B., & Bourrières, J.-P. (2007). Research and education in software engineering and production systems: A double complementary perspectives. In B. Wu, B. MacNamee, X. Xu, & W. Guo (Eds.), *Proceedings of the 3rd China-Europe International Symposium on Software Industry-Oriented Education* (pp. 145-150). Dublin, Ireland: Blackhall.

Chen, D., Vallespir, B., Tu, Z., & Bourrières, J. P. (2010, May). *Towards a formal model of UB1-HIT joint master curriculum.* Paper presented at the 6th China-Europe International Symposium on Software Industry Oriented Education, Xi'an, China.

Chickering, A. W., & Gamson, A. F. (1987). Seven principles for good practicals in undergraduate education. *The American Association for Higher Education Bulletin, 39*(7), 8–12.

Chinese Government Report. (2001). *File No. 2001(6).* Beijing, China: Ministry of Education.

Chua, C. (2004). Perception of quality in higher education. In R. Carmichael (Ed.). *Proceedings of the Australian Universities Quality Forum2004: Quality in a Time of Change* (pp. 181–187). Adelaide, Australia: Australian Universities Quality Agency.

Clark, N. (2005). Evaluating student teams developing unique industry projects. In A. Young, & D. Tolhurst (Eds.), *Proceedings of the 7th Australasian Conference on Computing Education* (pp. 21-30). Darlinghurst, Australia: Australian Computer Society.

Cole, M. (1989). *Algorithmic skeletons: Structured management of parallel computation*. London, United Kingdom: Pitman/MIT Press.

Crawley, E. F. (2001). *The Conceive, Design, Implement, Operate (CDIO) syllabus: A statement of goals for undergraduate engineering education*. MIT CDIO (Report No.1). Boston, MA: Massachusetts Institute of Technology.

Crawley, E. F. (2002). *Creating the Conceive, Design, Implement, Operate (CDIO) syllabus: A universal template for engineering education*. Paper presented at the 32nd American Society for Engineering Education/Institute of Electrical and Electronic Engineering (ASEE/IEEE) Frontier in Education Conference, Boston, MA.

Cross, K. P. (1999). *Learning is about making connections: The Cross Papers Number 3*. Mission Viejo, CA: League for Innovation in the Community College.

Culwin, F., Adeboye, K., & Campbell, P. (2006). POOPLEs: Pre-object-orientated programming learning environments. In *Proceedings of the 7th Annual Conference of the subject centre for Information and Computer Sciences of the Higher Education Academy* (pp. 59-63). Newtownabbey, Northern Ireland: Higher Education Academy.

Cunha, J. C., & Lourenço, J. (1998). *An integrated course on parallel and distributed processing*. In Association for Computing Machinery (ACM) Special Interest Group on Computer Science Education (SIGCSE 1998): 29th ACM Technical Symposium on Computer Science Education (pp. 217–221). New York, NY: Association for Computing Machinery.

Dahlgaard, J. J., & Dahlgaard-Park, S. M. (2006). Lean production, six sigma quality, TQM and company culture. *The Total Quality Management (TQM) Magazine*, *18*(3), 263–281.

Davenport, T. H. (1998). Putting the Enterprise into the Enterprise System. *Harvard Business Review*, (July-August): 1–11.

Davenport, T. H. (2000). *Mission critical: Realizing the promise of enterprise systems*. Boston, MA: Harvard Business School Press.

Davey, B. (2010). Special issue on information systems curriculum. *Education and Information Technologies*, *15*(4), 237–238. doi:10.1007/s10639-010-9143-7

Davis, C. H., & Comeau, J. (2004). Enterprise integration in business education: Design and outcomes of a capstone ERP-based undergraduate e-business management course. *Journal of Information Systems Education*, *15*(3), 287–299.

de Wit, H. (2005). *Higher education in Latin America: The international dimension*. Washington, DC: World Bank Publications. doi:10.1596/978-0-8213-6209-9

Dean, J., & Ghemawat, S. (2008). MapReduce: Simplified data processing on large clusters. *Communications of the ACM*, *51*(1), 107–113. doi:10.1145/1327452.1327492

Dean, J., & Ghemawat, S. (2004). *MapReduce: Simplified data processing on large clusters*. In Operating Systems Design and Implementation (OSDI)'04: Sixth Symposium on Operating Systems Design and Implementation (pp. 137–150). Berkeley, CA: USENIX Association (Advanced Computing Systems Association).

Dearing, R. (1997). *Higher education in the learning society*. London, United Kingdom: National Committee of Inquiry into Higher Education.

Delgado, J., & Marín, F. (2000). Evolución en los sistemas de gestión empresarial. Del MRP al ERP. *Economía Industrial*, *331*(1), 51–58.

Demirel, M. (2009). Lifelong learning and schools in the twenty-first century. *Procedia - Social and Behavioral Sciences, 1*, 1709–1716.

Dey, S. K., & Sobhan, M. A. (2007, December). *Guidelines for preparing standard software engineering curriculum: Bangladesh and global perspective*. Paper presented to 10th International Conference on Computer and Information Technology, Dhaka, Bangladesh.

Doherty, G. D. (2008). On quality in education. *Quality Assurance in Education, 16*(3), 255–265. doi:10.1108/09684880810886268

Dublin Institute of Technology (DIT). (2006). *Handbook for academic quality enhancement*. Dublin, Ireland: Dublin Institute of Technology.

Dublin Institute of Technology (DIT). (2007). *Regulations for postgraduate study by research* (4th ed.). Dublin, Ireland: Dublin Institute of Technology.

Duff, T., Hegarty, J., & Hussey, M. (2000). *The story of the Dublin Institute of Technology*. Dublin, Ireland: Blackhall.

Duff, T., Hegarty, J., & Hussey, M. (2000). *Academic quality assurance in Irish higher education: Elements of a handbook*. Dublin, Ireland: Blackhall.

EMERSION project management team. (2004). *EMERSION annual report to EU 2003/04*. Dublin, Ireland: Dublin Institute of Technology School of Computing.

EMERSION project management team. (2005). *EMERSION annual report to EU 2004/05*. Dublin, Ireland: Dublin Institute of Technology School of Computing.

EMERSION project management team. (2006). *EMERSION annual report to EU 2005/06*. Dublin, Ireland: Dublin Institute of Technology School of Computing.

Ertmer, P. A., & Simons, K. D. (2006). Jumping the PBL implementation hurdle: Supporting the efforts of K–12 teachers. *Interdisciplinary Journal of Problem-Based Learning, 1*(1), 40–54.

Esendal, T., & Rogerson, S. (2008, July). *Using technology to incorporate students' work-based experiences into a blended-learning environment*. Paper presented at the International Conference on Information Communication Technologies in Education (ICICTE 2008), Corfu, Greece.

European Association for Quality Assurance in Higher Education (ENQA). (2005). *Standards and guidelines for quality assurance in the European higher education area*. Helsinki, Finland: European Association for Quality Assurance in the European Higher Education.

European Commission. (2003a). *ATHENA - Advanced Technologies for Interoperability of Heterogeneous Enterprise Networks and their Applications: Integrated project proposal. European 6th Framework Programme for Research & Development (FP6-2002-IST-1)*. Brussels, Belgium: European Commission.

European Commission. (2003b). *INTEROP - interoperability research for networked enterprises, applications and software, network of excellence, proposal part B. European 6th Framework Programme for Research & Development*. Brussels, Belgium: European Commission.

European Commission. (2006). *Services directive*. Retrieved August 6, 2010, from http://ec.europa.eu/internal_market/services/services-dir/index_en.htm

European Community. (1986). *Single European Act*. Retrieved October 4, 2010, from http://eur-lex.europa.eu/en/treaties/index.htm

European Universities Association (EUA) Institutional Evaluation Programme. (2006). *EUA reviewers' report: Review of quality assurance in Dublin Institute of Technology*. Brussels, Belgium: European Universities Association.

Ewell, P. T. (1997). Organizing for learning: A new imperative. *American Association for Higher Education Bulletin, 50*(4), 3–6.

Fabra, E., & Camisón, C. (2009). Direct and indirect effects of education on job satisfaction: A structural equation model for the Spanish case. *Economics of Education Review, 28*(5), 600–610. doi:10.1016/j.econedurev.2008.12.002

Fagin, B. (2003). Ada/Mindstorms 3.0. *Institute of Electrical and Electronic Engineering Robotics & Automation Magazine, 10*(2), 19–24.

Fausser, J. (2008). *Maintenance of Oracle e-business suite V11 (Internal report of Internship of M2)*. Talence, France: University of Bordeaux.

Fekete, A. D. (2009). Teaching about threading: Where and what? *Association for Computing Machinery Special Interest Group on Algorithms and Computation Theory (SIGACT) News, 40*(1), 51–57.

Fenwick, J. B. Jr, & Kurtz, B. L. (2005). Intra-curriculum software engineering education. *Association for Computing Machinery Special Interest Group on Computer Science Education (SIGCSE) Bulletin, 37*(1), 540–544.

Finkelstein, A. (1993). European computing curricula: A guide and comparative analysis. *The Computer Journal, 36*(4), 299–319. doi:10.1093/comjnl/36.4.299

Fisher, S., Hunter, T., & MacRosson, W. (2001). A validation study of Belbin's team roles. *European Journal of Work and Organizational Psychology, 10*(2), 121–144. doi:10.1080/13594320143000591

Ford, G., & Gibbs, N. E. (1996). *A mature profession of software engineering* (Technical Report CMU/SEI-96-TR-004, ESC-TR-96-004). Pittsburgh, PA: Carnegie Mellon University, Software Engineering Institute.

Forfás. (2007). *5th report of the expert group on future skills needs- tomorrow's skills needs: Towards a national skills strategy*. Dublin, Ireland: Forfás.

Fouts, J. T., & Chan, J. C. K. (1997). The development of work-study and school enterprises in China's schools. *Journal of Curriculum Studies, 29*(1), 31–46. doi:10.1080/002202797184189

Friedman, T. L. (2005). *The world is flat: A brief history of the twenty-first century*. New York, NY: Farrar, Straus & Giroux.

Gamma, E., Helm, R., Johnson, R., & Vlissides, J. M. (1995). *Design patterns: Elements of reusable object-oriented software*. Boston, MA: Addison-Wesley Longman.

Garba, M., González-Vélez, H., & Roach, D. (2010). *Parallel computational modelling of inelastic neutron scattering in multi-node and multi-core architectures*. In Institute of Electrical and Electronic Engineering High Performance Computing and Communications (IEEE HPCC)-10: International Conference on High Performance Computing and Communications (pp. 509–514). Melbourne, Australia.

Garrison, D. R., Anderson, T., & Archer, W. (2000). Critical inquiry in a text-based environment: Computer conferencing in higher education. *The Internet and Higher Education, 2*(2-3), 1–19.

Garrison, D. R., Anderson, T., & Archer, W. (2001). Critical thinking and computer conferencing: a model and tool to assess cognitive presence. *American Journal of Distance Education, 15*(1), 7–23. doi:10.1080/08923640109527071

Gates, A. Q., Delgado, N., & Mondragon, O. (2000). A structured approach for managing a practical software engineering course. In *Proceedings of the 30th Annual Frontiers in Education Conference* (1, pp. T1C/21-T1C/26). Washington, DC: Institute of Electrical and Electronic Engineering Computer Society.

González-Vélez, H., & Cole, M. (2010). Adaptive structured parallelism for distributed heterogeneous architectures: A methodological approach with pipelines and farms. *Concurrency and Computation, 22*(15), 2073–2094.

González-Vélez, H., & Leyton, M. (2010). A survey of algorithmic skeleton frameworks: High-level structured parallel programming enablers. *Software, Practice & Experience, 40*(12), 1135–1160. doi:10.1002/spe.1026

Gorgone, J. T., Gray, P., Stohr, E., Valacich, J. S., & Wigand, R. (2006). Master of Science in Information Systems (MSIS) 2006: Curriculum preview. *Communications of the Association for Information Systems, 15*, 544–554.

Goth, G. (2009). Entering a parallel universe. *Communications of the ACM, 52*(9), 15–17. doi:10.1145/1562164.1562171

Guthrie, R. W., & Guthrie, R. A. (2000). Integration of enterprise system software in the undergraduate curriculum. *Proceedings of the Information Systems Education Conference (ISECON 2000), 17*(301).

Hacker, T. J., & Springer, J. A. (2008). *Meeting the data challenge: Curriculum development for parallel data systems*. In Special Interest Group on Information Technology Education (SIGITE)'08: 9th Association for Computing Machinery SIGITE Conference on Information Technology Education (pp. 153–156). New York, NY: Association for Computing Machinery.

Hao, Y. (2005). *A study of institutional alternative for hi-tech industry development of China's universities.* Unpublished doctoral dissertation, Huazhong University of Science and Technology, China. (in Chinese).

Hartman, J., & Sanders, D. (1991). *Teaching a course in parallel processing with limited resources.* In Association for Computing Machinery Special Interest Group on Computer Science Education (SIGCSE)'91: 22nd SIGCSE Technical Symposium on Computer Science education (pp. 97–101). New York, NY: Association for Computing Machinery.

Harvey, L. (2008). International network of quality assurance agencies in higher education. *Quality Control and Applied Statistics, 52*(6), 619–620.

Harvey, L., Green, D., & Burrows, A. (1993). Assessing quality in higher education: A transbinary research project. *Assessment & Evaluation in Higher Education, 18*(2), 143–148. doi:10.1080/0260293930180206

Harvey, L., & Knight, P. (1996). *Transforming higher education.* Buckingham, United Kingdom: Open University Press and Society for Research into Higher Education.

Hawking, P., McCarthy, B., & Stein, A. (2004). Second wave ERP education. *Journal of Information Systems Education, 15*(3), 327–332.

Hawking, P., Ramp, A., & Shackleton, P. (2001). Information systems IS'97 model curriculum and enterprise resource planning systems. *Business Process Management Journal, 7*(3), 225–233. doi:10.1108/14637150110392700

Hayes, J. H., Lethbridge, T. C., & Port, D. (2003). Evaluating individual contribution toward group software engineering projects. In *Proceedings of the 25th International Conference on Software Engineering* (pp. 622-627). Washington, DC: Institute of Electrical and Electronic Engineering Computer Society.

Hides, M. T., Davies, J., & Jackson, S. (2004). Implementation of EFQM excellence model self-assessment in the UK higher education sector: Lessons learned from other sectors. *The Total Quality Management (TQM) Magazine, 16*(3), 194–201.

Higher Education & Training Council (HETAC). (2008). Policy for collaborative programmes, transnational programmes and joint awards. Retrieved August 6, 2010, from http://www.hetac.ie/docs/Policy%20for%20 collaborative%20programmes,%20transnational%20 programmes%20and%20joint%20awards.pdf

Hilburn, T. B., Towhidnejad, M., Nangia, S., Li, S., & Hilburn, T. (2006, October). *A case study project for software engineering education.* Presented at the 36th Annual American Society for Engineering Education/ Institute of Electrical and Electronic Engineering (ASEE/ IEEE) Frontiers in Education Conference, San Diego, CA.

Hofstede, G. (1980). Culture and organizations. *International Studies of Management & Organization, 10*(4), 15–41.

Hogan, J. M., Smith, G., & Thomas, R. (2005). Tight spirals and industry clients: The modern software engineering education experience. In A. Young & D. Tolhurst (Eds.), *Proceedings of the 7th Australasian Conference on Computing Education* (pp. 217-222). Darlinghurst, Australia: Australian Computer Society.

Honey, P., & Mumford, A. (1992). *The manual of learning styles* (3rd ed.). Maidenhead, United Kingdom: Honey.

Horn, E., & Kupries, M. (2003). A study program for professional software engineering. In *Proceedings of the 16th Conference on Software Engineering Education and Training (CSEE&T 2003)* (pp. 298-308). Washington, DC: Institute of Electrical and Electronic Engineering Computer Society.

Huggins, K. (2004). Lifelong learning-the key to competence in the intensive care unit? *Intensive & Critical Care Nursing, 20*(1), 38–44. doi:10.1016/j.iccn.2003.10.001

Hunt, C. S., Regan, E. A., Everett, D. R., Green, D. T., Hunt, D., & Becka, P. (2010). Integrating enterprise systems concepts in the B-school: A regional university perspective. *Information Systems Education Journal, 8*(9), 3–13.

Huynh, M. Q., & Chu, H. W. (2010). Exploring the open-source ERP alternative for teaching business process integration in supply chain management. *Proceedings of the Academy of Information and Management Sciences, 14*(1), 32–36.

Huynh, M. Q., & Pinto, I. (2010). Open source ERP applications: A reality check for their possible adoption and use in teaching business process integration. *Information Systems Education Journal, 8*(69), 3–11.

Imai, M. (1986). *Kaizen: The key to Japan's competitive success*. New York, NY: McGraw-Hill.

Instructional Management Systems (IMS) Global Learning Consortium. (2003). *IMS learning design: Information model*, version 1.0 final specification. Retrieved October 15, 2010, from http://www.imsglobal.org/

Instructional Management Systems (IMS) Global Learning Consortium. (1999-2007). *Website*. Retrieved October 15, 2010, from http://www.imsglobal.org/

International Business Machines (IBM). (2010). *IBM academic initiative*. Retrieved October 15, 2010, from http://www.ibm.com/developerworks/university/academicinitiative

International Organization for Standardization (ISO DIS 16100). (2000). *Manufacturing software capability profiling - part 1: Framework for interoperability* (ISO TC/184/SC5, ICS 25.040.01).

International Organization for Standardization/International Electrotechnical Commission. (2001). *Software engineering - product quality - part 1: Quality model.* (ISO/IEC 9126-1).

International Project Management Association. (2006). *IPMA Competency Baseline (ICB) version 3.0*. Nijkerk, The Netherlands: International Project Management Association.

Ishiyama, J. (2010) What is the Impact of In-Class Active Learning Techniques? A Meta Analysis of the Existing Literature. *APSA 2010 Annual Meeting Paper.* 1-15

Iskanius, P. (2009, July). *The ERP project risk assessment: A case study*. Paper presented to the World Congress on Engineering, London, United Kingdom.

Ivanov, L., Hadimioglu, H., & Hoffman, M. (2008). A new look at parallel computing in the computer science curriculum. *Journal of Computing Sciences in Colleges, 23*(5), 176–179.

Jaakkola, H., Henno, J., & Rudas, I. J. (2006). IT curriculum as a complex emerging process. In [Washington, DC: Institute of Electrical and Electronic Engineering.]. *Proceedings of the Institute of Electrical and Electronic Engineering International Conference on Computational Cybernetics, ICCC,* 1–5. doi:10.1109/ICCCYB.2006.305731

Jæger, B., Rudra, A., Aitken, A., Chang, V., & Helgheim, B. (2010, January). *Teaching business process concepts using enterprise systems in a globalized context*. Paper presented to the 43rd Hawaii International Conference on System Sciences in Koloa, Kauai, Hawaii.

Jia, Z. (2008). *Pricing strategy for Point P based on analysis and comparison of commonly used pricing strategy (Internal report of Internship of M2)*. Talence, France: University of Bordeaux.

Joint Task Force on Computing Curricula. (2004). *Software engineering 2004: Curriculum guidelines for undergraduate degree programs in software engineering*. Washington, DC: Institute of Electrical and Electronic Engineering Computer Society, Association for Computing Machinery.

Joseph, G., & George, A. (2002). ERP, learning communities, and curriculum integration. *Journal of Information Systems Education, 13*(1), 51–58.

Kells, H. R. (1995). Building a national evaluation system for higher education: Lessons from diverse settings. *Higher Education in Europe, 20*(1), 18–26. doi:10.1080/0379772950200104

Kells, H. R. (1999). National higher education evaluation systems: Methods for analysis and some propositions for the research and policy void. *Higher Education, 38*(2), 209–232. doi:10.1023/A:1003704015735

Kitchenham, B., Budgen, D., Bereton, P., & Woodall, P. (2005). An investigation of software engineering curricula. *Journal of Systems and Software, 74*(3), 325–335. doi:10.1016/j.jss.2004.03.016

Knight, J. (1999). Internationalization of higher education. In *Quality and internationalisation in higher education* (pp. 13–28). Paris, France: Organisation for Economic Co-operation and Development (OECD) Publishing.

Knowledge Management Research Group. (2002). *Personalized access to distributed learning resources (PADLR)*. Retrieved October 15, 2010, from http://kmr.nada.kth.se/

Knowles, M. S. (1978). *The adult learner: A neglected species* (2nd ed.). Houston, TX: Gulf.

Kontagora, M., & González-Vélez, H. (2010, Feb). *Benchmarking a MapReduce environment on a full virtualisation platform*. In Complex, Intelligent and Software Intensive Systemsw (CISIS) 2010: 4th International Conference on Complex, Intelligent and Software Intensive Systems (pp. 433-438). Washington, DC: Institute of Electrical and Electronic Engineering.

Kornecki, A. J., Khajenoori, S., Gluch, D. P., & Kameli, N. (2003). On a partnership between software industry and academia. In *Proceedings of the 16th Conference on Software Engineering Education and Training (CSEE&T 2003)* (pp. 60-69). Washington, DC: Institute of Electrical and Electronic Engineering Computer Society.

Koska, D. K., & Romano, J. D. (1988). *Countdown to the future: The manufacturing engineer in the 21st century*. Dearborn, MI: Society of Manufacturing Engineers.

Kral, J., & Zemlicka, M. (2008). Engineering education - a great challenge to software engineering. In *Proceedings of the 7th Institute of Electrical and Electronic Engineering/Advanced Cellular Internet Service International Conference on Computer and Information Science (ICIS 2008)* (pp. 488-495). Washington, DC: Institute of Electrical and Electronic Engineering.

Kuchana, P. (2004). *Software architecture design patterns in Java*. New York, NY: Auerbach Publications. doi:10.1201/9780203496213

Kulmar, K., & van Hillegersberg, J. (2000). ERP - experiences and evolution. *Communications of the ACM, 43*(4), 23–26.

Kumar, V., Maheshwari, B., & Kumar, U. (2002). Enterprise resource planning systems adoption process: A survey of Canadian organizations. *International Journal of Production Research, 40*(3), 509–523. doi:10.1080/00207540110092414

Lawhead, P. B., Bland, C. G., Barnes, D. J., Duncan, M. E., Goldweber, M., Hollingsworth, R. G., & Schep, M. (2003). A road map for teaching introductory programming using LEGO Mindstorms robots. *Association for Computing Machinery Special Interest Group on Computer Science Education Bulletin, 35*(2), 191–201.

Lawless, D., Gordon, D., O'Leary, C., & Collins, M. (2004b, September). *Determining key skills for IT graduates in the emerging knowledge-based economy*. Paper presented at the Inaugural Conference of the All Ireland Society for Higher Education (AISHE), Dublin, Ireland.

Lawless, D., Gordon, D., O'Leary, C., Mtenzi, F., Xu, X., & Bechkoum, K. (2005, April). *Establishing undergraduate research communities*. Paper presented at the Computers and Learning 2005 Conference, Bristol, United Kingdom.

Lawless, D., Wu, B., Carroll, D., Gordon, D., Hussey, M., O'Leary, C., et al. O'Shea, B. & Xu, X. (Eds.). (2007). *An industry-oriented model for software education in China: Adapting an Irish model to Chinese conditions*. Dublin, Ireland: Blackhall.

Lawless, D., Wu, B., Xu, X., Yuan, C., & Bechkoum, K. (2004a, September). *Requirements for an industry-oriented IT education model to support the emerging knowledge economy in China*. Paper presented at the 2nd International Conference on Knowledge Economy and Development of Science and Technology, Beijing, China.

Lee, J., Siau, K., & Hong, S. (2003). Enterprise integration with ERP and EAI. *Communications of the ACM, 46*(2), 54–60. doi:10.1145/606272.606273

Lehtinen, E., Hakkarainen, K., Lipponen, L., Rahikainen, M., & Muukkonen, H. (1999). *Computer supported collaborative learning: A review of research and development. The J. H. G. I. Giesderbs Reports on Education, 10*. Nijmegen, The Netherlands: University of Nijmegen, Department of Educational Sciences.

Leijen, D., Schulte, W., & Burckhardt, S. (2009). The design of a task parallel library. *Association for Computing Machinery Special Interest Group on Programming Languages Notices, 44*(10), 227–242.

Lethbridge, T. C. (2000a). What knowledge is important to a software professional? *Institute of Electrical and Electronic Engineering Computer, 33*(5), 44–50.

Lethbridge, T. C. (2000b). Priorities for the education and training of software engineers. *Journal of Systems and Software, 53*(1), 53–71. doi:10.1016/S0164-1212(00)00009-1

Li, J. (2003). Exploration and practice in the construction of practical training bases in higher vocational education. [in Chinese]. *Vocational and Technical Education, 24*(22), 19–21.

Li, Z. (2008). *Data mining applied in cross-selling (Internal report of Internship of M2).* Talence, France: University of Bordeaux.

Lindoo, E., & Wilson, J. L. (2010). Offering process-centric education by way of an SAP simulator. *Journal of Computing Sciences in Colleges, 26*(2), 132–138.

Ling, F. Y., Low, S. P., Wang, S. Q., & Lim, H. H. (2009). Key project management practices affecting Singaporean firms' project performance in China. *International Journal of Project Management, 27*(1), 59–71. doi:10.1016/j. ijproman.2007.10.004

Maguire, B. (2010, April). Issues arising from qualifications frameworks in Europe. In the *Proceedings of the Irish Bologna Experts Conference.* Dublin, Ireland.

Major, C., & Palmer, B. (2001). Assessing the effectiveness of problem-based earning in higher education: Lessons from the literature. *Academic Exchange Quarterly, 5*(1), 4–9.

Mäkitalo, K., Salo, P., Häkkinen, P., & Järvelä, S. (2001, March). *Analysing the mechanism of common ground in collaborative Web-based interaction.* Paper presented at the European Conference on Computer-Supported Collaborative Learning (Euro CSCL 2001), Maastricht, The Netherlands.

Markus, M. L., Tanis, C., & van Fenema, P. C. (2000). Multisite ERP implementations. *Communications of the ACM, 43*(4), 42–46. doi:10.1145/332051.332068

Marshall, I. W., & Roadknight, C. M. (2001, October). *Management of future data networks: an approach based on bacterial colony behavior.* Paper presented at the Institute of Electrical and Electronic Engineering (IEEE) Conference on Systems, Man & Cybernetics, Tucson, AZ.

Mattson, T. G., Sanders, B. A., & Massingill, B. L. (2004). *Patterns for parallel programming.* Boston, MA: Addison-Wesley Longman.

McFarland, D., & Hamilton, D. (2006). Factors affecting student performance and satisfaction: Online versus traditional course delivery. *Journal of Computer Information Systems, 46*(2), 25–32.

McGettrick, A., Boyle, R., Ibbett, R., Lloyd, J., Lovegrove, G., & Mander, K. (2005). Grand challenges in computing education - a summary. *The Computer Journal, 48*(1), 42–48. doi:10.1093/comjnl/bxh064

McGourty, J., Dominick, P., & Reilly, R. R. (1998). Incorporating student peer review and feedback into the assessment process. In *Proceedings of the 28th Annual Frontiers in Education Conference* (1, pp. 14-18). Washington, DC: Institute of Electrical and Electronic Engineering Computer Society.

Meltzer, D. E., & Manivannan, K. (2002). Transforming the lecture-hall environment: The fully interactive physics lecture. *American Journal of Physics, 70*, 639–654. doi:10.1119/1.1463739

Microsoft. (2006). *Computer game production curriculum 2004 RFP awards.* Retrieved October 15, 2010, at http// research.microsoft.com/ur/us/fundingopps/Gaming_curriculumRFP_awards.aspx

Microsoft. (2006). *Microsoft robotics studio.* Retrieved February 14, 2008, from http://msdn2.microsoft.com/ en-us/robotics/aa731520.aspx

Ministry of Education. (2001). *China, File No. [2001] 3.* Beijing, China: Government of China.

Mishra, A., Cagiltay, N. E., & Kilic, O. (2007). Software engineering education: Some important dimensions. *European Journal of Engineering Education, 32*(3), 349–361. doi:10.1080/03043790701278607

Moller, C. (2005). ERP II: A conceptual framework for next-generation enterprise systems? *Journal of Enterprise Information Management, 18*(4), 483–497. doi:10.1108/17410390510609626

Moon, Y. B. (2007). Enterprise resource planning (ERP): A review of the literature. *International Journal of Management & Enterprise Development, 4*(3), 235–264. doi:10.1504/IJMED.2007.012679

Morris, I. (2009). *Resilience amid turmoil: Benchmarking IT industry competitiveness 2009*. The Economist Intelligence Unit. Retrieved October 15, 2010, from http://global.bsa.org/2009eiu/study/2009_eiu_global.pdf

Noguera, J. H., & Watson, E. F. (2004). Effectiveness of using an enterprise system to teach process-centered concepts in business education. *Journal of Enterprise Information Management, 17*(1), 56–74. doi:10.1108/09576050410510953

O'Leary, C., Lawless, D., Gordon, D., Haifeng, L., & Bechkoum, K. (2006a). Developing a software engineering curriculum for the emerging software industry in China. In *Proceedings of the 19th Conference on Software Engineering Education and Training (CSEE&T 2006)* (pp. 115-122). Washington, DC: Institute of Electrical and Electronic Engineering.

O'Leary, C., Lawless, D., Gordon, D., Carroll, D., Mtenzi, F., & Collins, M. (2006). *3D alignment in the adaptive software engineering curriculum*. Paper presented at the 36th Annual American Association for Engineering Education/Institute of Electrical and Electronic Engineering (AAEE/IEEE) Frontiers in Education Conference. San Diego, CA.

Oliveira, P. C., Oliveira, C. G., Neri de Souza, F., & Costa, N. (2006). Teaching strategies to promote active learning in higher education. In A. Méndez-Vilas, A. Solano Martín, J. A. Mesa González & J. Mesa González (Eds.), *Current developments in technology-assisted education volume 1: General issues, pedagogical issues* (pp. 636-640). Badajoz, Spain: Formatex.

Oracle. (1999). *Code convention for the Java programming language*. Retrieved October 12, 2010, from http://www.oracle.com/technetwork/java/codeconvtoc-136057.html

Oracle. (2010). *Javadoc – the Java API documentation generator*. Retrieved on October 12, 2010, from http://download.oracle.com/javase/1.4.2/docs/tooldocs/windows/javadoc.html

Organization for Economic Co-operation and Development (OECD). (1995). *Education at a glance*. Paris, France: Organization for Economic Co-operation and Development.

Organization for Economic Co-operation and Development (OECD). (2004). *Review of national policies for higher education: Review of higher education in Ireland, examiners' report, EDU/EC (2004) 14*. Paris, France: Organization for Economic Co-operation and Development.

Ortega-Arjona, J. L. (2010). *Patterns for parallel software design* (1st ed.). Chichester, UK: John Wiley & Sons.

Panorama. (2010). *2010 ERP report: Organizational change management*. Denver, CO: Panorama Consulting Group.

Pelagatti, S. (1998). *Structured development of parallel programs*. Bristol, UK: Taylor & Francis.

Peng, G. C., & Nunes, M. B. (2009). Surfacing ERP exploitation risks through a risk ontology. *Industrial Management & Data Systems, 109*(7), 926–942. doi:10.1108/02635570910982283

Petkovic, D., Thompson, G., & Todtenhoefer, R. (2006). Teaching practical software engineering and global software engineering: evaluation and comparison. In *Proceedings of 11th Annual Special Interest Group on Computer Science Education Conference on Innovation and Technology in Computer Science Education (ITiCSE).* (pp. 294-298). New York, NY: Association for Computing Machinery.

Pinto, Y. (2010). A strategy, implementation and results of a flexible competency based curriculum. *ACM Inroads, 1*(2), 54–61.

Pittarese, T. (2009). Teaching fundamental business concepts to computer science and information technology students through enterprise resource planning and a simulation game. *Journal of Computing Sciences in Colleges, 25*(2), 131–137.

Poole, B. (2010). Quality, semantics and the two cultures. *Quality Assurance in Education, 18*(1), 6–18. doi:10.1108/09684881011015963

Porter, M. E. (1996). What is strategy? *Harvard Business Review*, (November-December): 61–78.

Pressman, R. S. (2009). *Software engineering: A practitioner's approach* (7th ed.). Maidenhead, United Kingdom: McGraw-Hill.

Prey, J. C. (1995, November). *Co-operative learning in an undergraduate computer science curriculum.* Paper presented at the 25th Annual American Society for Engineering Education/Institute of Electrical and Electronic Engineering (ASEE/IEEE) Annual Frontiers in Education Conference, Atlanta, GA.

Price, B. A., Richards, M., Petre, M., Hirst, A., & Johnson, J. (2003). Developing robotics e-teaching for teamwork. *International Journal of Continuing Engineering Education and Lifelong Learning, 13*(1/2), 190–205.

Proceedings of the 2nd China-Europe International Symposium on Software Industry-Oriented Education. (2005). *Journal of Harbin Institute of Technology (New Series), 12 (Supplement).* Harbin, China: Harbin Institute of Technology.

Proceedings of the 4th China-Europe International Symposium on Software Industry-Oriented Education. (2007). *Acta Scientiarum Naturalium, 46*(2). Guang Zhou, China

Proceedings of the 6th China-Europe International Symposium on Software Industry Oriented Education. (2010). *Computer Education, 9*(117). Xi'an, China.

Protégé. (2000). *Protégé 2000 user guide.* Retrieved October 15, 2010, from http://protege.standford.edu/doc/users_guide/index.html

Quality Assurance Agency. (2004). *Code of practice for the assurance of academic quality and standards in higher education: Collaborative provision and flexible and distributed learning* (including e-learning). Retrieved August 6, 2010, from http://www.qaa.ac.uk/academicinfrastructure/codeOfPractice/section2/collab2004.pdf

Rabaa'i, A. A., Bandara, W., & Gable, G. G. (2010). Enterprise systems in universities: A teaching case. *Americas Conference on Information Systems (AMCIS 2010) Proceedings,* paper 171.

Rabhi, F. A., & Gorlatch, S. (Eds.). (2003). *Patterns and skeletons for parallel and distributed computing.* London, UK: Springer-Verlag. doi:10.1007/978-1-4471-0097-3

Reichlmayr, T. J. (2006). Collaborating with industry-strategies for an undergraduate software engineering program. In the *Proceedings of the 3rd International Summit on Software Engineering Education (SSEEIII)* (pp. 13-16). New York, NY: Association for Computing Machinery.

Reigeluth, C. M., & Darwazeh, A. (1982). The elaboration theory's procedure for designing instruction: A conceptual approach. *Journal of Instructional Development, 5*(3), 22–32. doi:10.1007/BF02905492

Reinders, J. (2007). *Intel threading building blocks: Outfitting C++ for multi-core processor parallelism.* Sebastopol, CA: O'Reilly Media.

Rompelman, O., & Vries, J. D. (2002). Practical training and internships in engineering education: Educational goals and assessment. *European Journal of Engineering Education, 27*(2), 173–180. doi:10.1080/03043790210129621

Saiedian, H. (1999). Software engineering education and training for the next millennium. *Journal of Systems and Software, 49,* 113–115. doi:10.1016/S0164-1212(99)00082-5

Sanders, L. (2004). Strategies for teaching something new. *Science Scope, 28*(1), 26–27.

Savin-Baden, M. (2000). *Problem-based learning in higher education: Untold stories.* Buckingham, United Kingdom: The Society for Research into Higher Education & Open University Press.

Schaller, N. C., & Kitchen, A. T. (1995). Experiences in teaching parallel computing - five years later. *Association for Computing Machinery Special Interest Group on Computer Science Education Bulletin, 27*(3), 15–20.

Scheer, A.-W. (1994). *Business process engineering: Reference models for industrial enterprises* (2nd ed.). Berlin, Germany: Springer.

Schmidt, A., & Kunzmann, C. (2006). Towards a human resource development ontology for combining competence management and technology-enhanced workplace learning. In *Lecture Notes in Computer Science (LNCS), 4278/2006* (pp. 1078–1087). Berlin, Germany: Springer Verlag.

School of Software at Harbin Institute of Technology. (2009). *White Paper on software industry oriented education.* Harbin, China: Harbin Institute of Technology. (in Chinese).

SEEK. (2004). *Curriculum guidelines for undergraduate degree programs in software engineering.* Retrieved October 20, 2010, from http//sites.computer.org/ccse/

Shackelford, R., McGettrick, A., Sloan, R., Topi, H., Davies, G., & Kamali, R. (2006). *Computing curricula 2005: The overview report.* In Association for Computing Machinery Special Interest Group on Computer Science Education (SIGCSE)'06: 37th SIGCSE Technical Symposium on Computer Science Education (pp. 456–457). New York, NY: Association for Computing Machinery.

Shaw, M., & Garlan, D. (1996). *Software architecture: Perspective on an emerging discipline.* Upper Saddle River, NJ: Prentice Hall.

Shaw, M., Herbsleb, J. D., & Ozkaya, I. (2005, May). *Deciding what to design: Closing a gap in software engineering education.* Paper presented to the 27th International Conference on Software Engineering (ICSE 2005), St. Louis, MO.

Shepherd, C. (2010). *Evaluating online learning.* Retrieved October 15, 2010, from http://www2.warwick.ac.uk/services/ldc/resource/evaluation/elearning/

Shi, Y., & Tsang, M. (2008). Evaluation of adult literacy education in the United States: A review of methodological issues. *Educational Research Review, 3*(2), 187–217. doi:10.1016/j.edurev.2007.10.004

Shtub, A. (2001). A framework for teaching and training in the enterprise resource planning (ERP) era. *International Journal of Production Research, 39*(3), 567–576. doi:10.1080/00207540010009714

Si, S. Z. (2004). Discussion on the role orientation and development model of school-running enterprise in our country. [in Chinese]. *Technology and Innovation Management, 25*(4), 53–55.

Sorbonne Joint Declaration. (1998). *Joint declaration on harmonisation of the architecture of the European higher education system.* Paris, France: Sorbonne University.

Sourceforge. (2006). *LeJOS: Java for Mindstorms.* Retrieved February 14, 2008, from http://lejos.sourceforge.net/p_technologies/rcx/downloads.php

Stirewalt, R. E. K. (2004). Teaching software engineering bottom-up. In *Proceedings of the 2004 American Society for Engineering Education Annual Conference & Exposition*, Session Number 3532 (pp. 13755-13763). American Society for Engineering Education.

Straeter, W., & Kuensting, B. (2007). *LMS-Lego Mindstorms simulator.* Retrieved October 31, 2007, from http://ddi.uni-paderborn.de/en/software/lego-mindstorms-simulator.html

Su, H., Jodis, S., & Zhang, H. (2007). Providing an integrated software development environment for undergraduate software engineering courses. *Journal of Computing Sciences in Colleges, 23*(2), 143–149.

Swebok. (2008). *Software engineering body of knowledge.* Retrieved October 20, 2010, from http://www.swebok.org/index.html

Takwale, R., Prasad, V. S., Koul, V., Sinclair, P. K., Misra, S., & Kumar, V. … Banerjee, S. (2007). *Open and distance education. Recommendations from the Working Group on Open and Distance Education.* New Delhi, India: National Knowledge Commission.

Theling, T., & Loos, P. (2005). Teaching ERP systems by a multiperspective approach. *Americas Conference on Information Systems (AMCIS) 2005 Proceedings*, paper 151.

Times Online. (2010). *Good university guide* (report). News International Limited, London, UK: Times Newspapers Ltd. Retrieved from http://www.timesonline.co.uk/tol/life_and_style/education/good_university_guide/

Toll, W. E. (1995). *Decision points in the introduction of parallel processing into the undergraduate curriculum.* In Association for Computing Machinery Special Interest Group on Computer Science Education (SIGCSE)'95: 26th SIGCSE Technical Symposium on Computer Science Education (pp. 136–140). New York, NY: Association for Computing Machinery.

Tomayko, J. E. (1987). *Teaching a project-intensive introduction to software engineering.* (Technical Report SEI-SR-87-1). Pittsburgh, PA: Software Engineering Institute, Carnegie Mellon University.

Torbert, S., Vishkin, U., Tzur, R., & Ellison, D. J. (2010). *Is teaching parallel algorithmic thinking to high school students possible? One teacher's experience.* In Association for Computing Machinery Special Interest Group on Computer Science Education (SIGCSE)'10: 41st SIGCSE Technical Symposium on Computer Science Education (pp. 290–294). New York, NY: Association for Computing Machinery.

Towell, E. (2003). Teaching ethics in the software engineering curriculum. In *Proceedings of the 16th Conference on Software Engineering Education and Training (CSEE&T 2003)* (pp. 150-157). Washington, DC: Institute of Electrical and Electronic Engineering Computer Society.

Trandafir, I., & Borozan, A.-M. (2007, March). *E-learning design based on personalization requirements*. Paper presented to the International Technology, Education and Development (INTED 2007) Conference. Valencia, Spain

Trevisan, M. S. (2004). Practical training in evaluation: A review of the literature. *The American Journal of Evaluation, 25*(2), 255–272.

Turner, S., & Hill, G. (2008). Robots within the teaching of problem-solving. *Subject Centre for Information and Computer Sciences of the Higher Education Academy, 7*(1), 108–119.

United Nations Educational, Scientific and Cultural Organization. (1996). *La educación encierra un tesoro. Informe a la UNESCO de la Comisión Internacional sobre la Educación para el siglo XXI*. Paris, France: United Nations Educational, Scientific and Cultural Organization.

United Nations Educational, Scientific and Cultural Organization (UNESCO)/Organization for Economic Co-operation and Development (OECD). (2005). *Guidelines on quality provision in cross-border higher education*. Retrieved August 6, 2010, from http://portal.unesco.org/education/en/ev.php-URL_ID=29228&URL_DO=DO_TOPIC&URL_SECTION=201.html

University of Minnesota. (2003). *Five steps in problem-solving*. Retrieved October 10, 2003, from http://cda.mrs.umn.edu/~fauxr/computing/problemsolve.html

UPV. (2005). *Proyecto general de la UPV para la promoción y dinamización de la convergencia europea*. Retrieved October 30, 2010, from http://www.upv.es/miw/infoweb/pace/ProyectoGeneral.pdf

Vallespir, B., & Doumeingts, G. (2006). *The GRAI (graphs of interlinked results and activities) method*. Talence, University of Bordeaux 1: Interop Network of Excellence Project tutorial.

Van Damme, D. (2002). Trends and models in international quality assurance in higher education in relation to trade in education. *Education Management and Policy, 14*(3), 93–136. doi:10.1787/hemp-v14-art21-en

Van der Wende, M. (1999). Quality assurance of internationalisation and internationalisation of quality assurance. In *Quality and internationalisation in higher education* (pp. 225–235). Paris, France: Organisation for Economic Co-operation and Development (OECD) Publications.

Vluggen, M., & Bollen, L. (2005). Teaching enterprise resource planning in a business curriculum. *International Journal of Information and Operation Management Education, 1*(1), 44–57. doi:10.1504/IJIOME.2005.007447

Waks, S. (1995). *Curriculum design: From an art towards a science*. Hamburg, Germany: Tempus.

Waks, S., & Frank, M. (2000). Engineering curriculum versus industry needs - a case study. *Institute of Electrical and Electronic Engineering Transactions on Education, 43*(4), 349–352.

Wang, Y. (2008). *Improvement and extension of professional search engine (Internal report of Internship of M2)*. Talence, France: University of Bordeaux.

Watson, P. (2002). The role and integration of learning outcomes into the educational process. *Active Learning in Higher Education, 3*(3), 205–219. doi:10.1177/1469787402003003002

Watts, H. (1989). *Managing the software process*. Reading, MA: Addison Wesley.

Wen, J. (2003). *Government work report*. 10th Chinese National People's Congress (NPC). Beijing, China: Government of China.

West, M. A. (2004). *Effective teamwork: Practical lessons from organizational research* (2nd ed.). Chichester, United Kingdom: Wiley-Blackwell.

Wilkinson, B., & Allen, M. (1999a). *Parallel programming: Techniques and applications using networked workstations and parallel computers*. Upper Saddle River, NJ: Prentice-Hall, Inc.

Wilkinson, B., & Allen, M. (1999b). A state-wide senior parallel programming course. *Institute of Electrical and Electronic Engineering (IEEE) Transactions on Education, 42*(3), 167–173. doi:10.1109/13.779894

Wilkinson, B., & Ferner, C. (2008). *Towards a top-down approach to teaching an undergraduate grid computing course.* In Association for Computing Machinery Special Interest Group on Computer Science Education (SIGCSE 2008): 39th SIGCSE Technical Symposium on Computer Science Education (pp. 126–130). New York, NY: Association for Computing Machinery.

Williams, A. B. (2003). The qualitative impact of using Lego Mindstorms robot to teach computer engineering. *Institute of Electrical and Electronic Engineering (IEEE) Transactions on Education, 46*, 206. doi:10.1109/TE.2002.808260

Wing, J. (2006). Computational thinking. *Communications of the ACM, 49*(3), 33. doi:10.1145/1118178.1118215

Wohlin, C., & Regnell, B. (1999). Strategies for industrial relevance in software engineering education. *Journal of Systems and Software, 49*(2-3), 125–134. doi:10.1016/S0164-1212(99)00085-0

Woodhouse, D. (1999). Quality and quality assurance. In *Quality and internationalisation in higher education* (pp. 29–40). Paris, France: Organisation for Economic Co-operation and Development (OECD) Publishing.

World Bank. (2000). *Constructing knowledge societies: Challenges for tertiary education.* New York, NY: World Bank.

World Trade Organisation. (1995). *General agreement on trade in services.* Retrieved August 6, 2010, from http://www.wto.org/english/tratop_e/serv_e/gatsintr_e.htm

Wu, B., & Bourrières, J.-P. (Eds.). (2010). Educate adaptive talents for IT applications in enterprises and interoperability. In *Proceedings of 5th China-Europe International Symposium on Software Industry Oriented Education).* Talence, France: University of Bordeaux.

Wu, B., MacNamee, B., Xu, X., & Guo, W. (Eds.). (2007). *Proceedings of the 3rd China-Europe International Symposium on Software Industry-Oriented Education.* Dublin, Ireland: Blackhall.

Xu, X. (2006). The approach and practice of software industry-oriented education in China. *Proceedings of the 2nd China-Europe International Symposium on Software Industry-Oriented Education.* [new series]. *Journal of Harbin Institute of Technology, 12*, 1–3.

Yang, W. (2008). *Monitoring work situation of servers in Saint-Gobain Point P (Internal report of Internship of M2).* Talence, France: University of Bordeaux.

Young, M. (2005). *National qualifications frameworks: Their feasibility and effective implementation in developing countries.* Geneva, Switzerland: International Labour Organisation.

Zuser, W., Hetzl, J., Grechenig, T., & Bernhart, M. (2006). *Dimensions of software engineering course design.* IEEE Computer Society 28th International Conference on Software Engineering (pp. 667-672). Washington, DC: Institute of Electrical and Electronic Engineering.

About the Contributors

Matthew Hussey: Emeritus Professor, Director of Faculty of Science of Dublin Institute of Technology, Ireland (1994-2007), Head of Department of Physics (1983-1994). B.E. (National University of Ireland, Dublin), M.Sc. and Ph.D. (University of Pennsylvania, Philadelphia) in 1963, 1967 and 1970 respectively. Main research and publication areas (over twenty books published and over 200 book chapters, peer-reviewed papers and conference proceedings): medical physics and bio-engineering, theory of ultrasound, ultrasound imaging and image analysis, theory of electrocardiography, science of biomaterials (dental, optometric and others), textbooks and other science publications in Irish language, higher education policies and procedures, including quality assurance, research development and links with industry.

Bing Wu: Head of the Computer Science Department at the Dublin Institute of Technology (DIT), Ireland. B.Sc. and M.Sc. in China, Ph.D from University of Manchester Institute of Science and Technology (UMIST), United Kingdom in 1996. Worked in the Department of Computer Science, Trinity College Dublin (1996-1998) and joined DIT in 1998. Research interests include knowledge representation and management, system engineering and re-engineering, and application of advanced computing techniques to real-world situations, such as healthcare informatics and bio-informatics, as well as industry-oriented software education. Served vice-chair of the project steering committee and general project manager for the EMERSION project, a 3-year EU Asia-Link funded project which was completed in 2006.

Xiaofei Xu: Professor and Dean of School of Software in Harbin Institute of Technology (HIT), one of Top-Nine Universities in China. B.S., M.S. and Ph.D. from HIT. Research interests include enterprise computing, interoperability, modelling, resource planning and supply chain management systems, service computing and service engineering, databases and data mining, knowledge management, software engineering, and others. Leader of more than thirty Chinese national research and international co-operation projects. Author or co-author of over 300 refereed papers, four academic books and on editorial boards of nine academic journals. A member of the Expert Group of Computer Science and Technology in the Academic Degree Committee of the State Council of China, a standing member of the Council of China Computer Federation, vice-chairman of the Council of the China ERP Technology Association and was a member of the Expert Committee of Chinese National High-Tech R&D Program on Computer Integrated Manufacturing Systems (1994-2004).

* * *

Thècle Alix: Associate Professor at the University of Bordeaux 4, France. Ph.D. on production planning and control in 2001 at University Bordeaux 1. Her research activities are now carried out at IMS laboratory (UMR CNRS 5218) in the «production engineering» research group and especially in the track «Enterprise Modelling and Performance». She now mainly focuses on the modelling and characterisation of services and service activities. She has been involved in European projects: CEN-NET (China Europe Network on the NET), INTEROP (IST 508011). She is currently responsible of the studies in a department of transportation and logistics management. She teaches quality management and information system modeling in an international joint master's degree programme led by Bordeaux 1 University in France and Harbin Institute of Technology in China.

Kamal Bechkoum: Dean of the School of Science and Technology at the University of Northampton, United Kingdom. Ph.D from Cranfield University in Software Techniques for Computer Aided Engineering. Over 20 years experience working in the United Kingdom higher education sector and joined the University of Northampton from the University of Derby where he was Head of the School of Computing and Assistant Dean of the Faculty of Business, Computing and Law. Prior to that, he was an Associate Dean of the School of Computing at the University of Wolverhampton. His contribution to the field of Computing Curriculum is recognised internationally and he has served as external examiner and advisor to many universities and higher education institutions both in the UK and abroad. Published over 50 papers. A Fellow of the British Computer Society, a member of the IEEE Computer Society and a Chartered IT Professional.

Constanta-Nicoleta Bodea: Professor in the Faculty of Cybernetics, Statistics and Economic Informatics, Economic Informatics Department at the Academy of Economic Study, Bucharest, Romania. Currently teaches artificial intelligence, data mining and project management. Coordinates numerous research projects at national level and achieved a high expertise in managing projects with multiple consortia. Author of eleven books and more than 50 refereed papers on project management, information systems, and artificial intelligence, being honored by IPMA (International Project Management Association) with the Outstanding Research Contributions in 2007.

Jean-Paul Bourrières: Professor at the University of Bordeaux 1, France, Director of Department LAPS (Automation and Production Science) of IMS, a research unit jointly attached to University Bordeaux 1 and CNRS (French National Centre for Scientific Research). Ingenieur Degree in Electronics and Automatic Control, Ph.D. in Theory of Control, State Docteur es Sciences Physiques. His scientific field is manufacturing science, discrete event systems and operations management in which he has published 100 refereed journal and conference papers. He was the project manager of Framework Project 6 INTEROP Network-of-Excellence on Interoperability Research for Networked Enterprises Applications and Software. In 2007 co-founded the laboratory on Enterprise Interoperability, INTEROP-VLab AISBL, Brussels, a large research network with 70 member organizations in Europe and in China, of which he currently is the president.

Andrés Boza: Lecturer in Management Information Systems at the School of Computer Science and the School of Industrial Engineering, Universidad Politécnica de Valencia (UPV), Spain. Ph.D. in Supply Chain Management and Enterprise Integration at the UPV. Member of the Research Centre on

Production Management and Engineering (CIGIP). He has participated in the doctoral programme and in national and international projects on information systems for production management, supply chain management and performance measurement. He has published several refereed papers in books, journals and international conferences in these fields.

David Chen: Full professor at the University of Bordeaux I, France and member of IMS Laboratory (Laboratory of Integration from Materials to Systems). Ph.D. from University Bordeaux 1 in Control Theory in 1988. His research interests include enterprise modelling, integration and interoperability. His main teaching domain deals with enterprise architectures and models, modelling techniques and production management methods. Since the 1990s he has been actively involved in European research projects and working groups (such as IMPACS, CIMOSA, CIMMOD, IDEAS, UEML, ATHENA, INTEROP...) and participated in several co-operation programmes between the European Union and China in the domain of enterprise modelling and integration. A member of CEN TC 310/WG1 and ISO TC184/SC5/WG1 (modelling and architecture) and involved in IFIP WG5.12 and IFAC WG5.3 (enterprise integration and networking). Published more than 80 refereed papers in international journals and conferences.

Llanos Cuenca: Assistant Professor in Enterprise Management and Management Information Systems at the Universidad Politécnica de Valencia (UPV), Spain. Ph.D. from the UPV. Member of Research Centre on Production Management and Engineering (CIGIP). Participated as a researcher in several Spanish and European projects. Has worked on issues relating to production management, supply chain, enterprise modelling and the use of IS/IT in industrial enterprises. Currently, her research lines focus on process management, enterprise architectures and the use of IS/IT in these areas. Published several refereed papers in international conferences and journals.

Tugrul Esendal: Senior lecturer in the Department of Computing Technology at De Montfort University, United Kingdom. After a very brief industrial career as a mechanical engineer, part of which he studied programming and data processing, he returned to computing full-time and specialised in applications development and software portability. He now combines teaching, research and consultancy in various aspects of software engineering. His current areas of interest for research are teaching and learning of programming languages, software quality and metrics, and learning support requirements. He is a founding member of two interest groups in the faculty: visual programming and special needs support requirements. He is also currently involved in knowledge transfer partnerships with industry.

Horacio González-Vélez: Lecturer with the School of Computing and a researcher with the IDEAS Research Institute of the Robert Gordon University in Aberdeen, Scotland, United Kingdom. Ph.D. in Informatics from the University of Edinburgh. Received the NESTA Crucible Fellowship for interdisciplinary research on computational science in 2009 and a European Commission award for work on scientific dissemination in 2006. His research encompasses parallel computing, multi-core technologies, cloud/grid computing, and computational intelligence in distributed environments. Spent over ten years in the ICT industry working for innovation-driven companies such as Silicon Graphics and Sun Microsystems, in different commercial roles in engineering and marketing. Enthusiastic about technology and its applications, he supports joint interdisciplinary research that motivates knowledge transfer, creative thinking, and innovative products. Has published several refereed scientific contributions and presented at numerous fora across the world.

228

Gary Hill: Head of Computing and Immersive Technologies at the University of Northampton, United Kingdom. His specialist area of interest/expertise is programming, with Java the preferred language. His particular passion is for Graphical Programming i.e. 2D/3D graphics, graphics & visualisation, 3D computer modelling and more recently programming mobile devices/smart phones. Having lectured programming to undergraduate and postgraduate students for the past 10 years he has always sought to make the subject as enjoyable as possible, whilst covering the key concepts required.

Deirdre Lawless: lecturer in Dublin Institute of Technology, Ireland, and chair of the MSc programmes in the School of Computing. She was the project manager for DIT on the EMERSION project, the 3-year EU Asia-Link project which was completed in 2006. EMERSION successfully developed an industry-oriented pedagogical model for software education in China. DIT was the lead partner of this project and was responsible for the design of the curriculum and quality assurance mechanisms and, in particular, for enshrining the industry orientation in the model. She is currently working on a range of projects including the development of a strategy for the provision of continuing professional development to industry by the School of Computing.

Alok Mishra: Associate Professor of Computer and Software Engineering at Atilim University, Ankara, Turkey. Ph.D. in computer science-software engineering, and dual M.Sc. degrees in computer science and applications and human resource management. His areas of interest and research are software engineering, information system, information and knowledge management and object oriented analysis and design. Published articles, book chapters and book-reviews related to software engineering and information system in refereed journals, books and conferences. Member of editorial board of many journals including *Computer Standards and Interfaces*, *Journal of Universal Computer Science*, *Computing & Informatics, Electronic Government - an International Journal*. Has extensive experience in distance education related to computers and management courses. Received an excellence award for online education from U21Global Singapore. Served as chief computer science examiner of the International Baccalaureate (IB) organization. Recipient of national merit scholarship and department of information technology scholarship of Government of India.

Deepti Mishra: Assistant Professor of Computer Engineering at Atilim University, Ankara, Turkey. Ph.D. in Computer Science (Software Engineering) and M.Sc. in Computer Science and Applications. Research interests include software process improvement, software quality, requirement engineering and databases. Published many refereed research papers and book chapters at international and national levels. Recipient of department of information technology scholarship of Government of India.

Ciarán O'Leary: Lecturer in the School of Computing in the Dublin Institute of Technology, Ireland. B.Sc. in Computer Applications from Dublin City University and M.Sc. in Computer Science from Trinity College, Dublin. Has been involved with several joint and franchised international programmes in the DIT over the past decade. Participated with colleagues in funded projects on international education models. Has also taught and delivered training in both China and Tanzania, and currently holds responsibility for the quality assurance of two international programmes involving partners in those countries.

Simon Rogerson: Professor Emeritus in Computer Ethics and former Director of the Centre for Computing and Social Responsibility at De Montfort University, United Kingdom. Following a successful industrial career where he held managerial posts in the computer field, he now combines research, lecturing and consultancy in the management, organisational and ethical aspects of ICT. He received the 2000 IFIP Namur Award for outstanding contribution to the creation of awareness of the social implications of ICT. In 2005 he became the first non-American to be given the prestigious SIGCAS Making a Difference Award by the Association for Computing Machinery. He is a Vice-President and the current Chairman of the Institute for the Management of Information Systems. He is editor of the Journal of Information, Communication & Ethics in Society.

Yushan Sun: Since 2002, Associate Professor at Harbin Institute of Technology at Weihai, China, and associate dean in the School of Software there since 2006. Obtained a Master's degree in Mathematics from Heilongjiang University in 1986. Worked as a lecturer at Harbin Institute of Technology (1988-1993) and in 1993 became Associate professor. Studied as a graduate student in North Dakota State University in the United States (1995-2000) and obtained two Master's degrees, one in Mathematics and the other in Computer Science. Worked as a software engineer for IBM (2000-2002).

Scott Turner: Pathway Leader for the B.Sc. Computing, a University Teaching Fellow, and a Teaching and Learning Co-ordinator at the University of Northampton, United Kingdom. His specialist areas are the teaching of problem-solving within computing and the application of artificial intelligence techniques.

Bruno Vallespir: Professor at the University of Bordeaux 1, France and member of IMS. Within this framework, he is manager of the «production engineering» research group (15 permanent researchers, 15 PhD students) of the IMS laboratory (UMR CNRS 5218). His research topics are production management, performance evaluation and enterprise modelling including modelling tools and design methodologies, and in particular, the research track «enterprise modelling and performance». This work rests on the research results obtained by the GRAI over the three past decades that have led it to the two methodological tools known worldwide: the GRAI model (generic architecture of control) and the GRAI method (enterprise modelling). This research track is concerned also with other concepts such as performance indicators and systems integration and engineering.

Yanqing Wang: Associate professor in the School of Management at Harbin Institute of Technology (HIT), China; previously was lecturer for seven years in the School of Software at HIT. Received B.A. and M.A. in computer science and Ph.D. in management science and engineering from HIT. In 2003, worked at Dublin Institute of Technology in Ireland as a visiting scholar. His general research interests include software quality assurance at source code level and software engineering education. Particular research projects include evaluation of coding standards, improvement in the process of peer code review, and pedagogical management information systems. His peer-reviewed papers have been published in journals such as *Asia-Pacific Management Review, Association for Computing Machinery Special Interest Group on Computer Science and Software Engineering Bulletin, China Soft Science Magazine* and elsewhere.

Index

Symbols

30-credit module 83

A

academia-industry gap 153
academic quality assurance 9-10, 30, 38
accreditation 6, 153, 159, 161-162, 164, 170, 173, 178, 209
active learning 138-139, 142-143, 149-152
advanced distributed learning (ADL) 193
advanced learning infrastructure consortium (Alice) 194
algorithmic skeletons 130, 133, 136
application-oriented activities 156
application service providers (ASP) 144
Association for Computing Machinery (ACM) 87, 98-99, 107-108, 126, 129, 133-137, 149-150, 156-157, 159, 162, 164
autonomous learning 139, 152

B

blended environments 90
blended learning 88, 96, 208
business value 40

C

CDIO education theory 39
CDIO syllabus 42
China-Europe International Symposia on Software Industry-Oriented Education (CEISIE) 3, 12, 21, 30, 36
chip multiprocessors 128
closed practicals 138-139, 142-148, 152
commercial software 41, 84
competency catalogue 191, 200-202, 206, 209
Computational Thinking 110, 112, 125-126

computer integrated manufacturing open system architecture (CIMOSA) 68
computer laboratories 144, 176
computer science curriculum 133, 135, 141, 164
Computing Curricula 2005 135-137, 159
conceive, design, implement, operate (CDIO) 21, 24, 39, 41-43, 55
Concurrency 128-129, 132-134, 136
containment area (B) 10, 13-22, 30, 37-38, 47, 55, 58, 60-62, 67, 70-71, 76-77, 80, 86, 93, 95, 100, 107, 112-116, 125-126, 129, 133-136, 146, 149-151, 156, 162-164, 187-188, 194, 198, 201, 206-208
content providers 191
control and information management (CIM) 68
convergence education 55
co-operation models 39
co-operation value chain 45-46
cultural interchange 29
curriculum development 16-17, 26, 28-30, 38, 134, 137, 158
customer relations management (CRM) 69, 148

D

Dual Master's Degree 57-58, 64, 79, 81
Dublin Institute of Technology (DIT) 1-4, 9, 12-18, 20, 23, 26-33, 35-37, 53, 160, 167

E

e-business 80, 140, 149
educational ontology 191, 195, 197, 201-202, 206
education model 2-3, 6, 10, 12-14, 16-17, 22, 26-30, 35-38, 107, 170
elaboration theory of instruction 23, 98, 103-104, 107-108
e-learning 4, 12-13, 23, 68, 90, 188, 191-195, 201, 204-209
e-learning tools 191